The Lindlahr VITAMIN COOKBOOK

By VICTOR H. LINDLAHR

Editor, JOURNAL OF LIVING

President, NATIONAL NUTRITION SOCIETY

Journal of Living
Subscriber Edition

National Nutrition Society, Inc., New York, N. Y.

CONTENTS

ACKNOWLEDGMENT

No book is ever the product of one man's endeavors. All the past centuries' accumulation of knowledge in the field is in part responsible. I should like to express my gratitude to the many food researchers whose contributions to modern nutrition science have helped make this book possible.

And in the same vein, I should like to thank particularly those who have actually helped bring this book into being — Ann White, Jeanne Delevie, Eunice Brokenshire, Frances Goodnight, Maxine Smith and Louis Biro.

V. H. L.

FOREWORD

TODAY the housewife is just as important as the nutrition expert to the health of the people. Today she must not only prepare appetizing meals for her family, but she must so prepare foods that their precious vitamin and mineral contents are not lost or destroyed. She must know how to use and conserve the natural health values in foods. Upon the shoulders of the housewife rests the responsibility of turning the discoveries of the nutrition experts into practical use and value. Ability to accomplish this task calls for a new understanding of cooking—a new kind of cookbook.

The Vitamin Cookbook by Victor H. Lindlahr is such a book. It is designed to bring the newer knowledge of cooking out of the laboratory and into the kitchen, and in this way help to advance what President Roosevelt has sanctioned as an important objective of the National Defense Program—*improved nutrition in the civilian population.*

It is a pleasure to recommend this book to the homemakers of America!

WALTER H. EDDY
Professor Emeritus,
Columbia University.

INTRODUCTION

You who cook can help yourself, and those who eat the foods you prepare, to extract a wealth of health from foods. Any one of a score of symptoms, a dozen diseases, may plague you if you don't get your daily requirements of the various vitamins— those food chemicals necessary to human life. But most important of all, an abundance of vitamins adds to your health and improves your well-being. Vitamin A can help you sail through a winter without colds or flu, Vitamin B₁ can help make you seemingly tireless, Vitamin C can help make you feel like a million. The fact that vitamins help give you health is the wonder of wonders in the vitamin story.

When you have read this book, you will know how to get enough of the known vitamins from foods. You will know how to use the *science* of cooking to obtain the utmost in taste and health value from the wonderful variety of foods this modern age of agricultural science has brought us. The more we find out about vitamins in foods, the more we realize that their welfare depends upon you who cook our foods.

The *art* of cooking has the wholesome purpose of bringing the pleasures of taste and enjoyment of eating to us human beings. But there is a *science* of cooking, too. It began 100 years ago when the genius of Justus von Liebig was turned to the problem of making foods more easily, quickly and completely digestible. Digestibility is still a primary objective of cooking.

Sixty years ago, the French chemist, Louis Pasteur, help us to understand how a science of cooking would enable us to destroy the germs, viruses, fungi and other factors for evil which may lurk in uncooked food. Then the vitamins were discovered, and a further, even more imperative, need for scientific cooking became apparent. Why? Because the vitamins aren't like so many grains of salt or pepper. They are little bits of life, some of them very delicate and fragile. Wrong cooking and inexpert handling damage them readily —in fact, certain of the vitamins may be entirely destroyed by what you do to foods in the kitchen, and all of them are too often murdered, mangled and wasted. Yes, our new food knowledge has shown dramatically that the deadliest menace to vitamin values may be some of our established cooking habits, customs and prejudices, handed down to us from past generations of cooks.

In short, we have come to recognize that one of the most important concerns in cooking is the *conservation* of the special chemicals in foods which help to give us life and health. A new science of foods is developing today. Research workers are discovering new health-bringing factors in the fruits, vegetables, meats and dairy products available to all. It is up to you to take advantage of this knowledge . . . to use it . . . to apply the lessons of science in vitamin cooking— for your health's sake!

Victor H. Lindlahr

Chapter One

VITAMINS AND
YOUR GOOD HEALTH

IN this day and age, you may see a business man lift a glass of orange juice to his lips and say, "Well, here goes for some vitamins." You may find a mother at the grocery store, selecting luscious red tomatoes with a little smile of satisfaction, secure in the knowledge that she is buying vitamins for her family. You may hear someone's secretary order a glass of milk at lunch because she has been told that milk contains vitamins. People are really beginning to understand that you can get vitamins from foods.

Think of yourself. All of your life you have probably eaten three times a day, day in and day out, year in and year out. When did you first begin to get some inkling of what you were doing for yourself when you ate foods?

Perhaps you began to get a hazy idea of the marvelous chemistry of foods, and of what special food factors may do for you in the way of bringing more abundant health and well-being, when you first grasped the significance of the word "vitamins." Today we can measure these all-important food elements, we test foods for them, we know the specific vitamin unit values of many foods. In addition, we have found out that vitamins are harmed by improper cooking. Thus even if you eat well-balanced meals, the vitamin value of your diet may be blasted all to smithereens by what is done to foods in your kitchen. That is why it is necessary now to present a way of cooking foods which takes the welfare of vitamins into consideration.

Think of your own plight, if you don't cook for yourself. Someone may be throwing away, burning up, or otherwise destroying the vital chemicals of your foods, thereby exposing you to premature aging, a half-dozen diseases and a score of symptoms. These evils may be the result of the foods you eat, when, by the goodness of Nature, your foods should be giving you health!

The plain, unvarnished truth is that probably not one woman in 500 who buys, prepares and serves food for her family has any idea about what she is doing nutritionally when she cooks foods. She knows her husband and children must eat, and she may be very much concerned with whether or not they like the food she prepares. But if she doesn't have some idea of food chemistry, she is meddling with health and disease, and with a blindfold over her eyes is influencing the physical welfare of those she feeds, blissfully unaware of whether she is doing right or wrong.

These mistakes are easily avoided. They don't have to occur, for cooking ways are easy to improve. Therefore, if we learn how to conserve and use the vitamin values in foods, we can help ourselves to abounding energy, vibrant well-being and longer years of life.

WHAT VITAMIN A CAN DO FOR YOU

Probably the most spectacular thing which Vitamin A can do for you is to supply your eyes with a substance called visual purple. This is a purplish coloring matter which behaves somewhat like the chemical used to coat a camera film. When you are in darkness, and light waves strike your eyes, the visual purple reacts and carries the impulse of light to your eye nerves, and they, in turn, enable you to see in dim light.

It follows that only with a sufficient supply of visual purple present in your eyes will you be able to see in dim light. And since each moment of dim-light seeing releases some Vitamin A, here is a vital reason why you constantly need a generous supply of this vitamin. When you are temporarily blinded by the headlight glare of an approaching car at night, some of the Vitamin A in the visual purple in your eyes is used up. If you have plenty of Vitamin A in your system, visual purple will be immediately restored, but if you are deficient in Vitamin A, your eyes will need a much longer time to function normally again. Such a deficiency is called night blindness, and it is a common cause of nighttime automobile accidents. If every car driver received enough Vitamin A in his diet, many motoring disasters might be avoided.

The entire chemistry of seeing is not yet completely understood, but we do know that the ability to see in daylight is a process similar to the one we described for night seeing. In bright-light seeing, a light-sensitive chemical called visual violet is involved, and apparently this, like visual purple, is composed partly of Vitamin A. It is likely that Vitamin A is as important to daylight seeing as to dim-light vision.

Another reason Vitamin A is so important for you is that it helps strengthen some of the most important tissues in your body. Among those tissues are your skin (including your hair and fingernails), the membranes of your nose, throat, lungs and digestive system, and the enamel of your teeth.

In other words, any part of your body composed of certain cells called epithelium depends largely upon Vitamin A for its welfare. If you don't get enough of this vitamin, such epithelial tissues may become weaker. They cannot develop or work as they should, and when that happens, symptoms and troubles occur.

Epithelial tissues act as a shield or produce fluids which help protect the body against certain infections and germ invasions. For example, the epithelial tissues in the wall of the stomach produce a protective fluid called mucus. If these cells get out of order, ulcers of the stomach may develop because the protecting mucus is lacking.

The epithelial cells of your eyes help keep the outer surfaces moist. When Vitamin A is lacking, your eyes may tend to become dry, with inflamed and itchy lids. You may have seen this condition in rheumy-eyed tramps or derelicts of the Bowery, or in the sore-eyed, homeless dog wandering around your neighborhood. They all are typical examples of Vitamin A deficiency.

A lack of Vitamin A may also affect the ears and produce what were once called aural changes—difficulties which may result in some degree of deafness. In the membranes of the nose, sinuses or lungs, defective epithelial cells may invite colds, sinus troubles and a form of bronchitis. Formation of tooth enamel is greatly influenced by Vitamin A. In women, a degeneration of the lining of the womb from lack of Vitamin A may lead to painful menstrual disturbances. In general, then, wherever epithelial tissue exists in the body, Vitamin A is essential to its welfare and health, and a lack of this food factor may cause symptoms ranging from kidney stones to pimples.

WHAT VITAMIN B₁ CAN DO FOR YOU

There is something about tired nerves which seems to make your disposition edgy, isn't there? The common phrase is, "My nerves are raw," and perhaps that is close to actual fact in your body chemistry. At least, as your nerves become tired or jumpy, your disposition tends to grow irritable, and your reactions to everyday happenings become distorted, just as the image of your face may be distorted in an amusement park trick mirror.

Your ordinarily even disposition may become excitable; your usually sound sleep, fitful; your normally calm view of what goes on, neurotic. When you are in this state, your hopeful and forward-looking bent of mind may turn depressed and anxious. Old-fashioned doctors used to call this condition "nervous irritability." Now physicians consider the possibility of a deficiency of Vitamin B_1.

Vitamin B_1 is as necessary to your nerves as electricity is to the filament of an electric light bulb. Vitamin B_1 is a nerve nourishment, and the way your nerves behave depends to a great extent upon the amount of this food factor they receive each day.

Vitamin B_1 is also one of Nature's best tonics, for it helps give you "pep" by helping to remove some of the acids of tiredness. A special type of power moves all the thousands of body muscles, from those which cause your hair to rise to those which pump the blood through your heart. It is this force which powers all the internal body activities, such as the churning of the stomach, the movement of the intestines, the rise and fall of the lungs, as well as the movements of muscles under the control of your will.

These body motions are made possible by the power produced when body sugar, called glucose, is broken up into gases and water. When this happens, a waste chemical called lactic acid results.

As lactic acid accumulates in body cells, tiredness begins. The more acid produced, the more tired and fatigued the tissues grow. This, of course, is Nature's way of preventing overwork, because the tired tissues become refreshed in the degree that fatigue acids are removed.

In this complicated body chemistry, lactic acid is first transformed into pyruvic acid, then into carbon dioxide and water—and here is where Vitamin B₁ comes in. Its rôle is to help change pyruvic acid into carbon dioxide and water, and it is as essential to the process as a spark is to ignite the gasoline in automobile motors.

Naturally, if your body doesn't get rid of the pyruvic acid its activities produce, you will tend to grow tired and weary. If enough of this acid of tiredness accumulates, you may become completely exhausted.

If you think of the process in terms of local body activities, you will begin to appreciate the incredible number of symptoms a lack of Vitamin B₁ may bring on. Each organ and tissue has a special work to do. Each tissue can become tired, and then it will tend to get out of order. It certainly will not work as it should, and that lag may bring on what physicians call functional symptoms!

For example, you may lose your appetite when you are lacking in Vitamin B₁ because stomach muscles which are tired will not contract as they should, and hence will fail to produce the juices and stimulations which give you an appetite. Vitamin B₁ insufficiency might cause you to get out of breath when you go upstairs, because your heart muscles are tired and unable to work as they should. From lack of enough Vitamin B₁ you might tend to be constipated, because the muscles of your thirty-two feet of intestines are just too tired to work as they should.

Yes, the influence of Vitamin B₁ upon your well-being and health is truly tremendous in scope and importance.

WHAT VITAMIN C CAN DO FOR YOU

Vitamin C is the vital chemical which helps to hold body cells together by forming a "glue" between them. Consider the small blood vessels—the capillaries. They twine their way through every tissue and structure in your body, and lie so close together that you cannot stick a pin into any part of your body without puncturing one and releasing a drop of blood. These little pipes are often just single layers of cells formed into a tube to distribute blood and nourishment to various tissues, but the cells which form capillaries must be cemented together with a glue-like substance. Vitamin C furnishes the "glueyness" to this intracellular material, essential to health.

When you are deficient in Vitamin C, capillaries will not form as they should in new tissues. That is why an up-to-date surgeon will prescribe Vitamin C for the patients he has operated on—Vitamin C helps to knit and heal cuts and wounds.

The gums, which are studded with minute capillaries, may grow pulpy and fragile when Vitamin C is lacking. Blood may ooze from them to make "pink toothbrush."

Some people who lack Vitamin C develop black and blue marks from even the slightest blow.

Body joints depend upon capillaries to produce the fluid (synovial) they require to work properly. Your joints may hurt, ache and later swell when you do not get enough Vitamin C. Probably the most usual cause of the symptoms we call rheumatism and arthritis is Vitamin C insufficiency.

Bones may not be able to utilize the lime they need to become hard if Vitamin C is absent. Soft tissues such as the tonsils, which should be firm and spongelike, may become pulpy, swollen masses if Vitamin C is lacking. There is evidence that a great many children who have "enlarged" tonsils might soon have normal tonsils if they were given the Vitamin C their body tissues need. In brief, almost any tissue in the body may develop some abnormal structural change if it does not get enough Vitamin C for its welfare.

There is still another consideration. Vitamin C controls the respiration of body cells, the oxygen exchange. This vital work, too, is upset by Vitamin C insufficiency, but its rôle in symptom production is of chief interest to the physician and physiologist.

You can, however, thoroughly appreciate the wonderful poison-locking power of Vitamin C. This food chemical is capable of neutralizing a great many poisons which may disturb body health, particularly toxins produced by certain infections, such as diphtheria, rheumatic fever and similar ailments. It does this by combining with the toxin or poison, embracing it and holding it in a vise-like grip that neutralizes its harmful effects.

Lead poisoning is a very common affliction, troubling house painters particularly, as well as anyone else who absorbs minute traces of lead for a long period of time. A man who has accumulated enough lead in his body to produce symptoms may be magically relieved by large doses of Vitamin C because the vitamin combines with lead particles to form an innocuous compound which is readily passed from the body through the bowels.

Vitamin C picks up certain poisons and toxins as a magnet picks up iron filings. That is why a person suffering from a toxemia of some kind, or pus absorption from bad teeth, may need double the normal requirement of Vitamin C a day. In turn, a person using a medicine which is poisonous or toxic will neutralize much Vitamin C. The habitual use of aspirin or headache powders tends to deplete the body of this vitamin.

Because Vitamin C enters into the oxygen exchange of body cells, fever consumes it in extravagant quantities. It is interesting that the old-time herb remedies which were used successfully in treatment of fevers are those which we now have found to be rich in the fever-fighting Vitamin C.

One of the most potent powers for good in Vitamin C lies in its ability to increase body immunity. The theory is that Vitamin C helps to build antibodies, but to try to explain our current immunity theory is like trying to explain the Einstein concept of relativity. We can rest content with the knowledge that the human body can acquire an immunity to or a tolerance for various ailments.

The millions who suffer from allergy symptoms have lost their immunity to some common substance. If they can restore their natural resistance, their annoying symptoms may be relieved. One of the most familiar allergy symptoms is hives, which some people develop when they eat strawberries. Such individuals have lost their natural immunity to some ordinarily harmless chemical in the fruit. An extra 1000 units of Vitamin C per day may restore their immunity to normal, enabling them to eat strawberries once again without fear of "breaking out."

The most spectacular allergy is hay fever. Each year, millions of Americans tear, sneeze, itch and wheeze at certain seasons because they have lost their natural immunity to some air-borne pollen.

The more Vitamin C hay fever sufferers get during this trying time, the less allergic they may become. A diet rich in the vitamin may mean less severe symptoms, as well as fewer attacks. In many instances, our radio listeners have reported that they avoided outbreaks of hay fever entirely by increasing their Vitamin C stores with foods rich in this factor for months preceding the hay fever season.

This, then, is a brief outline of what the three major vitamins can mean to you. The picture is complete enough, I am sure, to make you want to get all the health benefits from vitamin-rich foods that you possibly can. If you cook for your family, surely you don't want to hurt, destroy or lose those precious health-bringers, the vitamins, do you? Yet perhaps you are doing just that, unwittingly and un-knowingly, because you are an old-fashioned cook. Let's get a clearer understanding of this situation by looking for a moment at the story of how cooking developed.

Chapter Two

WHY YOU COOK AS YOU DO

A⊤ some time in the dim reaches of history, man learned to cook. There are only romantic legends as to how this first happened, but we do know that cooking is one of the oldest of all arts.

When man left the Garden of Eden, his need for preserving foods began, and he must have learned early that cooking was one way of saving foods from spoilage. That alone probably was the solid foundation for the beginning of the art of cooking. It is probable that primitive man preferred his foods, particularly meat, raw rather than cooked—even as some people do today.

The roots of American cooking lie mainly in England and her neighboring countries. Peoples native to those lands, the Angles, Saxons, Scots and Picts, lived mainly on meats and fish, and were great hands at roasting such foods.

But it wasn't every day that a man had luck at the hunt. Naturally, he and his family wanted to save what they could from the previous yield because it might be two days, three days or a week before another meal would come along, and empty, gnawing hunger was not pleasant. A way of keeping meat for several days was essential.

We can reason, then, that man first cooked from necessity—the downright, positive necessity of keeping putrefactive bacteria from making away with his meat. That is the reason why our remote forefathers roasted foods until they were charred. Later they boiled or baked them until they were grossly overdone by our standards.

If you think this strange, just imagine your kitchen without the advantages of a refrigerator or ice box, of canned goods, or even a bottle or a mason jar. Imagine yourself living in a city of 10,000 to 50,000 people, with none of these conveniences available, or on an isolated farm where meat and fish would have to be brought to you from some distance away.

Because of the lack of rapid transportation and refrigeration, foods in the "good old days" were bound to spoil, to become a trifle high in a very short time. Even thorough cooking can't do away with the aromas and flavors which taint partially decomposed animal food.

What did our ancestors do? They did exactly what some of our modern roadstand and "coffee pot" cooks do—they spiced up the evil-tasting food! Yes, they drowned the taste of taint by using spices with a heavy hand. That's why recipes in the time-worn, centuries-old cookbooks you see on book collectors' shelves read like the tickets on the drawers in a druggist's prescription nook.

Later, cooks learned to smoke, salt and pickle foods or dry them in the sun or oven. Some foods, of course, were particularly adapted to one method of preservation; others to another. Larders and pantries, even in comparatively recent times, were stocked mainly with salted, pickled or smoked foods and conserves. Cooking methods were fitted to the needs of a housewife who had only such foods to prepare most of the year.

That is the background of most of our commonly used recipes. Our cookbooks show the influence of another day, another time, another age in cooking needs. For example, the instructions given in many cookbooks for cooking cabbage were developed when the only cabbages available were the tough and leathery little seashore worts known to the wives of the Pilgrim Fathers. Such cabbages had to be boiled two, three or four hours—our modern cabbages don't need to be. And the same story could be repeated for many other foods.

An art of cookery did eventually develop. Its growth was slow, though, and certainly unknown to most people until the past 200 years. In fact, only within recent centuries has the great majority of human beings had a chance to learn that cooking could be an art. The rich and noble found out, but they were few and far between.

This small minority could pay handsomely for good cooks, could import foods from nearby countries, and could maintain hot houses, deer parks and game preserves. They had a royal time at their meals, but not so the Joneses and Smiths of yore. The latter were glad to get what little variety they could in foods; they had no opportunity to know about the frills and flourishes of cooking.

In those days, pots and pans were expensive. There were no gas or electric stoves, and a wood-, coal- or peat-burning stove had to be kept burning from morning until night, unless the cook was willing to build the fire anew three times a day. It could not be turned off and on at their convenience. Even great open fires required great houses, and few people lived in such.

So in the London, Paris or Berlin of long ago, most people took their foods to so-called "cook shops" to be cooked. And probably these common kitchens marked an all-time low in cooking. Even the cheapest greasy-spoon lunchroom in the slums of New York City would no doubt have been rated as a Waldorf-Astoria in comparison with those "cook shops."

In early times, as today, there were roadside inns for travellers. But the dining rooms they contained were not at all like the restaurants of today. There were no menus of any kind. The wayfarer ate what the landlord served—and paid his bill in advance.

In London, the start toward a better general appreciation of good cooking came about through the birth of eating clubs. In fact, that was the origin of clubs as we know them today. They were not conceived to satisfy the desire of men to get together, as some club historians would have us believe; they were purely a matter of digestive defense.

Picture a dozen or so shipowners or tea merchants with the problem of eating lunch every day. They could not afford the time to drive their carriages through the congested, crooked alleys called streets to homes miles away from their business. They grew very tired of box lunches, too. The only other choice was to patronize the food hawkers or food-stall merchants who roamed the streets—forerunners of our hot dog and popcorn venders of today.

So what did our forebears do? They banded together, rented a room and hired a first-class cook. That is the reason for being of many of the world-famed London clubs of today, and sound reason why Tom Jones and Bill Smith did not get a chance to sample good cooking for many a dreary century. Good cooking belonged to the wealthy.

In France, from the beginning of the seventeenth century, the rich and noble had gone in for fancy cooking in a big way. Louis XIV went so far as to cook personally many of his own dishes. The Duc de Richelieu, so legend has it, found time to invent mayonnaise.

This appreciation of cooking created—among those who could afford it—a demand for great chefs and masters of the culinary art. Nobles and rich commoners vied with each other to hire the best cooks, in order to impress their friends and entertain in a truly royal fashion. And so, for many decades, men skilled in cookery drew amazing salaries and were the pets of society, even as are our movie stars of today. Small chance did commoners have to sample such cooking. They were scarcely allowed to read about it.

But then came the French Revolution; the nobles had their heads chopped off; the rich, their estates scattered. What did the great chefs do? The obvious thing: They opened up restaurants.

No wonder the idea pleased the public. A restaurant was entirely different from any eating place ever seen before. The chefs provided a menu, and Mr. Citizen could take his choice of a dozen or two different foods. What's more, the foods tasted different because each chef, like the artist he was, put every talent he possessed into the preparation of the dishes he served.

And so came the days when Monsieur Reynaud and his cronies had a chance to sample tasty cooking—and grew dissatisfied with the cooking they had once known. Monsieur Reynaud fussed with his wife until she could duplicate in a measure what the great chef, Monsieur X, served in his restaurant. Then in time, when Monsieur Polette dined at Monsieur Reynaud's and tasted Veal So-and-So, he demanded of Madame Polette when they came home, "Why can't you cook like that?"

So Madame Polette had a new ambition . . . and thus the art of cookery spread until practically every household in France boasted a good cook.

The English who found time to trade with Frenchmen between their wars and political tiffs brought news and views of fancy cooking back to England, and the art spread across the Channel. It came to this country, too, by way of French visitors like Lafayette, and men like John Adams, James Madison and other of the great early Americans who took to French cooking like ducks to water. Delmonico opened up his famed establishment and taught the sons of liberty the delights of the culinary art. Yes, it had burst national boundaries, this art of cooking, and it has continued its progress ever since.

The people of England lived on a small island which couldn't possibly supply enough foods to feed its increasing population. Prior to 1850, when refrigeration and canning methods really began to be developed, it was impossible to import any quantity of fresh fruits and vegetables. So the English people became, in the main, a meat- and cereal-eating nation, and they learned how to cook these foods tastefully. Thus our common saying, "For meats and puddings, go to England."

The French, on the other hand, were chiefly a nation of small landholders, each cultivating every inch of his small plot of ground. Being thrifty, the Frenchman stretched out meats with vegetables— and his wife became expert in the preparation of stews and ragouts and similar combination dishes. Furthermore, she dropped every vegetable paring or leftover fragment into the always brewing stock pot on her stove, and thus always had the basic makings of tasty soup or a sauce. And that we express in the adage, "For soups and sauces, go to France."

The lands of the Germanic people bordered the Roman Empire in olden times, and there was constant war and intermingling between the two races. That explains why German cooking is essentially the cooking of ancient Rome. For example, the Caesars liked mixtures of sweet and sour, and sausages and sauerkraut were ancient Roman innovations. Such dishes became a part of German cooking.

America gave some new foods to the world—potatoes, tomatoes, beans, corn, squash and pumpkin, to name only a few. No other cooks in the world can bake corn bread or pumpkin pie to equal ours. The founders of our nation took a violent dislike to high-taxed tea; one result is that we do brew a better cup of coffee, on the average, than you find in England or France. But basically, American cooking is a combination of the three national types we have discussed, with Yankee and Dixie interpretations.

And so from this brief picture you can see that up until recently, our cooking ways were:

1. Concerned only with taste appeal, often sacrificing digestibility, vitamin value or nutritive benefit to appearance and taste.

2. Based upon needs and demands no longer pertinent in this day and age of scientific food preservation, refrigerators, and many other technological advances in cooking apparatus.

Today, you have dozens of ways of preserving foods which make the long cooking and overspicing of another day entirely outmoded and unnecessary. Today, farmers are growing foods whose flavors are enhanced by a short cooking time. Many of them may be eaten raw, now that sanitary regulations about food production and handling are enforced.

Many of the cooking ways you learned from your mother, or the traditions carried on in your cookbook recipes, are harmful and destructive to vitamin values. This fact could not have been determined until vitamin science was developed, but now that such development has taken place, "French" cooking, "English" cooking, and all other methods of cooking based upon national or sectional customs, prides and prejudices, must give way to cooking techniques from the land which has no boundaries—science. And the scientific way of cooking is vitamin cookery.

Chapter Three

HOW TO COOK THE VITAMIN WAY

VITAMIN cooking is a method of cooking designed to preserve the natural vitamin content of foods, to make foods more digestible and to enhance their natural taste and flavor. The basic principles are as follows:

1. To use the vitamins as a guide in the care, preparation and cooking of foods, because preservation of these delicate factors will best conserve all the nutritional qualities of foods.

2. To prepare and cook foods so as to promote the ease, rapidity and completeness of digestion, thus insuring the maximum health benefits from each and every nutrient factor.

Example

VITAMIN WAY OF COOKING SPINACH	PURPOSE
Cleanse thoroughly; store in hydrator.	Wilting destroys Vitamin A.
Tear leaves from tough stems; save stems for soup pot.	Shorter cooking time of tender leaves saves Vitamins B_1 and C.
Drop leaves immediately into $\frac{1}{2}$ inch boiling water.	Heat prevents enzymes from destroying Vitamin C.
Allow first steam to pass off.	Volatile acids destroy Vitamin A and color.
Cook briskly 5 minutes.	Overcooking destroys Vitamin B_1.

3. To fortify recipes with vitamin, mineral and other specific nutritional values.

Example

Beef liver is exceedingly rich in Vitamin A, averaging 7,100 International units per ounce. A quarter of a pound of beef liver mixed with two pounds of chopped steak would add flavor and 28,400 International units of Vitamin A.

PLAN YOUR DAILY VITAMIN INTAKE

Science has developed the unit value as a measuring rod for vitamins. We say that a person needs so many units of Vitamin A or so many units of Vitamins B_1 and C. When you know that an ounce of liver has so much Vitamin A, an ounce of egg yolk so much Vitamin B_1, a glass of orange juice so much Vitamin C, it becomes easy to fortify recipes scientifically and deliciously with the vitamins of health.

Such a mode of thinking, such an approach to your menu planning and your choice of recipes, is the essence of vitamin cooking—the selection of foods worth while in the vitamin sense.

On the average, you will want for each adult per day:

5,000 International units of Vitamin A
600 International units of Vitamin B_1
1,500 International units of Vitamin C

You will learn that there are some highly potent Vitamin A foods which can be used to make the diet amply fortified in this factor. A dish of greens or a bit of liver or cheese may easily and adequately take care of the Vitamin A quota.

The same story holds true for Vitamin C. There are quite a few foods superlatively rich in this factor. Salads and fruit juices or fruit desserts are convenient and tasty ways to provide the necessary number of units of Vitamin C every day.

However, supplying enough Vitamin B_1 is going to require the most thinking on your part. While this vitamin is the most widely distributed of all, no single food has a great deal, and we moderns require quite a large amount of Vitamin B_1. Your major concern in buying the day's foods should be to provide enough Vitamin B_1 to give the family a wide safety margin. Therefore, the Vitamin B_1 foods should be the fundamental foundation of your meal planning.

Your ideas of food selection should try to follow this pattern:

1. Vitamin B, foods should form the foundation of the diet.
2. Vitamin A foods, in the form of green vegetables, the dairy products and organ meats, should supplement them.
3. Vitamin C foods, in the form of fruit juices, salads and fruit desserts, should supplement both Vitamins A and B,.

It is a sensible and practical idea to check off the foods which your family likes, and best meet your budget, in each vitamin group. Make those "musts" on your marketing list, and henceforth let them be the five-star foods in your family's eating.

THE SELECTION OF VITAMIN FOODS

Now, then, after you have decided which foods you are going to select for your balanced menus, you must understand that the freshness, color and texture of food tell you much about the vitamin values they contain.

These features are explained to you in our charts and recipes. They will give you valuable clues as to how the farmer, the shipper and the merchant treat your vitamins, and will help you to become an expert buyer of these factors in foods.

FRESHNESS

Wilting destroys Vitamins A and C, and leafy greens turned brown are no bargain at any price from the vitamin viewpoint.

The vitamin value of beans depends upon the freshness and the degree of their maturity.

Vitamin C value of fruits is directly influenced by their degree of ripeness. A fully tree-ripened orange will have far more Vitamin C than a poorly ripened specimen.

The Vitamin C content and digestibility of bananas rise with the degree of ripeness. Bananas taken from the same bunch show progressive increase in vitamin content as they ripen.

TEXTURE

The "juiciness" of citrus fruits is an indicator of their vitamin values. Woody grapefruit has less Vitamin C than the juicy specimens.

Firm, plump apricots and peaches have far more Vitamin A than shrivelled ones; crisp lettuce, more Vitamin A than limp lettuce.

COLOR

Nature advertises vitamin values lavishly through color. The more yellow in corn, squash, melons or pumpkins, the more Vitamin A you get. Deep-colored Hubbard squash has far more Vitamin A than pale yellow summer squash. Reddish golden "yams" have far more than sweet potatoes. The more green in the Vitamin A-rich leafy vegetables, the better their vitamin values. Bleached asparagus, celery and lettuce contain very little Vitamin A.

CONSIDER THE COOKING TIME NEEDED!

You will remember also to keep your eyes on actualities. Meat is apparently a rich source of the Vitamin B complex, containing on the average more Vitamin B_1 to the ounce than vegetables and fruits. However, the advertised vitamin values of meat are based on analyses of raw steaks, roasts, chops, etc. Many cuts of meat must be cooked a considerably long time. Therefore the Vitamin B_1 value probably dwindles to one-half its original amount.

However, it should be pointed out that the less tender cuts, so full of other nutritional values as well as the flavor substances of meat, can be made tender and palatable by proper preparation and proper methods of cooking. It is equally possible to ruin the tenderest cuts by the wrong method. These points will be demonstrated in the recipes dealing with specific methods of meat cookery.

On the other hand, vegetables which you cook in just a few minutes (or actually eat raw) will give you almost all the Vitamin B_1 they originally contained. Remember, too, that the more calories you consume, the more Vitamin B_1 you need. Since most vegetables have a low calorie content, they give you far more Vitamin B_1 proportionately than any meat, which is higher in calorie content.

Example

Four ounces of roast pork contain 290 International units of Vitamin B_1 and 200 calories. Four ounces of cooked asparagus contain only 75 International units of Vitamin B_1, but they also contain only 22 calories, so the asparagus gives you 3.4 units per calorie, in contrast to the pork with 1.4 units per calorie.

Under any circumstances, never forget to take cooking time into consideration. You will get more Vitamin B complex from ground beefsteak patties (twenty minutes' cooking time) than in a pot roast (three and one-half hours' cooking time).

YOUR FOOD DOLLARS

Obviously you have to measure vitamins by your budget yardstick, too. Many of the foods richest in vitamins are very inexpensive, and it is possible to build vitamin-rich menus with little money.

But sometimes your judgment of what to spend for a food will have to be guided entirely by vitamin worth.

If your purse will not permit tree-ripened oranges, which you are sure will be rich in Vitamin C, it would be best to buy grapefruit in preference to color-added oranges which may have little Vitamin C value. In fact, you may find it more suitable to get your Vitamin C from cabbage than from the more expensive fruits.

American homemakers, on the average, spend about 35 per cent of their food money on meat. In a government survey, 50 per cent of the women questioned said that they bought the "best" grades, yet only 9 per cent of the meat produced in the United States is of the best grade. Very few women know enough about the various cuts of meat to buy intelligently.

For instance, do you know that the less tender cuts of meat may be more desirable from the point of both economy and nutrition than the so-called "select" cuts? Our charts will show the much greater value of a simple meat loaf over the more expensive "select" cuts of meat. Your choice, of course, is your own.

Most women are aware of the amount of wastage which bone, fat, gristle and skin in meat represent. They often forget that there may be an equally high wastage in commonly used vegetables. When you are vitamin-wise, you will use much of the "waste" in vegetables to make pot liquor and soups. Trimmings, peelings, etc., may represent, on the average, 35 per cent of your vegetable purchase dollar.

Millions of homemakers buy coffee, fancy specialty foods and little "luxuries" of eating when they should be buying vitamins in lowly foods with their money. If they have to spend more money for fillings in their teeth, or pay unnecessary bills because of food-deficiency symptoms, they have done themselves a double injustice.

More millions of homemakers on a limited budget make the mistake of buying filling foods which they believe are cheap. Foods which lack real nutritive value are never cheap. Spaghetti, white bread and such rib-sticking foods may stretch the stomach and send the family away from the table with a feeling of satiation after a meal, but they cannot satisfy the craving for vitamins and minerals.

Hungry bellies will continue to cry. Mother will buy more spaghetti and more bread, and the gnawing hunger will still go on. And so we see the parade of people "filled" with food yet hungry for more; of people on relief who are grossly overweight and hungry all the time. These individuals don't know that they are hungry for Vitamin A, Vitamin C or other essential food factors. A bunch of carrots, a head of cabbage, a quart of milk, or a handful of beet greens might satisfy such hunger and bring vitamin health. Without question, the people most in need of vitamin knowledge and vitamin cookery are those who are unhappily forced to get along on a minimum budget.

As you learn and appreciate the vitamin values of foods you can budget your food dollar more wisely. A head of cabbage is a Vitamin C bargain; a bunch of chard a storehouse of Vitamin A. The first expenditure of food money should be for the vitamin-rich protective foods. When these have been selected and purchased, proteins and energy foods should come next. Then, and only then, should coffee, tea and other luxuries be given a place on the marketing list.

It requires knowledge, study, planning and intelligence to spend a food dollar wisely. How much money you have to spend is not half so important as how you allocate the money.

Poverty is not the sole cause of malnutrition. Members of well-to-do families often suffer from food deficiencies. You might spend ten dollars per person on a meal and not get enough of the food essentials. Yet you might buy these for ten cents a person. It's up to you to learn how to buy vitamins in foods. The axiom that you can't buy health doesn't hold in nutrition science. You definitely can.

THE CARE OF VITAMINS

After you have received the most for your money in vitamin foods, it is up to you to take good care of the precious substances you have purchased. Learn by heart every technique of care which will save or preserve the vitamins you seek from a special food.

It would be poor economy, for example, to buy a large can of orange juice if your family can consume only one-third of it a day. Even if you put the unused portion carefully away in the refrigerator, it is likely that much of the vitamin value would be lost in the forty-eight hours elapsing before it would all be used.

Fresh vegetables of the flower, fruit, stem or leaf classification, when stored at room temperature, lose much of their vitamin value; when stored in a refrigerator, the loss is much less; when stored at temperatures below 48° F., there is comparatively very little loss.

VEGETABLES TO BE REFRIGERATED

Flower Class
  French Artichokes
  Broccoli
  Cauliflower

Fruit Class
  Cucumbers
  Melons
  Okra
  Peppers
  Tomatoes

Stems and Shoots
  Asparagus
  Celery
  Kohlrabi

Leaf Class
  Beet Greens
  Brussels Sprouts
  Cabbage
  Chard
  Collards
  Dandelion Greens
  Endive
  Kale
  Lettuce
  Mustard
  Parsley
  Spinach
  Turnip Greens
  Watercress

All leafy vegetables should be stored in hydrators or other closed containers in the refrigerator. Use as soon as possible. Deterioration of Vitamin C begins as soon as vegetables or leaves are picked.

Fresh green seed vegetables such as peas, lima beans and fresh corn, should be left in the pod or husk until used. If not used at once, they should be kept in a refrigerator or a very cool place and used as soon as possible.

Cereals used as vegetables include corn and rice. Rice, because it is dried, requires no special care except to store in a dry place. Fresh corn has been discussed.

Root Class
Beets
Carrots
Parsnips
Sweet Potatoes
Radishes
Rutabagas
Salsify
Turnips

Tuber Class
Jerusalem Artichokes
Irish Potatoes

Bulb Class
Chives
Garlic
Leeks
Onions
Scallions
Shallots

Roots, tubers and bulbs, with few exceptions, do not need refrigeration, but they should be stored in a cool place. However, radishes and salsify definitely should be refrigerated, and beets and carrots likewise keep better under refrigeration.

Further details of vitamin care will be more apparent as you become more food-wise, and as new, authentic research on the subject is made public. Watch for leads and clues as you learn the characteristics of various foods.

THE HANDLING OF FOODS BEFORE COOKING

In the process of getting foods ready for cooking and serving, their vitamin-mineral protective values may be seriously injured.

Scientific cooking tests, made quite some time ago, showed that the losses of dry matter in cooking vegetables was 15 per cent when cooked by steam, 30 per cent when cooked in a small amount of water, and 40 per cent when cooked in a large amount of water. The value of these generally accepted findings has been changed by the fact that the time of cooking is more important than has heretofore been acknowledged by most of the researchers in nutrition.

Therefore, the fineness of division of the vegetables you cook looms up as a very important point. Shredded beets, for example, will cook in five minutes; quartered Brussels sprouts in eight. Such consideration likewise demands that you break up cauliflower into flowerets, and that you cook the stems, stalks and leaves separately. You will slice okra into thin ringlets, dice parsnips and turnips, chop peppers fine, cut your string beans into slivers.

You must, however, arrange your kitchen schedule so that foods which you intend to shred or dice will be prepared at the last minute. This must be done particularly to preserve their Vitamin C values, because fracturing a food exposes it to oxidation, and oxidation is deadly to Vitamin C.

Salad vegetables should be allowed to stand in water just long enough to regain evaporated moisture and become crisp again. A few ice cubes in the water hasten this process. If crisping is done properly and carefully, the water-soluble elements will not be dissipated because of unnecessarily long soaking.

Oysterplant, parsnips and other vegetables which have the tendency to darken when pared or scraped will keep their natural color if they are dropped into water that has been acidulated with a teaspoonful of vinegar. Drain and cook in fresh water. The darkening usually means oxidation, which means vitamin loss.

Contrary to general opinion, long soaking does not improve the cooking quality of dried fruits. The washed fruit should be placed in a saucepan and simmered over a low heat (175° F.) so that the fruit may be hot without boiling. If this is done, the fruit will have time to plump (swell) and develop maximum flavor. Sugar should be added *after* cooking if needed.

Dried legumes (peas, lentils and beans) are hard because the fiber and cellulose in them are quite developed. Naturally, certain varieties are harder than others. They are softened to the degree that they absorb water. Some, such as black beans, and soybeans, should be softened before as well as during the cooking process; others, such as peas, lentils, lima beans, etc., need no soaking.

Adding baking soda does hasten water absorption but it destroys certain vitamins. Soft water helps absorption considerably. When you simmer beans in water below 180° F., the hardest varieties will become soft (take up their own weight in water) in five or six hours, whereas the less hard and more commonly used ones, such as peas, lentils, limas, etc., will become soft in 1½ to 2 hours. Soaking any legume for several hours will always decrease its cooking time. Never discard soaking water.

All these do's and don'ts sound rather formidable in the telling, but in practice they are not much extra trouble. Since you must handle foods in some fashion, it is just as easy to handle them right.

There is no getting away from the fact that you should take care of each vitamin-rich food with the same thoughtfulness, knowledge and skill that a pharmacist gives to his drug stock. Your recipes are just as important, for, after all, are not foods Nature's medicines?

THE PREPARATION OF FOODS FOR COOKING

You may take many wise precautions which will help to conserve the vitamin and other nutritive values of foods during actual cooking. When your great-grandfather killed a steer, he couldn't hang the carcass in a refrigerated shed to allow the tough beef to grow more tender by the orderly process of self-digestion which correct hanging insures. He had to use fresh-killed meat when the opportunity presented itself—and there are very few meats more tough than a fresh-killed ox, cow or bull. Here was an invitation, indeed a demand, to cook the beef long enough to make it tender and edible. Probably very little Vitamin B_1 remained in such meat.

However, if you will ask your meat dealer to keep a leg of lamb in his refrigerator for a week or so and allow it to ripen, you will cut the cooking time considerably, which in turn will save a corresponding degree of Vitamin B_1. This ripening of meat is a digestive process resulting from enzymic action, and it improves both tenderness and flavor. Ripened meats are juicier and better tasting. Perhaps your next-door neighbor prepares beef for a beef stew by cutting the meat into large chunks. If you will cut the beef for your stew into small pieces, you will get two or three times as much Vitamin B_1 value in your stew as she does from hers—because you need to cook yours only half as long.

Many vegetables require as preliminary preparation a thorough washing under running water, and a good going-over with a vegetable brush. Spoiled, wilted or discolored portions should be trimmed off, and undesirable leaves and coarse stems removed.

During this time of preparation you should also decide whether or not skins, stems, leaves, or other portions of the vegetable should be removed and saved for the soup stock pot. Your criterion should be the cooking time. Stems of spinach and stalks of cauliflower and broccoli haven't so much nutritional value as the leafy parts and may slow up cooking time. Why not save them for the stock pot? If stalks of some vegetables such as broccoli or chard are going to be used, it is best to cook them separately, because the time it takes to cook them will overcook the more tender flower or leaf parts.

The woody parts of some vegetables contain much woody fiber (lignin), which is undesirable, and cooking to get the hard part tender often results in overcooking the tender portion. For example, parsnips may have a hard core which should be removed and saved for the stock pot. Therefore, for the best results, always quarter parsnips, remove the core if present, and then dice or quarter the pieces to shorten cooking time still further.

Potatoes pared before cooking lose much more of their original mineral matter, solid matter and vitamin content than potatoes which have been cooked in their skins and peeled after cooking.

COOKING FROM THE VITAMIN VIEWPOINT

Cooking methods are divided into moist-heat and dry-heat methods, or a combination of the two.

Dry-heat cooking
1. Broiling
2. Pan-Broiling
3. Roasting
4. Baking
5. Sautéing

Moist-heat cooking
1. Steaming
2. Boiling
3. Simmering (not boiling)
   a. Stewing
   b. Fricasséeing

Combination moist- and dry-heat cooking
1. Braising
2. Pot-Roasting

These methods are described in detail on the pages immediately following. Before using any of the recipes contained in the latter part of this book, be sure to familiarize yourself with these definitions, as well as with those in the general list on pages 67 to 73, so that you may follow easily all directions to your best advantage.

Broiling means cooking a food before an open heat such as that produced by gas, coal, coke or electricity. Broiling temperatures called for in former days were often as high as 550° F. Today, such heat is considered too high a temperature to use, for it is destructive to Vitamin B_1. Place food about three and one-half inches from source of heat. Broiling times vary from 3 to 40 minutes, depending upon kind of food, its tenderness and thickness.

Pan-broiling, a variation of broiling, is a term usually used in meat cookery. The food is placed in a sizzling hot, ungreased skillet of heavy metal and cooked over direct heat. Bacon, pork or lamb chops are often pan-broiled. If meat, such as bacon, is very fatty, remove excess fat as it accumulates so food will not be fried.

Roasting and *baking* are really synonymous terms, although literally roasting applies to meats cooked before an open fire. Searing roasts at 500° F. does not prevent a loss of meat juice as is commonly thought. It does develop a brown layer, or outer coating, the flavor of which many people like, but the high cooking temperature is destructive to nutrients. A temperature of 300° F. produces a better-flavored, juicier meat, and results in far less cooking losses, but such a low temperature means longer cooking time. Therefore, we suggest using temperatures of 325° to 350° F. for roasts of five pounds or more.

If the brown outer layer is desired, it may be produced after the meat has cooked sufficiently by applying a quick spurt of heat, either by broiling or baking at a very high temperature for a short time. Generally speaking, meat is best when roasted in an open pan. The water evaporates but the minerals and extractives deposit on the surface of the meat and the pan.

The method of cooking meats by minutes-per-pound, or time-weight relation, is very inaccurate and always approximate because meat cuts vary so much in quality, degree of "ripening," thickness of cut, shape of roast and proportion of meat to fat or bone. The internal temperature of the roast is the only actual gauge of degree of doneness, so the best way to cook meat is to use a meat thermometer. For a further discussion of the value of a meat thermometer, read the Comments on Beef, in the recipe section of this book.

Before a roast is put into the oven, insert the thermometer in the meat so that the bulb reaches the center of the largest muscle (be sure that it does not touch bone or fat). As heat penetrates the meat, the internal temperature gradually rises and this registers on the thermometer.

When the inside of the meat has reached a temperature of about 140° F., the meat will be rare; at 150° F., medium; at 165° F. to 170° F., well done. When the thermometer registers the internal temperature which indicates doneness for the particular kind of meat, remove roast from oven.

The chief point to remember is this: The higher the temperature, the greater the vitamin destruction and the losses of weight, solids, moisture and volatile matter.

Sautéing means to cook in smallest amount of fat possible in a skillet over direct heat. This method of cooking, together with broiling and pan-broiling, has replaced frying in vitamin cooking.

The absorption of fat is very objectionable. To prevent it, shake skillet backward and forward or use wooden spoon or steel fork to move food occasionally from side to side of pan. The longer foods remain in the fat, the greater the fat absorption. The larger the proportion of the surface of the food cooked, the greater the fat absorption will be.

Always sauté over a low or medium heat. Never permit fat to sizzle or smoke because this is a definite indication that the fats have been broken down, and harmful chemicals produced.

MOIST-HEAT COOKING

Steaming means to cook over steam or surrounded by steam; to cook over boiling water in a double boiler (without liquid); or to cook in a steam or pressure cooker. The last-named method is particularly useful in cooking legumes such as lima beans and lentils. It is always applicable if it saves greatly in cooking time.

Boiling is to cook in a liquid at a temperature of 212° F. (at sea level). The liquid should bubble actively during the time suggested, and just enough heat should be used to keep the liquid in this state unless rapid boiling is specified in the recipe. (Slowly boiling water is just as effective, and prevents heat loss through steam.)

Simmering is to cook in liquid just below the boiling point, between 180° F. and 210° F. (Different altitudes cause slight variances in cooking temperatures.) In simmering there should be no active movement of the water except an occasional bubble which rises slowly to the surface. Simmering particularly applies to cooking meat by any moist-heat cooking method to make it more tender. Modern methods of moist-heat cooking of all meats call for low temperatures. High temperatures in moist-heat cooking, just as in dry-heat cooking, tend to toughen meats and cause excessive shrinkage.

Meats, like vegetables, when cooked in water tend to lose the water-soluble nutrients—minerals, Vitamins B₁ and C, and albumen. The more surface exposed, the greater the loss.

Simmering also applies in many other instances in cooking, such as coddling eggs, cooking organ meats (sweetbreads, brains, etc.), cooking legumes, etc.

Stewing is actually simmering. The difference is in the size of the pieces of meat, not in the cooking principle. A stew is a dish made of small uniform pieces of meat simmered in liquid with or without vegetables. It is a moist-heat method used chiefly in the preparation of less tender cuts.

Fricasséeing is a term describing the process by which small pieces of meat, usually poultry, are cut as for stew and cooked by moist heat in poultry stock.

MOIST-AND DRY-HEAT COOKING

Braising is to cook in a tightly covered kettle in a small quantity of liquid (water, milk, cream, stock or vegetable juices) at a low temperature, either over direct heat on top of the stove or in the oven. This method is suitable for veal, mutton and all cheaper (tough) cuts of meat.

Pot-roasting is essentially the method of cooking meat by braising.

YOUR CHEMICAL LABORATORY

You realize by now, don't you, that your kitchen is a food chemical laboratory, vital to your family? Your pots, pans and other cooking utensils are as specifically useful to you as the beakers and test tubes of a chemist are to him. If a particular pot or pan has a superlative value (from the nutrition viewpoint) in the preparation of some particular food, that pot or utensil is worth having.

If a pot with a tightly fitting cover will enable you to cook a Vitamin B_1-rich food in twenty to forty minutes' less time than another pot will, it is greatly worth while to own and use the former. For example, if a new-type pressure cooker will enable you to cook lima beans in four minutes, the investment will be good, for lima beans are extremely rich in Vitamin B_1.

Highly acid foods are better cooked in glass rather than aluminum utensils.

Vitamin C is destroyed when a food containing it is cooked in a copper pot. Also, other objectionable compounds may form when foods are cooked in copper. To offset this, iron-containing foods cooked in copper may be helped a bit.

KITCHEN EQUIPMENT

The array of kitchen equipment offered to the modern housewife savors of something Aladdin might have provided with his magic ring and lamp. As you become acquainted with the characteristics of the vitamins, you will find that many of our newer kitchen conveniences have an even greater value than their enthusiastic promoters claim for them.

If you can obtain prune nectar by putting uncooked prune pulp into an electric whirligig which makes a liquid of it, you will undoubtedly get more units of Vitamin B_1 from that nectar than you possibly could out of any produced from cooked, strained prunes. If you can reduce celery—as you can—to a liquid in a few minutes' time, and pour it into a suitable soup stock, you will have cream of celery soup which is rich in all the nutritive factors of celery.

A refrigerator skillfully used probably pays for itself in foods saved from deterioration, because good refrigeration keeps food safe. The coldest part of the refrigerator should be reserved for the most perishable foods. But in addition, refrigeration is essential to vitamin preservation. You will learn how cold inhibits the destruction of Vitamin C. If your refrigerator is equipped with a hydrator, Vitamin A- and C-rich vegetables can be spared nutritional loss from wilting.

Modern refrigerators now have three degrees of cold—the customary dry cold, the extreme cold for meat, and the latest improvement called moist cold for storing greens and vegetables.

Glass containers which can be covered and kept in the refrigerator will help to conserve and preserve the Vitamin C values of the foods you buy. All meats should be kept in the refrigerator. Ground meats should be used as soon as possible after grinding, and kept in the coldest part of the refrigerator until the moment of cooking.

The new types of stoves with their very efficient temperature regulators will save many thousands of units of Vitamin B_1 if you use the mechanical accuracy they provide to cook your foods to a proper degree of doneness and no longer. Stoves with special insulation for the conservation of heat not only pay their way in fuel, but they also cut cooking time as well as insure better texture of most dishes.

As your own experience has probably shown you, meats roasted at high oven temperatures in poorly insulated ovens may shrink as much as 40 to 60 per cent, as compared to the 15 or 20 per cent loss at lower temperatures in heat-controlled, properly insulated ovens.

For many reasons, then, modern scientific cooking is controlled cooking, and when you consider an investment in new kitchen equipment, remember that any device which helps to preserve, save or improve the vitamin value of a food you prepare is an asset. Acquire it; utilize to the full all its modern advantages.

Chapter Four

COOKING AND CARE OF VITAMIN A

THE food factor we call Vitamin A is classified by the scientist into two divisions: real Vitamin A, found only in animal products, such as liver, cream, cheese, eggs, etc.; and pro-Vitamin A or carotene, which is obtained from plants and turned into Vitamin A by the human body. However, it is much simpler to call both forms Vitamin A, since that is what both finally become.

Carotene, which is yellow, is manufactured by the action of the sun's rays on the chlorophyll in plants. Since carotene is yellow, the deepness in color of a Vitamin A-containing food is a good indication of its worth in that vitamin.

For example, dark green spinach has far more Vitamin A than light green spinach; reddish-yellow apricots, more than the pale yellow type; deep orange sweet potatoes, more than light yellow ones; Hubbard squash, more than summer squash. White corn has very little Vitamin A, while yellow corn is quite rich in the factor. The deep green outer leaves of lettuce are very rich in Vitamin A; the inner bleached leaves have practically none.

Vegetable-eating animals make Vitamin A in their livers from the carotene they find in grass and other plants. Foods or food derivatives of animal origin which are rich in Vitamin A give us color clues, too. Except when chickens have been regularly fed cod liver oil, the deeper the color of an egg yolk, the more Vitamin A it will usually be found to contain.

The lion, tiger or any other carnivorous animal accumulates Vitamin A only by eating other animal tissues, which probably explains the natural instinct of a wild animal to eat the liver of a kill first.

In all animals, birds or fish, the liver is the storehouse of Vitamin A. Approximately 90 per cent of the body's Vitamin A is concentrated in that organ, so when you eat liver, you are getting practically all the Vitamin A that the animal had stored.

The American Indians never heard of Vitamin A, but when they killed an animal in the hunt, one of the first portions they ate was the liver. They didn't eat the steaks or chops first, as we do. They ate these last, because they considered such cuts an inferior kind of meat. Modern food science has proved that their choice was right.

But the strangest thing of all is that the Eskimo in the Arctic, the savage in deepest Africa, or the native on some romantic South Sea isle, eats exactly the same way today when he makes a kill.

How could primitive peoples all over the world, thousands of miles apart, learn this basic, fundamental lesson in food values? The probable explanation is that they learned it by noting the habits of carnivorous animals, for the tiger in India, the wolf in Russia, or the wildcat in Montana, eats the vitamin-rich parts of its kill first. There you see the wonder-working hand of Mother Nature.

In this particular case, savages are wisely guided by instinct, because an ounce of beef liver has, on the average, 7,100 International units of Vitamin A—real, natural, honest-to-goodness Vitamin A—and the livers of other animals are correspondingly rich.

Indeed, if an animal has eaten green food and received some sunshine, its liver might contain as high as 11,500 International units per ounce. Compare that to beef steak, with 9 International units per ounce, or a chuck roast with similar value.

So under any circumstances, you can figure 7,100 International units of Vitamin A per ounce of beef liver over and above any other nutritional value the meat might have. Calf liver or lamb liver is even richer, and any type of liver is an excellent source of Vitamin A. Four centuries before the Christian Era, Hippocrates was curing night blindness by prescribing the livers of birds.

Stop now to think what the Vitamin A value in liver means. You are probably going to serve gravy with your roast next Sunday, aren't you? Chop up four ounces of sautéed beef liver and add it to the gravy. If you have a family of four, and each one takes an equal portion of the gravy, right then and there, each member of your family will receive 7,100 International units of Vitamin A in addition to any more they may obtain from the rest of the meal.

What happens to the livers of the chickens you serve? Does Peggy or Johnny get the liver, and the rest of the family do without? That means Vitamin A for Peggy and Johnny, and pot luck for all the others. When you become a vitamin cook, chicken livers will be cooked and chopped up with the stuffing of the chicken, or they will go into the gravy. Then the whole family can benefit from their Vitamin A richness.

Does your mind run to appetizers, hors d'oeuvres and other tasty tidbits? Next time you have the Tuesday Sewing Club over, mix some chopped cooked chicken livers with a little chicken fat, season the paste and serve the girls some chicken liver canapés. They will be getting valuable Vitamin A—and who's done so well "since when" by the Club as you will be doing next meeting?

When did you last serve a beef loaf? A long time ago? No particular reason to serve it . . . you forgot about it . . . you always thought it a poor dish at best?

Yet, if you mix a quarter of a pound of sautéed and chopped beef liver with the next beef loaf you prepare, it will add to the flavor, will make a much more appetizing beef loaf than any you have ever served before. And right there are 28,400 International units of Vitamin A. Where could you get an equal amount of this vitamin so pleasantly, so economically?

Common, ordinary yellow American cheese made with whole milk contains on the average 530 International units of Vitamin A per ounce. Many foods are improved in taste by the addition of cheese. This will mean *au gratin* to old-fashioned cooks; thousands of units of Vitamin A to us.

When you sprinkle grated yellow cheese on the mealy centers of stuffed baked potatoes, you add about 530 units of Vitamin A per potato. Then there is cheese sauce to serve with asparagus, cauliflower or sautéed tomatoes. In fact, there are dozens of delicious and delightful ways to fortify foods with Vitamin A.

Any cooking of cheese should be done at a low temperature for a short time, just until the cheese is melted. If you don't take care in cooking, the result will be an indigestible, stringy mess because a too high temperature or too fast cooking overcoagulates protein, making the cheese tough. When improperly cooked, any cheese dish is very indigestible as well as unpalatable, and at the same time its vitamin values are harmed.

To illustrate this principle of vitamin cookery, here are a few rules:

1. *Select* a cheese rich in Vitamin A (whole-milk type).

2. *Prepare* by grating or shredding so that it is finely divided; this makes blending (or creaming) easier and quicker.

3. *Cook* at low temperature, stirring constantly, just until cheese is smooth and well blended.

Like cheese, an egg is a protein food, and hardens or becomes firm when heat is applied. The chemist calls this process "coagulation." You use eggs as a thickening agent for a soufflé, custard, sauce or pudding, and to bind such foods as bread crumbs and ground meat. Careful handling and cooking at a low or medium temperature are essential to any phase of egg cookery.

But eggs are more than binders or thickening agents. An egg gives you 700 International units of Vitamin A in addition to its other excellent values. So think of eggs as vitamin fortifiers of recipes.

VEGETABLE SOURCES OF VITAMIN A

When you get your Vitamin A from peaches, spinach, broccoli, carrots or other fruits and vegetables, it comes to you in the form of carotene, which your liver must change into Vitamin A.

Right now, your liver may be in top-notch working condition; at other times, it may be functioning poorly. Generally speaking, your liver may do very well at its work. But if, for one reason or another, you develop a spell of constipation, the picture changes. If your liver is sluggish, it doesn't make carotene into Vitamin A so efficiently as it should. It begins to operate on the slow-down principle occasionally used in strikes, and sometimes lapses into an actual "sit-down strike," with all its attendant discomforts.

So at this time when constipation has slowed up the liver, a dish of spinach, well prepared, attractively dressed, and supposedly capable of giving you 13,175 International units of Vitamin A, becomes a snare and a delusion. Your torpid liver may produce only 100 units of Vitamin A from the carotene in spinach—sometimes even less, depending upon the condition it is in at the time.

For some people with liver disease, it is necessary to prescribe as many as 50,000 International units of Vitamin A daily (in the form of carotene) to enable them to absorb and use the 4,000 to 5,000 International units they must have if their eyes are not to show the effect of Vitamin A deficiency.

If you can't really get Vitamin A from the foods you eat, or the Vitamin A pills you take, it is a serious affair. Therefore, any slip-up in liver action, whether it results from overindulgence in alcohol, the use of harsh laxatives, an aggravating visit from Aunt Minnie, or a spell of constipation—*anything* which keeps the liver from working as it should—blights your chances to get Vitamin A. Don't ever forget that!

Thousands of letters received from listeners during twelve years of broadcasting experience have led me to one unalterable conclusion: i.e., that common constipation and haphazard use of harsh laxatives —particularly among people over the age of 35—are definitely complicating problems for nutritionists! The complex apparatus in the human body which extracts the vitamins from food must be working properly, or the whole promise of health from vitamins is *blitzkrieged* into oblivion. Common complaints such as constipation, or any other condition which may interfere with the digestion and absorption of foods, deserve serious consideration and competent attention, and should never be dismissed as unimportant.

The transformation of carotene into Vitamin A, then, depends upon liver function. Considering this, we recommend for safety's sake that you get your Vitamin A from both sources—the direct animal, and the indirect vegetable and fruit. In most cases, the proportion might be approximately one-third animal to two-thirds vegetable.

Eggs, butter, milk and cheese are the best animal sources of Vitamin A (except for liver). Children, however, should get more than one half of their Vitamin A from animal sources, particularly milk.

KITCHEN CARE OF VITAMIN A

Generally speaking, Vitamin A is a robust chemical, not easily destroyed by cooking. Heat hurts Vitamin A only when the food is exposed to air at the same time. In fact, the destruction of Vitamin A, from the cooking viewpoint, can come about only through oxidation, and you would have to heat food a long time at baking temperatures of 350° to 400° F. to oxidize the Vitamin A potency. Even then, the heating would have to be done in the presence of air. In other words, if you were to put a Vitamin A-rich food into a can or a mason jar which was sealed so that the air couldn't get to the food, you could heat it for a long time and not hurt the Vitamin A content. It withstands the pressure of preserving very well, but not entirely.

High temperatures, however, increase oxidation. For example, you will probably be very impressed with the Vitamin A value of butter. You may decide that from now on you will fry your eggs in butter. But you will have to change your mind on that score because frying or sautéing exposes butter simultaneously to air and high heat, and that combination at least partially destroys Vitamin A content. So you can confidently reckon that there is no great Vitamin A value left in the butter you use for sautéing.

This means that from the vitamin angle, sautéing may be done in vegetable and animal cooking oils instead of butter. Butter is too rich in Vitamin A to be subjected to any cooking hazards.

Foods which are *dried* by *long* application of mild heat, without protection against oxidation, may lose a great deal of their Vitamin A value. That lesson was learned dramatically during the first World War by the Austrians, who tried to feed their soldiers on dried, dehydrated foods. The sickness and debility which followed not only produced a sick army, but brought costly defeats as well.

However, the destructive effect of drying upon Vitamin A is being taken into consideration nowadays by many food processors. New methods which avoid oxidation have been developed, and many dried foods on the market have been protected against it.

Bleaching, of course, is destructive to Vitamin A. The very fact that color has disappeared announces the injury. Green celery has far more Vitamin A than bleached or white celery. Green asparagus is not only more tasty than the bleached variety—it has far more vitamin value as well. The outer green leaves of lettuce may have thirty times the Vitamin A content of the pale inner leaves.

You can understand better now why vegetable leaves which have begun to turn brown have lost a large part of their Vitamin A. Any fading or browning of color tells you unmistakably that oxidation has taken place and Vitamin A has deteriorated.

Staleness in vegetables also gradually destroys the Vitamin A. This is because of the effect of certain chemicals (enzymes) contained within the plant itself. The destruction takes place only after the plant is picked, which means that we should hurry the Vitamin A vegetables and fruits to the cook or the table as soon as we can after they are picked.

A similar enzymic process takes place in animal sources of Vitamin A through the development of rancidity. Rancid butter is a negligible source of Vitamin A, as is any leftover dish which has begun to grow rancid to any degree.

We are strongly inclined to suggest that a green vegetable cooked so that it loses its color has been mismanaged in such a way that its carotene will not readily be made into Vitamin A.

As you remember, the Vitamin A-potent carotene in vegetables is manufactured from chlorophyll. There is an average proportion of carotene to chlorophyll of about one to three and a half. In other words, the green leaf on the tree in front of your house has a proportionate amount of carotene to chlorophyll, but you won't know this until fall when the chlorophyll disappears and the leaf begins to show its yellow color.

If you cook a green vegetable so that the chlorophyll is damaged, it will turn to a bronze color—the yellow carotene pigments have now appeared. Theoretically, no harm has been done to the carotene, but practically speaking, the vegetable has been made less palatable and, too often, indigestible as well.

Many experiments have shown that even people with normal, "strong" digestions cannot readily digest this sort of badly cooked vegetable. When you remember that carotene must be converted into Vitamin A by the processes of digestion, it is not unreasonable to insist that the Vitamin A vegetables must be carefully cooked.

Our grandmothers kept their pickles and green vegetables green by cooking them in copper vessels. This added to the green color of the vegetables because the vegetable acids united with copper and thus did not destroy the chlorophyll. However, such a practice is not permissible in scientific cooking because of the drastic effect copper has on Vitamin C—which is very abundant in most green foods.

VITAMIN A DISSOLVES IN OIL

The vitamins have very individual physical characteristics. Vitamins B_1 and C, for example, dissolve readily in water. Vitamin A is distinguished by the fact that it dissolves in oil.

That is interesting for a number of reasons, particularly because the presence of some oil or fat seems necessary to convert carotene into Vitamin A efficiently. Laboratory animals on a fat-free diet appear able to assimilate only a small part of the carotene they are fed, yet they turn all of it into Vitamin A with 100 per cent efficiency when they are given a diet containing 10 per cent fat.

If you stop to think about it, you will realize that all the animal sources of Vitamin A—milk, cream, butter, liver and eggs—are well endowed with fat. Even the Vitamin A we get from sea sources comes to us in fish oils.

We recognize this association of Vitamin A with oil perhaps instinctively when we add butter to spinach, chard and other green vegetables. Broccoli deserves to be dressed with Hollandaise on this score. A salad rich in Vitamin A foods is helped by French dressing or mayonnaise. We have good reason, too, to pour cream on peaches and use a bit of butter on squash, yellow turnips, sweet potatoes and corn. All of these practices provide a fat or oil medium into which Vitamin A may dissolve.

You can take it as a good sound rule that you will always help the absorption and assimilation of Vitamin A by using a dressing containing butter or oil on any vegetable which contains the factor. This does not mean that fatty dressings should be used with a lavish hand. It requires but little fat, certainly not more than 10 per cent, to insure a better use of Vitamin A.

You who are concerned with calories and must keep your weight down need not furrow your brows now. In the first place, if you follow a well-thought-out reducing regimen, you will be amply supplied with carotene-containing vegetables. Your own body stores of fat may supply the amount needed to convert sufficient carotene into Vitamin A because body fat droplets float in the blood, and there is always a supply of fat in the liver. When you are not on a strict reducing diet, the amount of fat you can scarcely avoid in ordinary foods will keep you from Vitamin A deficiency. A pat of butter will go a long way.

These considerations, then, complete our general rules for Vitamin A management. Let us point out again that you can easily and generously fortify a diet with Vitamin A. Even a modest amount of parsley (11,000 International units per ounce) sprinkled on carrots, string beans, potatoes and other foods will put you over the top with Vitamin A for the day.

Chapter Five

THE CARE AND PRESERVATION OF VITAMIN B₁ IN COOKING

In 1898, a Dutch scientist—Christian Eijkman —discovered that people with a paralyzing disease called beriberi could be cured by eating small amounts of the outer hulls of rice. In 1911, this curative substance in rice hulls was extracted, and it was called Vitamin B.

In 1926, it became clear that more than one vitamin existed in the extract that had originally been called Vitamin B. To date, ten or eleven different factors have been isolated and the group is now called the Vitamin B complex.

For all practical purposes, in balancing your diet, you should learn to think of the Vitamin B group as a family. A carrot contains so much of the Vitamin B complex, so does a piece of meat.

Each particular vitamin in this family, when separated and analyzed, has something different to do; each provides some different health benefit. But Nature does not make our getting enough of each and every one of these a separate job. She does not produce Vitamin B_1, or any other vitamin of the B complex, singly as such, in foods. She gives us foods which contain the entire family of B vitamins in various quantities as part of the B complex.

It is necessary in the scientific work of the food chemist, or the physician who treats abnormal conditions, to deal with these separate components of the Vitamin B group. But you do not have such problems. If you see to it that you and each member of your family get enough Vitamin B_1 every day from natural foods, you will know that at the same time you have been given a corresponding amount of the Vitamin B complex. Thus, by using a variety of foods you will automatically receive enough of Vitamin B_2 or G, nicotinic acid and all the other members of the B complex, whatever their names or purposes may be.

If you cook a food so that its Vitamin B_1 is not destroyed or hurt by what you do to it, you will automatically protect and save all the vitamins in the B family. Using Vitamin B_1 as your guide, then, is by far the most practical plan to help you act and save all of the B group of vitamins in foods. Use it to save yourself confusion.

THE SELECTION OF VITAMIN B₁ FOODS

You will remember from page 14 how necessary Vitamin B_1 is to turn the starch and sugar you eat into body energy. It is an integral part of this life process, so every hour which passes means that some Vitamin B_1 is used up in your body chemistry. Yet Vitamin B_1 is not stored in your body to any great degree, so you must constantly be supplied with this vitamin.

You will find when you study the Vitamin B_1 value of foods that some cuts of meat contain an excellent amount of Vitamin B_1. You'll find that the whole grain cereals seem to be rich in this vitamin. Then, when you turn to the vegetables and fruits, it may appear that they are not very well endowed with Vitamin B_1. Offhand, you may say to yourself, "Well, gracious, the fruits and vegetables are only a fair source of Vitamin B_1."

But don't make that mistake. You're wrong if you do. Intrinsically, and for all practical purposes, the fruits and vegetables are the best sources of Vitamin B_1 in all foods! And this startling fact hinges upon the use of Vitamin B_1 in the energy chemistry of the body.

For every 100 calories of food you eat, you require 30 International units of Vitamin B_1. That is the accepted, standard figure. Your Vitamin B_1 requirements are based on the number of calories of food you take in each day. Cereals have a high calorie content; so do meats. Vegetables usually are low in calorie content.

Meats average approximately 60 International units per 100 calories. Whole grain cereals average approximately 40 International units per 100 calories.

Protective vegetables average approximately 160 International units per 100 calories.

Protective fruits average approximately 150 International units per 100 calories.

Thus, when you obtain Vitamin B_1 from vegetables and fruits, you are receiving a lavish amount of the vitamin for body requirements.

For most modern people, dinner has always been the chief meal of the day, but in 13th century England, 9 o'clock in the morning was the dinner hour; a century later, it was 10 o'clock; in Queen Elizabeth's time, it reached 11 o'clock; by the year 1700, it had moved to 2 o'clock; by 1740, 3 o'clock; then, as the industrial age with its factories and offices came into being, the accepted hours for dinner changed from 6 to 8 o'clock.

The English worker of Elizabeth's time lived on a simple diet of unrefined bread and dairy products. Beer was his drink, meat his luxury. Careful study shows that average people in bygone days received perhaps two to three times the Vitamin B_1 that we modern Americans do. But we will not munch a two-pound loaf of whole rye bread per day, or make a dinner of bread, cheese, milk and whey. We have found a tremendous variety of new foods to please our palates, many of them very poor sources of Vitamin B_1. Yet the pace of today's living burns up more of this vitamin than ever before.

Nowadays most of us eat a small breakfast from 7 to 9 A.M. and a fairly light lunch from 12 to 2. Dinner at 6 to 8, is the main meal of the day. These mealtime bells are rung by the school bus, factory bell, office routine—we have adjusted our mealtimes to demands of society, not physiology.

We can't set our dinner time back to 11 or 12 o'clock in the morning, or make it a Vitamin B_1 masterpiece, as our great-grandfathers did. We can, though, replace the simple, perhaps humdrum, "daily bread" with equivalent Vitamin B, values in foods. A bit complicated, yes, but that's the penalty for forsaking simple ways.

As it stands, you should sharpen your pencil, and wits, survey your eating habits, and if possible, plan roughly to get:

> Half your units of Vitamin B, at breakfast and lunch.
> Half your units if Vitamin B, at dinner.

VITAMIN B, AND COOKING TIME

Whatever we have said about the saving of cooking time applies particularly to foods with any significant Vitamin B, value. The precautions apply with increasing importance to restricted budgets. The less money you have to spend for foods, the more necessary to conserve Vitamin B,.

Consider carefully, when you purchase various cuts of meat, the cooking time involved and the nutritional advantages of stews, patties and meat loaves over roasts. When you are figuring your Vitamin B, menu estimates, remember always to make a probable estimate as to how much of the vitamin is lost in the cooking of a Vitamin B,-rich food. Remember, also, to estimate which members of your family require more Vitamin B, than others, and tempt them to eat enough by providing it in dishes they like.

Keep in mind all the vitamin-sparing methods of preparation for cooking. Cutting meat into little pieces will hurry the diffusion of the Vitamin B, into the juice of your stew or soup stock. Mashing beans and forcing them through a sieve or ricer will help to diffuse practically all of the Vitamin B, out of them into the soup or stock. If you cut string beans into little slivers, you will not only cook them more quickly but you will also saturate the water you cook them in with Vitamin B,—which is fine, if you see to it that the pot liquor is consumed.

Cooking beans, prunes or other foods in the water you soak them will save the water-soluble B complex.

Pastries, pies and cookies for families with restricted food budgets cannot be used as luxury tidbits. They must be selected for their nutritive value because they *can* add real Vitamin B complex contributions to the day's eating if they are made from unrefined flour—either whole wheat, rye, corn or any kind you may desire.

Whole wheat bread is an excellent source of the Vitamin B complex. Breadmaking was a laborious process for grandma, but in this day, when we really understand yeast, when the "setting of the sponge" can be avoided, and when electric mixers, temperature controlled ovens and so many other kitchen improvements are available, breadmaking at home is easy. What a wholesome revival it would be!

Homemade frozen desserts—ices, sherbets and particularly ice creams —may offer excellent Vitamin B_1 values with selected ingredients. No harm comes to Vitamin B_1 by cold.

Salads made of leftover meats, poultry or fish are excellent main course dishes in which possible B_1 sources are not further damaged by cooking the food a second time in an attempt to disguise it.

VITAMIN B₁ IS WATER-SOLUBLE

Vitamin B_1 dissolves in water even more readily than does the coloring in ground coffee. This easy diffusion makes the water in which you stew a meat, and cook or can a vegetable, a rich source of Vitamin B_1. At least 30 per cent of the Vitamin B_1 in any food will dissolve into the cooking water. If you fracture the cells of the food by cutting or crushing, leakage of Vitamin B_1 may be higher.

For this reason, you should not throw away any cooking or canning waters. Vegetables should be served in individual side dishes and the family should be instructed to eat the pot liquor which you have tastefully seasoned. Any pot liquors not served with the vegetables themselves may be used to make sauces or soups, or they may be refrigerated in a tightly closed jar and combined to make vegetable cocktails, which are rich in all water-soluble vitamins and minerals. The addition of a bouillon cube, tomato juice or other flavorful fluids to these pot liquors makes them even more delicious.

In the days before oil, gas and electric stoves, the soup stock pot was an important source of bone and blood nourishment, as well as Vitamin B_1, in American households. The stove was always going, and the soup stock pot always waiting for scraps of vegetables, potato parings and other odds and ends.

Here was a safety box for all pot liquors. It would be a valuable addition to modern apartment kitchens, for hundreds of units of Vitamin B_1 can be extracted from the food parings most housewives throw away because they cannot be used for ordinary eating.

In our test kitchen, wastage averages, from the old-fashioned house-wife's viewpoint, ran about as follows:

Broccoli, leaves and tough stalks	50 per cent
Cabbage, outer leaves and core	25 per cent
Brussels sprouts, stalks and outer leaves	25 per cent
Carrots, tops and scrapings	35 per cent
Cauliflower, leaves and stalks	50 per cent
Celery, stalks and trimmings	35 per cent
Cucumbers, parings	30 per cent
Lettuce, outer leaves	25 per cent
Green peas, pods	50 per cent
Potatoes, parings	15 per cent
Spinach, stalks and wilted leaves	15 per cent
Beets, tops and skins	25 per cent
Asparagus, butt ends	25 per cent

These do not represent waste to us, for we salvage thousands of units of Vitamins B_1, C and G, and tremendous amounts of valuable food minerals, from these sources. They become pot liquors, soup stocks and the bases for many fine dressings.

The varied selection of canned soups we now have available would be much more worth while if they were fortified with all the water-soluble Vitamin B_1 and minerals left in canning and cooking waters. That is where pot liquors belong—not down the kitchen sink drain.

Esau traded his birthright for a thick red lentil soup. Oatmeal gruel was the chief sustenance of the Greek and Roman commoners. Hippocrates spoke highly of barley broth, and prescribed it frequently. All these forms of soup furnished wonderful Vitamin B_1 values, and we can use selected soups for that excellent purpose today. The advantages of a meal planned with a substantial soup lie in the ease with which the nourishment is digested and absorbed, and the sureness with which all elements that make up the soup are eaten.

BAKING SODA AND VITAMIN B_1

Vitamin B_1 is destroyed in any alkaline medium. For that reason, adding baking soda to vegetables to preserve their color is a major nutritional crime. Adding soda to beans to soften them is equally pernicious, for these legumes are an important source of the Vitamin B complex which the soda is bound to harm or destroy.

In the baking of cakes, biscuits and breads, the batter or dough is usually lightened (leavened) by:

(1) Fermentation (yeast)
(2) Chemicals (baking soda or powders)

Either method produces carbon dioxide gas which lightens and makes spongy the flour mixture. At one time, the yeast method (which is wholesome and adds the Vitamin B complex) was the only method in use. Then when chemists got busy with the problem, the use of baking soda and baking powders began. Such chemicals are easier for the housewife to use, but they are destructive to Vitamin B_1. In flour mixtures where a proportionately large amount of baking soda or powder is used, you can reckon that most of the Vitamin B_1 has been destroyed. See page 83 for a fuller discussion of this problem.

A food like hominy, which is produced by adding lye to corn, is a double abomination from the vitamin viewpoint.

It is even of concern that you treat the water you use in cooking, if it happens to be of the decidedly alkaline type. You are bound to lessen the Vitamin B_1 value of any food you cook in such water, and an investment in a water modifier would be worth while.

By the same token, wherever it is practicable, the addition of a drop or two of lemon juice or vinegar to any food you cook will help it to hold on to its Vitamin B_1.

All vegetables contain acids (volatile) which pass easily into the air in the presence of heat. When you drop a vegetable into hot water, a good deal of the volatile acid content escapes in the first few whiffs of steam that arise. If you are cooking a vegetable to conserve its color, you may be glad to get rid of the volatile acids, but if trying to conserve Vitamin B_1, you want to hang on to these acids. For that reasons, we will sometimes suggest, particularly in the cooking of dried beans, that you keep the pot tightly covered from the moment cooking begins until the beans are finished.

THE REFINING OF GRAINS AND CEREALS

Nature placed a generous portion of the Vitamin B complex in grains and cereals. The Vitamin B_1 they contain helps to transform their starch into body energy, and the Vitamin B_1-calorie ratio is adequately maintained by the fine B complex value if the grains and cereals are in their natural state. However, we have upset that picture by the many processes of refinement in use today.

FLOURS

Wheat and rye are ground and crushed to make our most commonly used flours. In olden days this was accomplished by grinding the grain between stones and, generally speaking, the flour was used in its entire state. But for about seventy-five years, roller mill processes have been in use. This means that the grain passes from one roller to another to be more finely pulverized and sifted as it progresses. The sifting finally removes all the bran, the germ and a good part of the protein, leaving a highly refined white flour. Because of public demand, even this is usually bleached to make it whiter.

Residues from the different stages of rolling are blended to make various grades of flour, such as bread ("family"), pastry or cake types. Each blend has characteristics which adapt it to a special purpose. Pastry flour makes good pie crust because it is softer. Cake flours are very fine and velvety; hence make a better cake.

The point is that these qualities are concerned only with the adaptability of the flour to baking techniques—the vitamin value of the product is entirely disregarded. When the bran, middlings and germ are removed from grains, the Vitamin B complex is removed in exact proportion.

But the fact that white bread is a pauper in the Vitamin B complex isn't its greatest evil. What is worse is that the slices of white bread you eat actually steal Vitamin B_1 from other foods to complete their starch chemistry in the body. That is why the vitamin-wise person will demand whole grain products and use whole grain flour whenever feasible.

By a recent Federal ruling, the terms whole wheat, Graham and entire wheat flour must henceforth by applied only to products made of the whole wheat kernel, with nothing removed.

For those people who cannot tolerate whole wheat or rye, new processes of milling have produced:

(1) A whole wheat flour with the bran very finely divided.
(2) A flour in which the germ has not been removed.

Also wheat germ may be purchased in various forms, and added to cakes, cookies, biscuits and quick breads to fortify them with the Vitamin B complex. If baking powders are not used, a fine Vitamin B potency can be assured.

Rice and potato flours are pure starch, adding no vitamin value to breads although they help to vary flavors.

CEREALS

When the germ is removed, cereals or grains have good keeping qualities and can be stored or held in reserve. This fact is what led to the development of clever and ever more clever methods of refinement. Man did not suddenly rise up and demand refined cereals—he liked them in their natural state, and, generally speaking, still does. But they grew rancid and spoiled in storage. At one time, this characteristic may even have led to famines—it certainly prevented the development of milling and baking industries such as we know today. However, modern packaging, milling and distributing methods could help to replace many of the refined cereal products on the market with the infinitely more valuable whole grain types.

Cereals are an economical source of energy. In addition they are a fine source of the Vitamin B complex if they are not refined. They are even an important source of protein, and when used with milk represent a good all-around nourishment.

There are so many varieties of breakfast food cereal preparations on the market that they cannot adequately be discussed. In general, their vitamin worth depends upon the kind of grain used, the part used, and the method of milling and preparation.

Suffice it to say, only whole grain products should be used. Butter on hot cereal will add Vitamin A; milk, substantial protein, mineral and vitamin values. Cooking methods, of course, depend upon the type of cereal used and the manner in which it has been milled.

It is well to remember that ready-to-eat cereals have already been processed and cooked at the factory. Read the labels of such cereals carefully to check on their vitamin values.

Spaghetti, macaroni and similar pastes are cereal in origin because they are made from a special high-gluten wheat called durum. Fortunately, the bland taste of these products usually calls for the addition of tomatoes, cheese and other valuable vitamin foods.

THE CASE FOR WHOLE GRAIN CEREALS AND BREADS

Today, some familiar arguments against the use of these foods are, "People no longer depend upon cereals for their sustenance," and, "Bread is no longer the staff of life." Because we moderns eat a variety of foods, certain individuals seem to believe that it really doesn't make any difference if the Vitamin B$_1$ is taken from refined cereals and grains.

All such statements and beliefs are false and misleading, for cereals and bread still form a considerable part of most American diets, and there is no reason why these foods should not be stellar sources of the greatly needed Vitamin B complex.

As we have seen, it is necessary to protect every possible source of this vitamin if we are to obtain as much as we need of it every day. There are no common foods outstandingly rich in the B complex, and the amount which you should receive each day may prove difficult to get. Thus, when a fifth or a sixth of the food budget goes for breads, cereals, pastes and such like, the loss of even a little Vitamin B complex from these sources becomes a matter for concern.

In most families with restricted budgets, cereal foods—because of their "filling power"—are a most important item of diet. Here the Vitamin B loss through refinement borders on tragedy. Such people, least of all, can afford the cost of sickness or vitamin concentrates.

Whole wheat flour contains 49 International units of Vitamin B$_1$ per ounce; white flour, 8. Whole wheat bread has 27; white bread, 4. Whole rice has 32; white rice, 2.

And so we could go through the whole list of cereal products, pointing out the tremendous Vitamin B$_1$ difference between the refined and the whole grain products. In every instance, the difference will be proportionately the same.

The same story holds for all the cereals. You will certainly come to the sensible conclusion that you cannot afford to use the refined types, for you need all the Vitamin B$_1$ you can get!

Chapter Six

VITAMIN C

Vitamin C is technically called ascorbic acid. It is not stored in seeds, as is Vitamin B₁, but develops in plants as soon as they germinate and begin to grow. Put any seeds into waters in a warm, moist place, and from the minute they start to sprout, they contain Vitamin C.

You amateur gardeners can now understand why soaking flower seeds in water for twenty-four hours before planting them spurs their growth so tremendously. You start the production of Vitamin C when you start germination. In turn, the Vitamin C spurs growth. If there ever was a Jack and his bean stalk, that nursery-tale bean must have been a veritable bomb of Vitamin C.

The vitamin occurs, then, in *growing* plants. Grains, cereals and nuts are not likely sources of Vitamin C; neither are eggs, milk (except human), cheese or meats. These foods have reached their growth and development, and whatever Vitamin C they contain is purely incidental.

Vitamin C is a powerful stimulus to the growth of any aggregation of living cells. That is why it is so necessary in large amounts for growing children and expectant or nursing mothers.

The relationship of Vitamin C to the growth of living tissues explains why fruits develop more Vitamin C as they ripen. For example, if you do not allow bananas to ripen fully, you may fail to get 30 or 40 per cent of the Vitamin C value they were capable of developing. Never refrigerate bananas.

An orange picked before it is fully ripe may have only 60 or 70 per cent of the Vitamin C value it would have contained a day later. Even the last few hours of ripening make a difference.

By following this same trail carefully, we find that all leafy vegetables are richest in Vitamin C during their early stages of growth. Young spinach, for example, has far more Vitamin C than old spinach; a young, tender head of cabbage, far more than an old head; young tender leaves of kale, 30, 40 or 50 per cent more than old kale.

When the kernels of corn are ripening, they have a good Vitamin C content. The nearer the growth is to completion, the less Vitamin C the kernels will have. This holds for peas, and all forms of beans. Likewise, a new potato has more Vitamin C than an old one. Remember this point carefully: Vitamin C gradually diminishes in vegetables once they reach maturity, or are cut from the growing plant. Its job—that of promoting growth—has been done.

VITAMIN C IS WATER-SOLUBLE

Vitamin C, like Vitamin B_1, is water-soluble. It must circulate in the sap of plants; it has to reach every cell in the living structure it serves. As a result, it is intimately associated with the juices and juiciness of a fruit or vegetable.

You know by experience that a very ripe orange will be juicier than an immature orange. It will also have a higher Vitamin C content. We just noted that young spinach, cabbage, beet greens, kale, lettuce, etc., contain more Vitamin C than the more mature leaves. They are not so dry. And the same thing is true of corn, peas and all kinds of beans. As these foods mature, they grow drier—and contain less Vitamin C.

The juiciness of fruits advertises their Vitamin C worth. Woody, pulpy, dried-out oranges, lemons and limes have less Vitamin C than plump, juicy ones.

Whatever we have already said in our remarks on Vitamin B_1 about saving pot liquors, cooking waters and canning liquids holds for Vitamin C as well. This important fact bears constant repeating.

When you are cooking a fruit or vegetable rich in Vitamin C, you must give thought to the possibility of using the cooking water as a Vitamin C source. This may require a little different treatment and care than that indicated for Vitamin B_1, because Vitamin C is even more sensitive to heat, more liable to destruction by exposure to air, by staleness and delay in using, than Vitamin B_1.

If it is at all possible to use cabbage water or potato water at once as a sauce or as an addition to a vegetable cocktail, do so. When the Vitamin C content of a pot liquor is not impressive, save it for soup stock to salvage the Vitamin B_1.

Pot liquors rich in Vitamin C to be used immediately:	*Pot liquors which need not be used for Vitamin C:*
beet greens	asparagus
broccoli	bean (all varieties)
brussels sprouts	carrot
cabbage	cauliflower
kale	parsnip
kohlrabi	pea
mustard greens	squash
potato	
spinach	
tomato	
turnip greens	

Of all the properties of Vitamin C, its solubility in water is most significant to the vitamin cook. This quality is far from being the disadvantage some nutritionists consider it. It is true that most American housewives throw much of the Vitamin C they buy down the kitchen sink—but that is because they discard the water in which Vitamin C-rich foods have been cooked or canned.

On the other hand, the informed housewife, who is aware of nutritional values, can turn the solubility of Vitamin C to many an advantage, as you will find when you study our recipes.

We discussed the saving of the 30 to 50 per cent vegetable residue wastage from the economy viewpoint. Considered in terms of Vitamin C salvage, some of these vegetable residues will provide, when prepared as sauces or pot liquors, as much Vitamin C as the average housewife gets from the vegetables she cooks.

EXPOSURE TO AIR HURTS VITAMIN C

When Vitamin C is exposed to air, it is destroyed by oxidation, which is the chemical equivalent of rusting. The skin of a fruit or vegetable protects its Vitamin C content from such destruction. Therefore, if you shred cabbage or dice apples or do anything which breaks or cuts the protective covering of vegetables or fruits, you at once begin the oxidation of Vitamin C.

That is why you must cook your shredded vegetables as quickly as possible, and protect them from air. Heat and light increase oxidation; therefore, allowing your fruits and vegetables to take quick refuge in covered vessels in the refrigerator helps save Vitamin C tremendously.

The common practice of dicing or slicing vegetables, and allowing them to stand for hours before cooking, greatly damages the Vitamin C. A vegetable of any Vitamin C worth at all should not be given such treatment.

If you allow tomato juice, or any other juice containing Vitamin C, to stand in a room in an open vessel, the Vitamin C will rapidly be destroyed by oxidation. This is an outstanding example of the disregard of Vitamin C conservation.

Some vegetables and fruits contain a special oxidizing enzyme which has a good purpose in plant chemistry but complicates the task of the housewife who wants to preserve Vitamin C. Cabbage and apples are good examples of this type of food.

Oranges, grapefruit and limes do not contain the oxidizing enzyme. Their Vitamin C keeps comparatively well on exposure. Potatoes are free of the enzyme, too, so their Vitamin C oxidizes very slowly.

Under any circumstances, the action of the enzyme is inhibited by cold and halted by heat. Thus, you see again the importance of refrigerating Vitamin C foods until they are used. And when you understand that heat/will also halt this action, you will appreciate why we say in our recipes that vegetables containing Vitamin C should be dropped quickly into boiling, bubbly water when they are cooked.

For this reason, among others, our technique of cooking the valuable Vitamin C-rich vegetables calls for the use of considerably more water than actual quick-cooking requires. Spinach cooked in a half-inch of boiling water only five minutes will have even more Vitamin C than spinach cooked without water for only three minutes. There is comparatively little exposure to air—and there is immediate contact with heat.

CHEMICALS AND VITAMIN C

The action of soda and other alkalies is even more destructive to Vitamin C than to Vitamin B$_1$. Even a slightly alkaline water will tend to destroy Vitamin C too rapidly. Therefore, we often add a few drops of lemon juice or vinegar to the better Vitamin C foods to slow up such destruction. Vitamin C is always protected to some extent when heated with natural acids such as tomato, pineapple and rhubarb.

In addition, alkali added to cooking water breaks up the vegetable cellulose and tends to produce a mushy, soft texture. On the other hand, acids help to retain firmness of texture.

Certain copper compounds completely destroy Vitamin C. Therefore, any pot made of copper or a copper alloy should not be used to cook valuable Vitamin C foods. Naturally, this rule applies only when the copper is in a position to come in direct contact with the foods. Pans made of other metals, with a heating base of copper (for better heat conduction) are excellent.

The oxidation menace to Vitamin C explains why many home-canned foods may be inferior sources of Vitamin C. The cold-pack methods avoid this danger, but you probably do not have the facilities to prevent oxidation which a canning company can command.

As a matter of fact, a great many commercially canned fruit juices are now made by a process entirely excluding oxygen. Such a method is a number one asset to Vitamin C protection.

FORTIFYING RECIPES WITH VITAMIN C

The same plans of deliberate fortification we outlined for Vitamin A may be followed in principle with Vitamin C foods. Green and red peppers contain more than 1,350 International units of Vitamin C per ounce. Chopped green peppers cooked with corn will not only add to the taste of the dish—they will also change it from a poor to a good source of Vitamin C.

Green peppers will likewise add liberal quantities of Vitamin C to any salad or coleslaw, and together with tomatoes, can supply interest —and much Vitamin C—to bland-tasting vegetables such as the various types of summer squash, or the familiar eggplant.

Parsley averages 1,050 International units of Vitamin C to the ounce. Thus, parsley potatoes or parsley carrots are doubly endowed with vitamin virtues.

Lemon juice, with 360 International units of Vitamin C to the ounce, is our choice for preparing salad dressings. It has all of the zip of vinegar, besides fortifying the dish it dresses with valuable Vitamin C. In addition, lemon juice not only gives character to a fish dish— it also adds Vitamin C. Lime juice is only slightly less serviceable. Use them both as often as you can.

As you become familiar with the Vitamin C-rich vegetables and fruits, attractive and delicious combinations of foods will suggest themselves. There is really no good nutritional reason for serving individual vegetables. alone. We can take a valuable lesson from the Chinese, whose ancient civilization has taught them that vegetables should be mixed. They should indeed, and Nature's wide variety of vegetables is probably a broad hint to this effect.

SOME PLEASING POSSIBILITIES

A great many factors influence the Vitamin C content of foods. One of these is the heredity of plants. A Baldwin apple, for example, will have far more Vitamin C than a Delicious or a McIntosh. What's more, a Baldwin with more Vitamin C will have a better taste than a Baldwin with less. Thus, as we begin to buy our apples on a vitamin basis farmers will undoubtedly try to supply the demand.

The same story holds for many other foods and for each vitamin. In the future, undoubtedly, strains of various foods will be developed, just as strains of cattle, chickens or hogs have been. Americans like broilers, and an entirely new and different strain of chickens had to be developed to supply this demand. They had to be raised differently, fed differently, treated differently. Similarly, when it becomes known that the beefsteak type of tomato has much more Vitamin A and C value than the scrubby little wart tomato, housewives will probably refuse to buy the inferior types of foods.

In brief, better strains of food plants will be developed because they are better nutritional bargains, they taste better and look better. Even today, canners and quick-freezing food packers are distributing seeds to farmers, and growing vegetables by contract. It pays them to do so in many ways.

The kind of soil in which a food is grown helps greatly to determine its vitamin content. Even now, methods of soil development and fertilization are being developed which endow the foods grown in such soil with much more Vitamin C. And even if you know nothing about vitamins, you can understand that foods grown in proper soil taste better, look better and are more disease-resistant.

You have been told that unwilted vegetables have more Vitamin A than the fading ones; tender cabbage, more Vitamin C than the tough type.

All these vitamin comparisons are even more marked by taste. Isn't a bright green, tender leaf of spinach infinitely better tasting than an acrid old tough leaf of this green? Isn't coleslaw made from tender cabbage a treat, and a concoction made from a tough old head an abomination?

These and many other vitamin considerations demonstrate clearly that the science of eating and cooking will eventually lead to the highest expression of the art of cooking and selecting foods. For *taste* is the appeal Nature uses to lure us into eating vitamins!

And so we have charted our course for Vitamin Cooking—this new science, which influences our health and well-being so profoundly! Each week and month that passes brings new discovery and progress in the study of the vitamins. It is our hope that you will keep abreast of this science for better living, for each advance will help to free you from the miseries of ill health and to win you the pleasures of longer, healthier years of life.

When you know what foods can do for you and to you, your kitchen becomes a wondrous laboratory of life. You will take pride in the responsibilities that are yours; you will thrill over the health and well-being your thoughtfulness, skill and judgment bring to your family through foods—through diet knowledge, learned and applied!

Chapter Seven

MEASUREMENTS
AND COOKERY TERMS

Our recipes are designed to provide 6 medium-sized servings. Where there are 3 or 4 in the family, there will be second helpings, and if there are only 2 in the family, most of the recipes may be halved. Each recipe has been tested to insure proper preparation of materials and correct handling of them to insure utmost preservation of vitamin and mineral contents, and to make the dish digestible and attractive. No changes need be made in the proportions of shortening, flour, baking powder or liquid. The only changes permissible would be more, less or contrasting seasonings. If use of a certain ingredient is optional or substitution of a similar choice is possible, recipe so states. In preparing ingredients, use standard measuring cups and measuring spoons and measure accurately. In recipes specifying dry ingredients, liquids and fats, measure in the order given, thereby using only one cup. Always use a wet cup or spoon for measuring fats, molasses and syrups to avoid need for scraping and to prevent sticking. The same spoon may be used for measuring dry ingredients if dark ones such as cocoa or spices are measured last.

To Measure Dry Ingredients: Before actual measuring, sift flour, and powdered and confectioners' sugar; loosen soda, baking powder and mustard in container by stirring; and break up lumps in salt or brown sugar. To measure granulated sugar or flour, fill cup to desired level with tablespoon and do not pack or shake. Pack brown

67

sugar firmly into cup. To measure by tablespoon or teaspoon, place spoon in ingredient, fill, and level with straight edge of knife. To measure half-spoonfuls, divide lengthwise of spoon with knife. To measure quarters, divide halves crosswise; crosswise again for eighths. Less than one-eighth is considered a dash or a few grains.

To Measure Liquids:

Use measuring spoon of size specified. A spoonful is all the spoon will hold. Fill cup to level indicated.

To Measure Fats:

Butter or other fats should be soft enough to pack for accurate measurement. Pack solidly into wet cup or spoon and level with knife. If part of a cupful is specified, fill cup with enough water to complete a cupful, put in fat by spoonfuls until cup is full (water rising to the 1 cup level) then pour off water. For example, to measure 2/3 cup shortening, fill cup 1/3 full of water, add shortening by spoonfuls until water in cup rises to 1 cup level, then pour off water. The 1-pound cartons of butter or fat may be measured without packing into a cup as the required amount may be easily marked off. Quarter-pound prints of butter are still more convenient for measuring, as ¼-pound print equals ½ cup or 8 tablespoons, and 2 tablespoons (1 ounce) equal ¼ of ¼-pound print.

Equivalent Measures

A dash (or few grains)	Less than ⅛ teaspoon
3 teaspoons	1 tablespoon
4 tablespoons	¼ cup
5 1/3 tablespoons	1/3 cup
2 cups	1 pint
2 pints	1 quart
4 quarts	1 gallon
8 quarts	1 peck
4 pecks	1 bushel
1 fluid ounce	2 tablespoons
16 ounces (dry measure)	1 pound

Cooking Temperatures

Simmering (water)	180° F.
Boiling (water)	212° F.
Soft-ball stage (frostings, etc.)	234° F.

Very slow oven	250° F.
Slow oven	275° to 325° F.
Moderate oven	350° to 375° F.
Moderately hot oven	400° to 425° F.
Hot oven	450° to 475° F.
Very hot oven	500° to 550° F.

CONTENTS OF THE MORE COMMONLY USED CONTAINERS OF CANNED FOODS

Size of Can	Contents
8 ounce	1 cup
Buffet or picnic	1¼ cups
No. 1	2 cups
No. 2	2½ cups
No. 2½	3½ cups
No. 3	4 cups
No. 10	13 cups

PREPARATION AND COOKERY TERMS

Bake—To cook in an oven. This term applies to all oven-cooked foods except meats, which are known as roasts when baked.

Baste—To pour small amounts of liquids or melted fat over food while cooking. This term is usually applied to oven-cooked foods such as roast meats or poultry or baked fish. Purpose is to prevent burning or add flavor.

Beat—To whip with spoon, fork, wire whisk, rotary or electric beater to enclose air by turning ingredients over and over, continually bringing contents at bottom of bowl to the top.

Blanch—To drop into boiling water just long enough to loosen skins as in the case of peeling tomatoes or removing skins of almonds.

Boil—To cook in a liquid at a temperature of 212° F. at sea level. The liquid should bubble actively during the time suggested and just enough heat should be used to keep the liquid in this state, unless rapid boiling is specified in the recipe. Slowly boiling water is just as effective as rapidly boiling liquid, because of heat loss which occurs through the escape of steam when liquids boil rapidly.

Braise—To cook tightly covered in a small quantity of liquid at a low temperature, either over direct heat on top of stove or in the oven. Meat is generally seared (browned) before braising to prevent escape of too much juice in the gravy and to give a richer color and flavor to both meat and gravy. When vegetables are cooked with meat which is to be braised, they are usually sautéed before combining with the meat. This is to shorten their cooking time and enhance their flavor.

Broil or *Grill*—To cook under, over, or in front of direct heat by gas, electricity or live coals. Place food on a greased broiling rack or in a greased broiler. During first part of cooking time, turn to sear both sides to prevent escape of juices. Use broad spatula or pancake turner for turning to prevent loss of juices by piercing with a fork.

Chop—To cut in small pieces with sharp knife or chopper.

Cream—To blend together shortening and sugar, or to soften fat by working or pressing it with wooden spoon in round-bottomed bowl or using an electric beater until smooth and creamy and free of lumps. This creaming process will be much easier when shortening stands at room temperature until slightly softened.

Crumbs—Soft bread crumbs are prepared from bread at least 24 hours old but not dry. It may be rubbed against a coarse grater or crumbled with the fingers. Dry bread crumbs may be prepared by grinding in a food chopper, or rolling with a rolling pin, any dry bread, crackers or corn flakes. Should a very fine crumb be desired, sift crumbs through a coarse sieve.

Cut in Shortening—A mixing process used to blend cold shortening with flour. This is accomplished by cutting the fat into the flour with a knife, two knives, or a pastry blender, until the fat is distributed throughout the flour in as small pieces as desired. When pieces of certain size are required, recipe will so state, as in the case of "fine as cornmeal" or "the size of navy beans."

Dice—To cut vegetables such as onions and potatoes into small squares. Pare, remove 1 slice, and cut across in both directions, making ⅛-inch squares, being careful not to cut entirely through or too deep into the vegetable. Hold firmly on cutting board and slice. Celery, rhubarb, and asparagus may be diced by holding several stalks together and cutting with a sharp knife into desired pieces.

Dot—To scatter bits, such as butter, over surface of food to be cooked.

Eggs, slightly beaten—Whole eggs beaten until well blended and slightly thickened. The beating of eggs, whole or separately, may be done with a steel fork, rotary beater or electric whipper. The last two are most successful for stiffly beaten eggs.

Egg Whites, stiffly beaten—Egg whites beaten until they will stand in peaks, but still remain moist and shiny.

Egg Whites, slightly beaten—Egg whites beaten just until foamy.

Egg Yolks, well beaten—Egg yolks beaten until thick and creamy.

Fold In—A mixing process whereby ingredients are blended by a cutting and folding motion to prevent the escape of air or gas bubbles that have already been introduced into either part of the mixture. This process is accomplished by two definite motions with a wooden mixing spoon; cutting, which is a repeated downward motion, and folding, which is using the bowl of the spoon to touch the bottom of the dish each time it carefully turns the mixture over and over until the mixing is complete. Whipped cream, beaten egg whites, sugar or flour, etc., are the more common ingredients used in this process.

Fillet—A piece of fish or meat which has had the bone removed.

Garnish—To add an accessory to a food when served for additional flavor or more appetizing appearance.

Grate—To rub or press against a grater—a utensil with a rough surface.

Knead—A mixing process applied to dough when more flour is added to a mixture than can be either stirred or beaten into it. Press dough firmly with palms of hands and fold once, repeating this motion and turning between foldings until dough is smooth and even in consistency. Often in addition to kneading, bread dough is dropped from a height to break the bubbles, allowing the gas caused by fermentation to escape. In kneading any type dough, do not use additional flour unless dough sticks to the board, in which case add only as much as needed.

Lard—To insert strips of fat in surface of meat with larding needle or skewers, or to cover surface of meat with strips of fat.

Marinate—To cover with French dressing for a period of time.

Mince—To chop very fine with a chopper or dice very fine as in the case of an onion. (See *Dice*.) Parsley, watercress or mint should be washed thoroughly and dried on a towel before mincing. Another method for cutting these greens, if fine mincing is not required, is to hold sprigs firmly between thumb and fingers, and cut with sharp knife on cutting board or use kitchen scissors.

Pan-broil—To cook bacon or meat such as pork chops in dry, hot skillet, pouring off fat as it cooks out of meat.

Parboil—To cook in slowly boiling water until food is partially cooked.

Pare—To remove skin or rind by cutting off with a knife.

Peel—To remove skin or rind by pulling or rubbing off. To start free skin by making a small incision with point of knife. To peel tomatoes more easily, blanch them first.

Poach—To cook in hot liquid below the boiling point.

Pot Liquors—The liquid in which vegetables have been cooked.

Purée—To force or press food through a coarse sieve.

Rice—To force or press food through a ricer.

Roast—To cook by dry heat in an oven.

Sauté—To cook in a small amount of fat in a pan over direct heat. To prevent absorption of fat, use wooden spoon or steel fork to keep moving food from side to side of pan. "Sauter" is the French word meaning "to jump," and French cooks usually shake the pan backward and forward constantly, thus preventing the food from remaining in one spot.

Scald—To heat liquid, usually milk, until hot but definitely not boiling. Milk scalds at 196° F., and the best way to scald milk is to heat covered in a double boiler over boiling water until milk around edge of pan has a bead-like appearance and is lukewarm to the touch when a small amount is dropped on the wrist.

Score—To make shallow lengthwise and crosswise cuts across surface (usually of meat) with a sharp knife.

Sear—To brown meat by applying intense heat.

Shortening—Any cooking fat.

Simmer—To cook in liquid just below the boiling point, between 185° F. and 210° F. There should appear only an occasional bubble which slowly rises to the surface.

Skewer—To fasten poultry or meat with thin wooden or metal pins. Small pieces of meat, fish or vegetables are often broiled on a metal skewer.

Steam—To cook over or surrounded by steam or over boiling water in a double boiler.

Stew—To cook in a small amount of water.

Stock—The liquid in which poultry, meat or fish has been cooked.

HOW TO READ THE CHARTS
ON THE FOLLOWING PAGES

The main charts at the beginning of each section represent a dish typical of the food discussed. It indicates how many vitamins, minerals, calories and proteins are contained in one portion of that recipe.

The smaller vitamin chart at the beginning of a recipe indicates only the vitamins contained in one portion of that recipe.

The height or length of the black bar in each chart shows how much of each nutrient you are getting from one portion of that recipe in relation to your daily need.

Abbreviations used are as follows

I.U.—International units   cal.—calories
mgs.—milligrams   gms.—grams
calc.—calcium   phos.—phosphorus
                prot.—protein

Where space limitations prevent the use of charts, the vitamin values are listed under the recipe title.

BEVERAGES

This Chart Gives Approximate Food Values for ORANGE JUICE.
For Vitamin Values of Other Beverages, See Recipes.

	VITAMINS	A	B	C	G	MINERALS	CALC.	PHOS.	IRON	ANALYSIS	CAL.	PROT.
1 PORTION CONTAINS APPROXIMATELY		447 I.U.	57 I.U.	1643 I.U.	.02 MGS.		34 MGS.	23 MGS.	.4 MGS.		68 CAL.	GMS.
BLACK PART OF COLUMN SHOWS HOW MUCH OF DAILY NEED IS SUPPLIED BY ONE PORTION												
AVERAGE DAILY NEED		5000 I.U.	600 I.U.	1500 I.U.	2.7 MGS.		800 MGS.	1320 MGS.	12 MGS.		2000-3000	70 GMS.

Water is second only to oxygen in importance to the welfare of the body. For that reason, beverages are an essential part of everyone's daily diet. In addition, Nature has contrived to make it easy and pleasant for us to derive quantities of vitamins from the fluids we drink, such as milk, fruit juices, etc.

THE VITAMIN C BEVERAGES

Six-ounce portions will yield the following units of Vitamin C:

Fresh Orange Juice	1714 International units
Fresh Grapefruit Juice	1371 International units
Canned Grapefruit Juice	1080 International units
Canned Tomato Juice	900 International units
Fresh Pineapple Juice	857 International units
Fresh Lemonade	368 International units
Canned Pineapple Juice	360 International units
Fresh Limeade	191 International units

ORANGE JUICE: In large measure, you can judge the nutritional value of orange juice by its sweetness and natural color. When you squeeze pale, acrid-tasting juice from an orange, you are not getting much more than a citric acid—and possible heartburn. It is unpleasant to drink—and you had better look elsewhere for Vitamin C.

74

Nowadays, canned orange juice is likely to offer a better nutritional bargain than inferior fresh orange juice, because modern methods of canning protect vitamin quality. Oranges, as a general rule, are selected for canning at the peak of their ripeness, and processed within a matter of hours. It is worth while to sample several brands to find the most palatable. Usually canned orange juice is standardized as to citric acid content.

Any so-called "canny" taste may be eliminated by exposing canned juice to the open air for fifteen or twenty minutes before using. Taste may be further improved by mixing a small quantity of good fresh citrus fruit juice with the canned product. A combination of canned orange juice and fresh grape-fruit juice is excellent.

Always use both fresh and canned orange juice as soon as possible after it has been squeezed or poured from can. If storing is necessary, place juice in tightly covered jar in refrigerator.

In buying oranges, or any other citrus fruit, select by weight rather than size. The fruit will feel heavy and be plump if it is juicy. Oranges which are light for their size usually have thick skins or pulpy interiors.

If at all possible financially, try to provide no less than 1,000 International units of Vitamin C (two-thirds of the day's requirement) in your breakfast fruit beverage or fruit. Approximately 1,000 International units of Vitamin C are contained in the following orange juice beverages:

$3\frac{1}{2}$ ounces tree-ripened orange juice
4 ounces Grade A canned orange juice
$3\frac{3}{4}$ ounces an equal mixture of above
6 ounces average "color-added" orange juice
5 ounces equal mixture canned and "color-added" juices

LEMON JUICE: Although not adapted for use undiluted and unsweetened in the way orange juice is, lemon juice is extremely valuable in plain lemonade, in combination fruit juice punches, and for adding to vegetables (especially greens), sauces, soups and salad dressings. Use lemon juice with any dish it will improve, and treat it with respect as a remedy of value in any sickness characterized by fever. Of even higher Vitamin C content than orange juice, it is still potent when diluted.

In most of the recipes in this book which call for lemon juice, the directions specify that the juice be added just before the sauce, soup or dressing is served. This precaution improves flavor, and protects Vitamin C from destruction by cooking and long exposure to air. Use lemon wedges or lemon juice as soon as possible after cutting or squeezing.

LEMONADE

INGREDIENTS:
  juice of 1 lemon
  1 cup cold water

  sugar syrup or honey to taste

DIRECTIONS: Combine juice and water. Sweeten to taste and serve cold. (Use boiling water for hot lemonade.) Yield: 1 serving.

Approximately 1,000 International units of Vitamin C are contained in the following lemon juice beverages:

- 1½ tablespoons lemon juice (juice of ½ lemon)—276 I.U.—and 4⅞ ounces grapefruit juice—800 I.U.

- 1½ tablespoons lemon juice (juice of ½ lemon)—276 I.U.—and 14 ounces canned pineapple juice—800 I.U.

- 1½ tablespoons lemon juice (juice of ½ lemon)—276 I.U.—and 5 ounces canned tomato juice—724 I.U.

LIME JUICE: Limes contain considerably less Vitamin C than lemons but are still an eminently worthwhile source. Besides, they contain at least one-third more fruit acids, which makes them more sour. Thus, they are adapted to making "ades," non-alcoholic drinks and salad dressings when an aromatic, sour flavor is desired, and for tartness yielded are less expensive than lemons.

LIMEADE

INGREDIENTS:
  juice of ½ lime
  juice of ½ lemon

  1 cup cold water
  sugar syrup or honey to taste

DIRECTIONS: Combine juices and water and sweeten to taste. Garnish with mint or maraschino cherry. Yield: 1 serving.

Approximately 1,000 International units of Vitamin C are contained in the following lime juice beverages:

- 1½ tablespoons lime juice (juice of 1 lime)—137 I.U.—and 6 ounces canned tomato juice—863 I.U.

- 1½ tablespoons lime juice (juice of 1 lime)—137 I.U.—and 30 ounces apple juice—863 I.U.

GRAPEFRUIT JUICE: The grapefruit is not a cross between lemons and oranges, as some people believe. It is a true citrus fruit in its own right, and from the economy viewpoint, it is often the best source of Vitamin C among fruits.

A half-grapefruit makes a splendid first course for any meal, and it is a wise selection as a dessert for any heavy or rich meal. The grapefruit is "tops" for people who wish to stay slim. Many people who do not tolerate orange juice well may drink grapefruit juice without fear of a stomach upset. Diluted grapefruit juice much more preferable for babies than the sharp acids of inferior orange juice.

All citrus fruit juices are converted by body chemistry into acid-neutralizing carbonate salts which swell the body's alkaline reserves. There is no better way to alkalinize than with grapefruit juice.

Approximately 1,000 International units of Vitamin C are contained in the following grapefruit juice beverages:

4⅘ ounces fresh grapefruit juice
5⅙ ounces canned grapefruit juice
3½ ounces canned grapefruit juice—600 I.U.—and 1⅘ ounces fresh orange juice—400 I.U.
4½ ounces canned grapefruit juice—771 I.U.—and 4½ ounces canned pineapple juice—257 I.U.

PINEAPPLE JUICE: For centuries, tropical peoples used the fruit we now call pineapple in dozens of ways medicinally. It was an unfailing worm remedy for their children. It healed common sore throat, and helped to allay fever.

Modern science has demonstrated why fresh pineapple possesses these virtues. The fruit not only has a generous quantity of Vitamin C, but in addition it contains, when fresh, a chemical called bromelin, which is a powerful digestant.

Bromelin actually destroys many types of intestinal parasites, yet it is entirely agreeable to the human body. It also helps in the digestion of protein (egg, cheese and meat) dishes. For this reason, fresh pineapple cannot be used in gelatin, which is a protein substance.

Fresh or canned unsweetened pineapple juice is of especial service to sufferers from gastric ulcers. Many of these individuals cannot tolerate orange juice or grapefruit juice, and since they need extra quantities of Vitamin C to help heal their eroded tissues, pineapple juice becomes doubly important to them.

Approximately 1,000 International units of Vitamin C are contained in the following pineapple juice beverages:

    7 ounces fresh pineapple juice
17½ ounces canned pineapple juice
16⅙ ounces canned pineapple juice—931 I.U.—and ¾ tablespoon lime juice (juice of ½ lime)—69 I.U.

TOMATO JUICE: Since most of the tomato juice now consumed in this country is bought in cans, it is comforting to know that this popular beverage retains most of its natural vitamin content. The canning methods of earlier days did destroy much Vitamin C, but the canning industry has since become extremely vitamin-conscious, and canned tomato juice today is a particularly valuable source of vitamins. Besides, it is inexpensive. The housewife on a food budget will find tomato juice provides impressive quantities of vitamins and other nutritive essentials per penny spent.

For reducers, tomato juice is an escape from the ever-inviting but fattening hors d'oeuvres or cream soups which introduce so many American meals. As a between-meal beverage for children, or for adults with that "letdown feeling," the refreshing qualities of tomato juice are unequalled. In all, it is a bright red reminder that foods are man's real medicines.

Approximately 1,000 International units of Vitamin C are contained in the following tomato juice beverages:

    7 ounces canned tomato juice
    5 ounces canned tomato juice—724 I.U.—and 1½ tablespoons lemon juice (juice of ½ lemon)—276 I.U.
6½ ounces canned tomato juice—928 I.U.—and 3½ ounces sauerkraut juice—75 I.U.

COMPLEMENTARY BEVERAGES

APPLE JUICE: Although apple juice is really an old-fashioned American beverage, it may seem new to many people because methods of canning it have only recently been perfected.

The familiar sweet apple cider is apple juice which has been left unfermented (or had the fermentation checked at an early stage). Hard apple cider is that which has been fermented to the stage where alcohol is produced.

While apple juice is not particularly rich in Vitamin C, it is a good alkalinizer and an excellent source of food minerals. It is very helpful to the digestive system, because apple pulp contains a great deal of pectin, which is soothing in various digestive inflammations. To fortify apple juice in Vitamin C content, mix it to suit your taste with orange, lemon, lime or grapefruit juice.

FRESH APPLE JUICE

INGREDIENTS:

8 apples   sugar to taste (optional)
lemon (or orange) juice to taste

DIRECTIONS: Wash apples, quarter and put into saucepan with water to cover. Cover pan and cook until apples are very soft. Strain through sieve lined with wet cheesecloth or a wet jelly or sugar bag. Chill and sweeten if desired. Add lemon or orange juice before serving. Yield: 1 quart. Remaining apple pulp may be put through a ricer, sweetened to taste and used as applesauce. (A few raisins or chopped nuts make the applesauce more interesting.)

APPLE JUICE AND GRAPE JUICE

INGREDIENTS:

$\frac{1}{2}$ cup chilled apple juice $\frac{1}{3}$ cup water
$\frac{1}{3}$ cup chilled grape juice   1 tablespoon lemon juice

DIRECTIONS: Combine apple juice, grape juice and water. Add lemon juice and sugar syrup to taste and mix well. Yield: 1 serving.

Approximately 1,000 International units of Vitamin C are contained in the following apple juice beverages:

25 ounces apple juice—726 I.U.—and 3 tablespoons lime juice (juice of 2 limes)—274 I.U.

16 ounces apple juice—448 I.U.—and 3 tablespoons lemon juice (juice of 1 lemon)—552 I.U.

14 ounces apple juice—400 I.U.—and 2 ounces orange juice—600 I.U.

GRAPE JUICE: Grape juice is particularly valuable because it contains acid potassium tartrate which is readily converted by body chemistry into splendid acid-neutralizing salts. In addition, it is a gentle stimulant to digestive action and kidney function.

The minerals, particularly iron, which grapes contain, are in a form which the body can use with extreme ease. Since grapes are a good source only of Vitamin B$_1$, their juice is even more serviceable when fortified with the citrus fruit juices rich in Vitamin C. The following beverage is excellent for convalescents and anyone with gastric ulcer or other inflammatory disturbances of the digestive tract.

GRAPE JUICE PUNCH

INGREDIENTS:

1 pint chilled grape juice
juice of 1 lemon

1 quart chilled gingerale

DIRECTIONS: Add gingerale to combined fruit juices just before serving. Garnish with lemon slices. Yield: 8 servings.

DRIED FRUIT NECTARS: It is scarcely appropriate to give the name "juices" to beverages made from dried apricots and prunes. When dried fruits are converted to liquid form, they should be called nectars, as they are when canned. Such nectars are inexpensive and easy to prepare, have delightful flavors, and are eminently worth while from the vitamin and mineral viewpoints. Naturally they do not have the concentrated consistency of commercial nectars, but many people really prefer the homemade drinks.

PRUNE OR APRICOT NECTAR

INGREDIENTS:

2 cups dried prunes (or apricots)
8 cups water

1½ tablespoons lemon juice
sugar to taste (optional)

DIRECTIONS: Wash prunes (or apricots). Put into saucepan with water, cover pan and simmer until fruit is very soft, about 45 minutes. Strain through sieve lined with wet cheesecloth or wet jelly bag. Add sugar, if desired, just before removing from heat, and stir until sugar is dissolved. Chill thoroughly. Stir in lemon juice just before serving. Cooking time may be shortened by soaking fruit in hot water about 2 hours. Cook in same water. Yield: 6 cups nectar.

Contrary to previous belief, sulphured fruit is really higher in vitamin content than unsulphured. However, anyone who is sensitive to sulphur should buy unsulphured variety. Packaged dried fruit preferred for reasons of sanitation and more uniform quality.

RESTORATIVE BEVERAGES

Beverages which contain considerable amounts of milk or eggs are fully entitled to be called restorative because they contain the Class A proteins as well as large amounts of minerals and vitamins.

The time-honored eggnog probably ranks first among such drinks. Eggs are the most nearly perfect of all foods nutritionally. Milk ranks second, so it is not surprising that a union of these two foods, whipped into a more easily digested form, should prove the king of the "building-up" foods.

For anyone with impaired digestive powers, it is best to make eggnog with only the yolk of the raw egg because egg white is less digestible than egg yolk, and contributes almost nothing nutritionally to the dish.

VITAMINS	1 PORTION CONTAINS APPROXIMATELY	DAILY NEED	
A	1055	5000 I.U.	EGGNOG
B	57	600 I.U.	
C	82	1500 I.U.	
G	.64	2.7 MGS.	

INGREDIENTS:

1 egg, separated	¼ teaspoon vanilla
2 teaspoons sugar (or honey)	dash of nutmeg
1 cup chilled milk	

DIRECTIONS: Separate egg and beat egg white until stiff. Beat egg yolk until light, and add sugar, milk and vanilla. Beat until sugar is dissolved. Fold in egg white and sprinkle with nutmeg. Serve at once. Yield: 1 serving.

VEGETABLE JUICES

It is a well-known fact that some of the vitamins, notably B_1, C and G, are destroyed when the foods containing them are heated. Vegetables, for example, probably lose 20 per cent of their B_1 value and 30 per cent of their C value when cooked.

But what many people forget is that these same vitamins—as well as the minerals iron, calcium, phosphorus and certain trace minerals—*dissolve* in water. When a vegetable is cooked or canned, perhaps a third of its entire content of Vitamin B_1 or Vitamin C will be dissipated throughout the cooking or canning water. Such water, then, is extremely valuable. It should be carefully saved and unfailingly used.

Store these pot liquors, if not served immediately with the vegetable, in tightly covered jar in refrigerator. Use sometime within the next two days after cooking, as juices are perishable. Liquors from strongly flavored vegetables such as turnips and cabbage must be used the day they are cooked. To give pot liquors extra flavor, combine them with tomato or sauerkraut juice, and serve with lemon wedges.

Here is a list of some of the commonly available pot liquors in any household. Note their richness in Vitamins B_1 and C. (All are derived from 1 cup of the vegetable, quick-cooked.)

Pot Liquor	Vitamin B	Vitamin C	
cabbage	11	286	International units
potato	7	68	International units
string bean	6	50	International units
cauliflower	14	151	International units
beet	7	16	International units

Sauerkraut juice is somewhat different from ordinary pot liquor, but if made properly it contains a good percentage of the soluble mineral salts and the Vitamin C present in sauerkraut. It may be combined tastily (if not too salty) in the following ways:

Sauerkraut-Tomato Cocktail: one-third sauerkraut juice, two-thirds tomato juice.

Sauerkraut-Potato Cocktail: one-third sauerkraut juice, two-thirds potato pot liquor.

Sauerkraut-Clam-Tomato Cocktail: ¼ cup sauerkraut juice, ¼ cup clam juice, ½ cup tomato juice.

BREADSTUFFS

This Chart Gives Approximate Food Values for 100 PER CENT WHOLE WHEAT BREAD. For Vitamin Values of Specific Recipes, See Charts Accompanying Them.

1 PORTION CONTAINS APPROXIMATELY	VITAMINS	240 I.U.	49 I.U.	4 I.U.	.07 MGS.	MINERALS	69 MGS.	130 MGS.	2 MGS.	ANALYSIS	204	7 GMS.
		A	B	C	G		CALC.	PHOS.	IRON		CAL.	PROT.
BLACK PART OF COLUMN SHOWS HOW MUCH OF DAILY NEED IS SUPPLIED BY ONE PORTION												
AVERAGE DAILY NEED		5000 I.U.	600 I.U.	1500 I.U.	2.7 MGS.		800 MGS.	1320 MGS.	12 MGS.		2000-3000	70 GMS.

COMMENTS: Breads are divided into two classifications: yeast breads and quick breads. The first uses yeast to make the dough light and spongy; the second employs some other leavening agent, such as baking powder, baking soda, acid, steam or air.

Yeast breads made with whole wheat flour a superior source of the Vitamin B complex, including the nerve and morale vitamin—B_1. Agents used to prepare quick breads, however, may destroy all but a tiny fraction of Vitamin B_1, so that any bread or flour product made with baking soda, baking powder, cream of tartar, etc., may not be a good source of this vitamin regardless of how rich in it the ingredients were before cooking. The quick breads included in this group of recipes are valuable for other nutritional or taste reasons than their content of Vitamin B_1, even though they are made with whole wheat flour.

However, if baking powder is used, it should be the best type—tartrate baking powder, containing pure cream of tartar made from the crystals of grapes. May cost more, but you need less of it than of the cheaper grades, so it is actually economical.

A small quantity of wheat flour must always be included in bread recipes (except Johnnycake), even though large quantities of rye, corn or oat meals are used to give the bread its character. Wheat flour adds to lightness of dough, since wheat is the only grain containing large amount of gluten (its chief protein), which gives dough elastic quality.

As texture of bread will depend upon action of yeast—and activity of yeast depends upon proper warmth, moisture and food—the proper use and handling of all ingredients play an important part. Care must be taken to give yeast plants the proper temperature for action (between 75° and 80° F.). Too high temperature will kill the plants and too low temperature will retard their growth. If bread is raised overnight, set bowl in warm place where it will neither be overheated nor be in a draught. Moisture is furnished by the liquid with which the flour is mixed, and for best results warm the flour and be sure milk or water is lukewarm. The micro-organisms of yeast reproduce rapidly when given food in the form of sugar (or starch which is convertible into sugar).

For all yeast breads, compressed yeast of moist cake type the purest. Most readily available, easiest and quickest to work with, and promises more consistent results. Follow all recipes exactly. Maintaining an even temperature (around 80° F.) throughout rising period most important so as not to kill action of yeast. Bread should rise exactly the right length of time—long enough, yet not too long. Dough must always be of proper consistency and texture and baked at correct heat if bread is to be successful.

Despite enrichment of white flour, which has taken place during last year, whole wheat flour is still a better source of vitamins, minerals and cereal protein than highly milled flour. For that reason, only whole grain yeast bread recipes are given here. Enriched white flour contains about as much Vitamin B_1 and iron as whole wheat, but the other members of the Vitamin B complex (including as yet unknown ones) are in greater concentration in the whole, unrefined flour. Thus whole wheat bread, as well as whole rye bread, highly nutritious foods from vitamin, mineral, protein and carbohydrate viewpoints. However, all whole grain products, including bread, may be contraindicated in ailments where roughage must be avoided (colitis, ulcers, etc.). In such instances, use only enriched white flour products.

One slice of whole wheat or rye bread goes considerably farther than a slice of ordinary, commercial white bread, since it is a fairly concentrated source of many nutrients. Use the bread to accompany lunch or supper dishes, like vegetable casseroles, rarebits, soups, etc., or in small quantities (one or at most two slices) with the main dinner meal. It may be desirable not to serve bread at meals containing both potatoes and a cake or pastry dessert, to avoid overbalancing meal on carbohydrate side.

100%
WHOLE WHEAT BREAD

INGREDIENTS:

2 cups milk, scalded
1/3 cup molasses or ¼ cup sugar
2 tablespoons butter (lard, margarine, vegetable fat)

2 teaspoons salt
1 yeast cake
¼ cup lukewarm water
4¾ cups whole wheat flour

DIRECTIONS: Scald milk and add molasses, shortening and salt, stirring until shortening is melted. Cool to lukewarm. Crumble yeast cake into bowl and slowly add lukewarm water, stirring until yeast cake is dissolved. Combine dissolved yeast and lukewarm milk mixture, and add flour gradually, a small amount at a time, beating thoroughly with rotary egg beater until mixture is smooth. This beating process is very important to distribute yeast (dough is not kneaded). An electric mixer may be used if available.

After about 3 cups have been added, remaining flour will have to be stirred into mixture with wooden spoon, as dough will be too stiff to use beater. Stir vigorously until all flour disappears and dough is smooth. Cover bowl with clean towel, and set in warm place (around 80° F.). Let rise until it has doubled its size, about 2 to 2½ hours. (If you wish to let bread rise overnight, use only ¼ yeast cake; if you wish to shorten the total bread-making time from 5 to 3 hours, use 2 yeast cakes.)

Again beat thoroughly with wooden spoon about 1 minute, and turn dough into 2 greased 8"x4" bread pans, having pans half full. Brush loaves with melted shortening, cover with towel, and let rise again until they have almost doubled in size, about 1 hour. Bake in moderately hot oven (400° F.) 15 minutes, then reduce heat to moderate (375° F.), and bake 45 minutes longer. Bread is done when it shrinks from sides of pan. Remove from oven, turn out on wire tray to cool and spread top and sides with melted butter. Cover with towel during cooling. When cool, wrap in waxed paper, *not* cloth, to store in tightly covered breadbox or stone jar.

Raisin Bread—Add 2 cups raisins to basic recipe for bread mixture after first rising. Beat or stir until raisins are evenly distributed throughout dough, and proceed as in basic recipe. *The raisins add 5 I.U. of Vitamin B₁ and .04 mg. of Vitamin G to Whole Wheat Bread.*

85

Whole Wheat Rolls—Follow directions in basic recipe up to the point of the end of first rising. Then, instead of turning dough into bread pans, fill greased muffin pans ½ full. Drop dough from spoon, as mixture is spongy and not stiff enough to handle. If dough sticks to spoon, use small amount of flour on finger tips to remove dough more easily. Brush with melted shortening, cover and let rise until almost double in bulk. Bake in moderate oven (375° F.) about 20 to 25 minutes.

RYE – CARAWAY BREAD

VITAMINS	1 PORTION CONTAINS APPROXIMATELY	DAILY NEED
A	74	5000 I.U.
B	17	600 I.U.
C	4	1500 I.U.
G	.07	2.7 MGS.

INGREDIENTS:

2 cups milk, scalded
2 tablespoons sugar
2 tablespoons shortening
1 teaspoon salt
1 yeast cake

½ cup lukewarm water
6 cups rye flour
1½ cups whole wheat flour
2 tablespoons caraway seeds

DIRECTIONS: Follow directions for Whole Wheat Bread (page 85), kneading in whole wheat flour and caraway seeds after first rising. If desired, caraway seeds may be omitted. Dough may be shaped into loaves and baked on a flat baking sheet, rather than baked in a loaf pan.

QUICK BREADS

COMMENTS: Although use of baking powder or soda destroys almost all Vitamin B_1 in quick breads requiring these chemicals as leavening agents, a few recipes are included here because of other nutritional values they supply to the diet. Thus it is always wise to use whole wheat rather than white flour in bread recipes, even though the primary nutrient (Vitamin B_1) of the whole wheat is destroyed. Whole wheat contains more Vitamin G, better protein and other members of the Vitamin B complex (including as yet unknown ones) than does white flour.

Griddle cakes and waffles included here, for example, should not be relied upon to supply the Vitamin B_1 their flour originally contained, but should be considered a good source of other members of Vitamin B complex. They contain, in addition, valuable vitamin and mineral elements of eggs and milk used. Cottage Cheese Crêpes a particularly valuable source of Vitamin A, egg protein and iron; provide an excellent way of incorporating eggs into menus.

All quick breads good for growing children as well as those wishing to gain weight, as usually eaten with butter and jam (or syrup), which make total dish a weight-producing combination of carbohydrates and fats. Reducers should not eat muffins, cakes or waffles often.

Quick breads usually served hot and, contrary to general belief, are perfectly digestible when properly mixed and thoroughly baked. It is important for good results that recipes be followed explicitly. Once liquid or moisture is added to dry ingredients of quick bread batter, gas formed by leavening agent begins to escape. Hence, should be placed in oven at once.

Use for breakfast, lunch or supper, always serving without other carbohydrate food at the meal. Best balanced with salad, soup or fruit.

V I T A M I N S	1 PORTION CONTAINS APPROXIMATELY	DAILY NEED
A	473	5000 I.U.
B	72	600 I.U.
C	22	1500 I.U.
G	.19	2.7 MGS.

SOUR MILK GRIDDLE CAKES

INGREDIENTS:

2 cups whole wheat flour
2 teaspoons tartrate baking powder
1 teaspoon baking soda
½ teaspoon salt

1 tablespoon sugar
1 egg, slightly beaten
2¼ cups sour milk or buttermilk
1 tablespoon shortening, melted

DIRECTIONS: Heat griddle slowly and evenly. Mix and sift dry ingredients. In a separate bowl, combine slightly beaten egg and milk, and stir into dry ingredients, stirring only until smooth. Do not overbeat. Stir in melted shortening. Pour batter from tip of spoon onto hot, ungreased griddle. Bake, turning each cake when it is puffed up, full of bubbles, cooked on the edges and browned on the underside. Turn only once, and continue cooking until other side is evenly browned. Serve immediately on warm plate.

JOHNNYCAKE

INGREDIENTS:

1½ cups yellow corn meal	2 egg yolks, beaten
1½ cups milk, scalded	2 egg whites, stiffly beaten
¼ cup butter	¼ cup sugar
1 teaspoon salt	

DIRECTIONS: Measure corn meal by lifting lightly by tablespoonfuls into cup. Sift gradually into milk that has been heated to scalding, stirring constantly to keep smooth. Remove from heat, and add butter and salt. Stir until butter melts, then add beaten egg yolks. Beat egg whites until stiff, then add sugar and again beat until smooth. Fold lightly into corn meal mixture, and turn batter into large shallow buttered pan or baking dish that has first been heated. Bake in hot oven (400° F.) until golden brown, about 20 to 25 minutes. (The thinner the johnnycake, the less baking time needed.) Yield: 5 to 6 servings.

WHOLE WHEAT WAFFLES

INGREDIENTS:

2 cups whole wheat flour	3 egg whites, stiffly beaten
5 teaspoons tartrate baking powder	3 egg yolks, well beaten
½ teaspoon salt	2 cups milk
1 tablespoon sugar	4 tablespoons melted shortening

DIRECTIONS: Heat waffle iron. Mix dry ingredients thoroughly. Beat egg whites just stiff enough to stand in peaks, but not dry. In separate bowl, combine well-beaten egg yolks and milk and add to dry ingredients gradually, stirring just until well blended and smooth. Do not overbeat. Stir in melted shortening. Fold in stiffly beaten egg whites. Bake at once in hot waffle iron, filling each compartment only two-thirds full. Waffles are baked when no steam escapes from edges of waffle iron. Do not attempt to lift upper side of iron until you are reasonably sure waffles are done, as you will tear waffle, ruining possibility of perfect texture of finished product. Waffle iron must be thoroughly heated before batter is poured in. If uncertain about proper preheating time, place 1 teaspoon cold water inside cold iron. Put top down and turn on electric current. When it stops steaming, iron is at correct temperature for baking waffles.

RAISIN WHOLE WHEAT GRIDDLE CAKES

Each portion contains approximately:
Vit. A—637 I.U.; B₁—79 I.U.; C—19 I.U.; G—.24 Mgs.

INGREDIENTS:

2 cups whole wheat flour	½ cup seedless raisins
½ teaspoon salt	2 egg yolks, slightly beaten
2 teaspoons tartrate baking powder	2 cups sour milk or buttermilk
1 teaspoon baking soda	2 tablespoons shortening, melted
1 tablespoon sugar	2 egg whites, stiffly beaten

DIRECTIONS: Heat griddle slowly and evenly. Mix dry ingredients and stir in raisins. Combine beaten egg yolks and milk and stir into dry ingredients, stirring only until smooth. Stir in melted shortening. Fold in stiffly beaten egg whites. Bake on hot, ungreased griddle until golden brown on both sides, turning only once.

COTTAGE CHEESE CREPES

Each portion contains approximately:
Vit. A—927 I.U.; Vit. B₁—37 I.U.; Vit. G—.29 Mgs.

INGREDIENTS:

4 eggs	¾ cup flour
1 cup cottage cheese	1 tablespoon sugar
1 cup sour cream	¼ teaspoon salt

DIRECTIONS: Heat griddle slowly and evenly. Beat eggs thoroughly. Add cottage cheese and sour cream and beat until well mixed. Mix dry ingredients. Stir into egg mixture gradually, beating well after each addition. Drop three tablespoons on medium-hot, lightly greased griddle and bake on each side until delicately brown. Serve at once with jelly or preserves. These crêpes are like French egg pancakes in texture and flavor.

BALANCED MEAL SUGGESTIONS: *Breakfast*—Tall Glass Orange Juice; *Raisin Griddle Cakes;* Milk (or Coffee).

CANAPÉS & SANDWICHES

This Chart Gives Approximate Food Values for TOASTED CHEESE CANAPES. For Vitamin Values of Specific Recipes, See Charts Accompanying Them.

1 PORTION CONTAINS APPROXIMATELY	VITAMINS	829 I.U.	152 I.U.	I.U.	.23 MGS.	MINERALS	303 MGS.	299 MGS.	.9 MGS.	ANALYSIS	243	9 GMS.
		A	B	C	G		CALC.	PHOS.	IRON		CAL.	PROT.
BLACK PART OF COLUMN SHOWS HOW MUCH OF DAILY NEED IS SUPPLIED BY ONE PORTION												
AVERAGE DAILY NEED		5000 I.U.	600 I.U.	1500 I.U.	2.7 MGS.		800 MGS.	1320 MGS.	12 MGS.		2000-3000	70 GMS.

COMMENTS: Canapés, in contrast to sandwiches, require only one slice of bread or toast, which is covered with any suitable vegetable, fruit, egg, cheese, fish or meat spread. For normal persons, who usually eat more than enough carbohydrate foods anyway, canapés are preferable to sandwiches for use at lunch or supper.

Canapés made with whole grain bread can be a real nutritional contribution to the diet. The bread supplies a reliable amount of the Vitamin B complex, as well as minerals and cereal protein. Canapé spreads, made of fruit, vegetable or cheese mixtures are not only delicious—they also add substantial amounts of all the vitamins, minerals and (with cheese and eggs) Grade A protein.

Always slice bread thin, and spread mixture so that it is twice as thick as bread slice. This makes a better-tasting canapé, besides increasing its protective quality. All canapé and sandwich recipes yield approximately 1¼ cups spread—enough for 6 large (24 tiny) canapés or 6 sandwiches. Use whole wheat, rye, brown, fruit or nut bread, according to taste. Unless mixture to be used is very moist, spread bread first with a thin covering of softened or Flavored Butter (page 96) to improve taste of canapé.

Canapés need not be the customary tiny, paper-thin affairs associated with cocktail parties, but may be made in the same size and with the same heartiness as ordinary sandwiches, minus the covering slice of bread. Such hearty canapés are also called open-faced sandwiches. They are especially valuable for children's home lunches or after-school snacks.

If large quantity is to be prepared, labor and time will be saved by using unsliced loaves of bread and cutting them lengthwise. Spread desired mixture over length of slice, then cut into desired canapé size. Canapés may be made attractive by cutting with a cookie cutter or knife into strips, diamonds, triangles, etc. Pinwheel canapés (or sandwiches) may be made by rolling the long spread slices like a jelly roll, wrapping in dry towel and placing in refrigerator to become firm, and then slicing as one slices a jelly roll.

For convenience in eating, canapés are always made with actual spreads; sandwiches with slices of meat, leaves of lettuce, etc.

VITAMINS	1 PORTION CONTAINS APPROXIMATELY		DAILY NEED
A	88		5000 I.U.
B		272	600 I.U.
C	143		1500 I.U.
G	.05		2.7 MGS.

PEANUT BUTTER-PINEAPPLE CANAPÉS

INGREDIENTS:

⅔ cup peanut butter
⅔ cup drained, crushed pineapple

5 teaspoons lemon juice
6 slices whole wheat bread

DIRECTIONS: Mix peanut butter with pineapple. Moisten with lemon juice and stir until well blended. Spread mixture on bread.

VITAMINS	1 PORTION CONTAINS APPROXIMATELY		DAILY NEED
A	286		5000 I.U.
B		206	600 I.U.
C	107		1500 I.U.
G	.08		2.7 MGS.

DRIED FRUIT CANAPÉS

INGREDIENTS:

½ cup raisins
½ cup figs (or dates)
¼ cup nut meats

2 tablespoons lemon juice
6 slices whole wheat bread
3 tablespoons softened butter

DIRECTIONS: Combine raisins, figs and nut meats. Put through meat grinder, using medium blade, or chop very fine. Moisten with lemon juice. Spread mixture on buttered bread.

TOASTED CHEESE CANAPÉS

V I T A M I N S	1 PORTION CONTAINS APPROXIMATELY	DAILY NEED
A	829	5000 I.U.
B	152	600 I.U.
C		1500 I.U.
G	.23	2.7 MGS.

INGREDIENTS:

6 slices whole wheat or whole rye bread
4 tablespoons softened butter

6 slices American cheese
1½ teaspoons paprika (or 2 tablespoons prepared mustard)

DIRECTIONS: Toast slices of bread on one side. Spread untoasted side with softened butter and cover with cheese slices. Either spread with prepared mustard or sprinkle with paprika or use both. Place on broiler rack toasted side down, about 3 inches below medium heat, and broil until cheese is melted and lightly browned, about 5 minutes. Serve hot.

CHEESE-ONION CANAPÉS

INGREDIENTS:

1 cup (½ pound) cottage cheese
2 tablespoons minced onions (or chives)
1½ teaspoons paprika

2 tablespoons cream (approximate)
6 slices whole wheat bread
3 tablespoons softened butter

DIRECTIONS: Combine cheese with onion, season with paprika and moisten to spreading consistency with cream. Spread mixture on buttered bread. (These canapés are especially good when toasted bread is used.)

PINEAPPLE-CHEESE CANAPÉS

INGREDIENTS:

1 cup (½ pound) cream or cottage cheese
¼ cup drained, crushed pineapple

2 tablespoons ground nut meats
6 slices brown bread
3 tablespoons softened butter

DIRECTIONS: Combine cheese, pineapple and nut meats, and cream until well blended. Spread mixture on buttered bread.

Cheese-Jam Canapés—Follow directions in basic recipe but omit nut meats and replace pineapple with ¼ cup fruit jam, fruit butter or jelly.

92

CHEESE-EGG CANAPÉS

Each portion contains approximately:
Vit. A—922 I.U.; Vit. B₁—29 I.U.; Vit. C—261 I.U.; Vit. G—.2 Mg.

INGREDIENTS:

¾ cup American cheese
2 hard-cooked eggs
½ small onion
1 pimiento
¼ teaspoon salt

1 teaspoon paprika
3 tablespoons mayonnaise
6 slices whole rye bread
3 tablespoons softened butter

DIRECTIONS: Put cheese, eggs, onion and pimiento through meat grinder, using finest blade. Mix and season with salt and paprika. Moisten with mayonnaise and spread mixture on buttered bread.

EGG-CELERY CANAPÉS

INGREDIENTS:

4 hard-cooked eggs, chopped
¼ cup minced celery
2 tablespoons minced parsley
2 teaspoons onion juice

3 tablespoons mayonnaise
  (approximate)
6 slices rye bread
3 tablespoons softened butter

DIRECTIONS: Combine chopped eggs, celery and parsley. Season with onion juice and moisten with mayonnaise. Spread mixture on buttered bread. Garnish with small sprinkling of minced parsley in center.

SALMON CANAPÉS

INGREDIENTS:

1 cup flaked salmon
2 tablespoons minced parsley
3 tablespoons minced pimiento
1 tablespoon minced onion
2 tablespoons mayonnaise
  (approximate)

⅛ teaspoon celery salt
pepper to taste
6 slices whole wheat bread
3 tablespoons Lemon Butter
  (page 96)

DIRECTIONS: Combine all ingredients except bread in small bowl. Blend thoroughly with fork so that mixture forms a thick spread. Chill. Spread bread with Lemon Butter, then with salmon mixture. Cut into desired shapes. Garnish each canapé with minced parsley, bits of pimiento or a sliced stuffed olive in center.

LIVER CANAPÉS

V I T A M I N S	1 PORTION CONTAINS APPROXIMATELY	DAILY NEED
A	9910	5000 I.U.
B	228	600 I.U.
C	107	1500 I.U.
G	1.3	2.7 MGS.

INGREDIENTS:

1 cup finely chopped cooked beef liver (or chicken livers)
3 hard-cooked egg yolks
¼ cup chopped watercress
1 tablespoon onion juice

3 tablespoons mayonnaise (or chili sauce)
salt and pepper to taste
6 slices whole wheat bread
½ cup softened butter

DIRECTIONS: Combine all ingredients but bread and butter. Mix well. Chill. Toast and butter one side of bread, and spread mixture on untoasted side. Lemon Butter (page 96) may be used to add flavor.

CHICKEN CANAPÉS

V I T A M I N S	1 PORTION CONTAINS APPROXIMATELY	DAILY NEED
A	783	5000 I.U.
B	196	600 I.U.
C	536	1500 I.U.
G	.07	2.7 MGS.

INGREDIENTS:

1 cup minced cooked chicken
2 tablespoons minced pimiento (or parsley)
1 small onion, minced
¼ cup minced celery

3 tablespoons mayonnaise (approximate)
1 teaspoon lemon juice
6 slices whole wheat bread
½ cup softened butter

DIRECTIONS: Combine chicken, pimiento (or parsley), onion and celery. Moisten with lemon juice and mayonnaise to taste. Spread mixture on buttered bread. (Flaked cooked or canned lobster meat, crab meat, tuna or salmon may replace chicken.) If used as sandwich filling, cover chicken with lettuce leaf and another slice of bread.

BALANCED MEAL SUGGESTIONS: *Lunch*—Cream of Spinach Soup; *Dried Fruit Canapés* (or any fruit or vegetable canapé); Stewed Rhubarb or Baked Custard; Milk.

Supper—Cabbage, Pimiento and Carrot Salad; *Toasted Cheese Canapés* (or any cheese, egg, meat or fish canapé); Baked Apples; Milk.

SANDWICHES

This Chart Gives Approximate Food Values for LETTUCE-TOMATO SANDWICH.
For Vitamin Values of Specific Recipes, See Charts Accompanying Them.

1 PORTION CONTAINS APPROXIMATELY	VITAMINS	1763 I.U.	391 I.U.	475 I.U.	.17 MGS.	MINERALS	59 MGS.	189 MGS.	2 MGS.	ANALYSIS	242	6 GMS.
		A	B	C	G		CALC.	PHOS.	IRON		CAL.	PROT.
BLACK PART OF COLUMN SHOWS HOW MUCH OF DAILY NEED IS SUPPLIED BY ONE PORTION												
AVERAGE DAILY NEED		5000 I.U.	600 I.U.	1500 I.U.	2.7 MGS.		800 MGS.	1320 MGS.	12 MGS.		2000-3000	70 GMS.

COMMENTS: Read Comments on Canapés for discussion of values and uses. Sandwiches are just canapés with second slice of bread to cover filling. All canapé spreads may be used as sandwich fillings. Properly made sandwiches are a decided contrast to the usual counter-luncheonette affairs, made of two thick slices of white bread with an infinitesimal amount of filling.

Sandwiches preferred to canapés for growing children and underweight persons. Those wishing to lose weight will do well not to eat either.

Use sandwiches for lunch or supper, balanced with salad (or a light soup, fruit juice or vegetable juice), fruit or egg dessert and milk. Spread bread with softened or Flavored Butter (page 96) and if sandwiches are not served immediately, wrap individually or in pairs in waxed paper and place in covered container in refrigerator. If lettuce or moist filling is used, sandwiches should be served immediately. Do not wrap this type sandwich as bread will become soaked and lettuce will wilt.

Always prepare sandwiches rather than canapés for picnic or lunch boxes. If canapés are preferred, wrap buttered bread and carry canapé mixtures in a tightly covered jar to be spread just before serving.

FLAVORED BUTTER SPREADS

For six servings of each of the following Flavored Butters, cream ½ cup butter until soft and then stir in suggested ingredients until thoroughly blended. All vegetables should be minced as fine as possible or put through the meat grinder, using the finest blade.

Lemon Butter—Add 2 tablespoons lemon juice. *This increases Vitamin C content by 285 I.U.*

Mustard Butter—Add 2 tablespoons prepared mustard.

Parsley Butter—Add ½ cup minced parsley (or watercress), 1 teaspoon lemon juice and 1 teaspoon onion juice. *This yields: Vitamin A—4485 I.U.; Vitamin C—351 I.U.*

Pimiento Butter—Add 3 tablespoons minced pimientos and 1½ to 2 tablespoons lemon juice.

LETTUCE-TOMATO SANDWICH

VITAMINS	1 PORTION CONTAINS APPROXIMATELY	DAILY NEED
A	1762	5000 I.U.
B	391	600 I.U.
C	475	1500 I.U.
G	.17	2.7 MGS.

INGREDIENTS:

12 slices whole wheat bread or toast

3 tablespoons softened butter

18 slices of medium-sized ripe tomatoes

12 lettuce leaves

salt and pepper

2 tablespoons Mayonnaise (optional)

DIRECTIONS: Butter 6 slices of bread. Cover each with crisp lettuce leaves and sliced tomatoes. Season tomatoes lightly and cover with remaining lettuce leaves. Spread remaining bread with mayonnaise (or butter) and cover sandwiches. Serve immediately.

TONGUE SANDWICHES

Each portion contains approximately:
Vit. A—460 I.U.; Vit. B₁—39 I.U.; Vit. C—10 I.U.; Vit. G—.07 Mg.

INGREDIENTS:

¾ cup ground cold boiled tongue

½ cup finely diced celery

2 sweet pickles, minced

3 tablespoons mayonnaise

½ cup softened butter

12 slices whole rye bread

DIRECTIONS: Put cold tongue through meat grinder, using finest blade, and mix with celery and pickles. Moisten with mayonnaise. Butter bread and spread 6 slices with tongue mixture. Cover with remaining slices of bread. The addition of lettuce leaves and sliced tomatoes makes this a very filling sandwich.

DESSERTS

This Chart Gives Approximate Food Values for CITRUS FRUIT CUP. For Vitamin Values of Specific Recipes, See Charts Accompanying Them.

	VITAMINS				MINERALS			ANALYSIS	
	A	B	C	G	CALC.	PHOS.	IRON	CAL.	PROT.
1 PORTION CONTAINS APPROXIMATELY	22 I.U.	27 I.U.	1200 I.U.	.15 MGS.	31 MGS.	27 MGS.	.52 MGS.	67	1 GMS.
BLACK PART OF COLUMN SHOWS HOW MUCH OF DAILY NEED IS SUPPLIED BY ONE PORTION									
AVERAGE DAILY NEED	5000 I.U.	600 I.U.	1500 I.U.	2.7 MGS.	800 MGS.	1320 MGS.	12 MGS.	2000-3000	70 GMS.

COMMENTS: Lunches, dinners and suppers need some form of dessert—a "sweet" to complete the meal and give a feeling of satisfaction. Of all desserts, best from nutritive standpoint are simple fruit dishes, such as those suggested, or various fresh fruits arranged attractively as a centerpiece, from which everyone can help himself. These recommended for entire family, because they are low in calorie content and high in protective values.

Fruits rich in vitamins and minerals, as well as natural sugars. Choice may be made among fresh fruits in season, canned or quick-frozen fruits or stewed dried fruits. Fresh fruits slightly more desirable from standpoint of both taste and vitamin-mineral contents, but good grades of processed fruit are excellent substitutes.

The heavier the meal, the lighter the dessert should be. Fruit best choice. Recipes given are only representative; each cook can devise her own combinations.

Be sure that all fruits are chilled before being peeled, segmented, taken from can, etc. (Of course, cooked fruit desserts should be chilled before serving.) Vitamin loss begins as soon as fruit is deprived of its natural covering or exposed to air when can or package is opened. If chilling is done beforehand in making cups, etc., fruit can be prepared, mixed and served as cold as it should be without further exposure.

Crushed or finely chopped mint, contrasting fruit juices, particularly lemon juice, or nut meats and raisins may be added to most fruit cups for extra flavor. Do not sweeten fruit unless necessary, as in the case of rhubarb or baked apples (for increased palatability).

CITRUS CUP

INGREDIENTS:
1½ cups diced, seeded orange (or tangerine) segments

1½ cups diced, seeded fresh (or canned) grapefruit segments

DIRECTIONS: Combine chilled fruit; serve in individual dessert dishes with diced, unpeeled red apple or a few mint leaves to give color, if desired.

DATE CUP

VITAMINS		1 PORTION CONTAINS APPROXIMATELY	DAILY NEED
	A	30	5000 I.U.
	B	12	600 I.U.
	C	362	1500 I.U.
	G	.07	2.7 MGS.

INGREDIENTS:
12 dates (¼ package), quartered
1 medium-sized grapefruit, peeled and segmented

3 slices pineapple, diced
12 cherries, cut into halves
6 sprigs mint

DIRECTIONS: Prepare thoroughly chilled fruit as directed, combine all ingredients and serve.

GRAPEFRUIT-STRAWBERRY CUP

Each portion contains approximately:
Vit. A—71 I. U.; Vit. B₁—9 I. U.; Vit. C—783 I. U.; Vit. G—.09 Mg.

INGREDIENTS:
3 small grapefruits (or 1 No. 2 can unsweetened grapefruit segments)

1½ cups fresh sliced strawberries
2 tablespoons sugar (optional)

DIRECTIONS: Cut grapefruits in halves. Carefully remove membrane, seeds and grapefruit sections, reserving shells to use as cups. Combine grapefruit sections and berries, and refill grapefruit shells with mixture. Sprinkle fruit with sugar just before serving, unless fruit is naturally sweet enough. If canned grapefruit is used, serve in individual dessert dishes. In winter, Cranberry Sauce may replace strawberries; in that case, omit sugar.

QUICK-COOKED RHUBARB

INGREDIENTS:

2 pounds rhubarb (5 to 6 cups, diced)

1 cup sugar (or more)
½ cup boiling water

DIRECTIONS: Remove leaves and stem ends of stalks, wash and cut into 1-inch pieces. Place rhubarb and sugar in saucepan with boiling water. Cover and cook over medium heat just until tender, about 6 to 8 minutes. Fruit should be soft but still in pieces and not strings. Chill before serving. Serve in individual dishes and garnish with a sprig of mint, if desired.

Stewed Rhubarb—Prepare as directed in basic recipe. Omit water. Place rhubarb with sugar in top of double boiler and cook, covered, over hot water until rhubarb is soft, about 30 to 40 minutes. Absence of water gives this dish better color and flavor than Quick-Cooked Rhubarb, but more of the vitamins are lost in longer cooking.

Baked Rhubarb—Prepare as directed in basic recipe. Omit water. Place rhubarb with sugar in baking dish, cover and bake in moderate oven (350° F.) about 30 to 40 minutes, just until rhubarb is soft.

APPLESAUCE

Each portion contains approximately:
Vit. A—43 I.U.; Vit. B₁—10 I.U.; Vit. C—28 I.U.; Vit. G—.07 Mg.

INGREDIENTS:

6 to 8 tart cooking apples
1 cup water

½ cup sugar (approximate)

DIRECTIONS: Wash and quarter apples. Place in saucepan with water. Cover, bring to boil, reduce heat to medium, and simmer until apples are tender, about 8 to 15 minutes, depending upon variety of apple. Force through a coarse sieve or ricer and add sugar to taste to strained pulp. Return to heat and stir just until sugar is dissolved, about 1 minute. (Do not sweeten apples until they have cooked; sugar prevents their breaking apart.) For additional flavor, add a few drops of lemon juice or a sprinkling of nutmeg or cinnamon. Chill thoroughly before serving.

BAKED APPLES

	1 PORTION CONTAINS APPROXIMATELY	DAILY NEED
A	43	5000 I.U.
B	10	600 I.U.
C	28	1500 I.U.
G	.07	2.7 MGS.

INGREDIENTS:

6 medium-sized cooking apples   1½ teaspoons cinnamon
12 tablespoons sugar or honey   raisins

DIRECTIONS: Wash apples and remove cores. Pare 1 inch of skin around top of each and place in baking dish. Put 2 tablespoons desired sweetening into cavity of each apple. (If desired, mix cinnamon or a few raisins or nut meats with the sweetening.) Add just enough boiling water to cover bottom of dish. Cover and bake in hot oven (400° F.) about 30 to 40 minutes, just until apples are soft. Serve hot or cold, with or without cream.

STEWED APPLES

Each portion contains approximately:
Vit. A—43 I.U.; Vit. B₁—10 I.U.; Vit. C—28 I.U.; Vit. G—.07 Mg.

INGREDIENTS:

6 medium-sized apples   1 cup sugar
6 whole cloves (optional!)   1½ cups water

DIRECTIONS: Core, pare and quarter apples. Stick cloves into apples. Boil sugar and water 5 minutes, and add apples. Reduce heat to medium, cover pan and simmer just until apples are tender, about 8 to 15 minutes, depending upon variety of apples. Do not overcook.

STEWED FRUIT WHIP

INGREDIENTS:

⅔ cup stewed dried fruit   ½ cup sugar
4 egg whites   ½ teaspoon lemon juice (or more)

DIRECTIONS: Rub stewed fruit through coarse strainer or put through ricer. Beat egg whites until stiff. Stir in sugar and lemon juice gradually. Fold in strained fruit. Mix well and chill thoroughly before serving. Serve with whipped cream or Soft Custard, if desired.

BALANCED MEAL SUGGESTIONS: *Lunch*—Cottage Cheese Salad; Potatoes; Chard; *Baked Apples.*

FROZEN AND GELATIN DESSERTS

COMMENTS: Simple fruit ice and gelatin desserts provide an excellent way of serving Vitamin C in a cooling, appetizing fashion. The light ices, such as orange, lemon and pineapple, are especially good sources of this vitamin, are very high in water content and low in protein, carbohydrates and fats. Thus they are ideal desserts for heavy or concentrated meals, and are especially valuable to reducers at all times, since they are low in calorie content. Use ices often in summer, as they are cooling foods—not only because of their appetizing, refreshing qualities, but because they contain few heat-producing calories.

Ice creams and mousses are, of course, higher in fat and calorie content than simple ices. Apricot Mousse is an especially valuable source of Vitamin A because of its combination of cream and apricots, and is recommended as a very pleasant way to get more of this vitamin. All these ice creams, made with heavy creams, are ideal for adding pounds to underweight persons and growing children. Should be avoided by reducers.

Gelatin desserts are fairly high in protein, because of the gelatin used. Outside of that, they are similar to the simple fruit ices in nutritive value. Low in calorie content, they are good dessert fare for reducers.

VITAMINS	1 PORTION CONTAINS APPROXIMATELY	DAILY NEED	
A	199	5000 I.U.	ORANGE ICE
B	26	600 I.U.	
C	960	1500 I.U.	
G	.01	2.7 MGS.	

INGREDIENTS:

2 cups boiling water

2 cups sugar

1 orange rind, grated

1/3 cup lemon juice

2 cups orange juice

DIRECTIONS: Combine water and sugar and stir constantly until sugar is dissolved. Boil 5 minutes without stirring. Cool, then add fruit juices and orange rind. Strain, pour in freezing trays of automatic refrigerator and freeze until firm, stirring occasionally.

Lemon Ice—Omit orange rind and juice and increase lemon juice to 3/4 cup. For a more definite lemon flavor, add 1 tablespoon grated lemon rind.

101

QUICK VANILLA ICE CREAM

INGREDIENTS:

⅔ cup (1 7½-ounce can) condensed milk

½ cup water

1½ teaspoons vanilla extract

pinch of salt

1 cup heavy cream, whipped

DIRECTIONS: Mix water with milk, blending thoroughly. Stir in vanilla extract and salt. Chill. Whip cream and fold into chilled mixture. Turn into freezing trays of automatic refrigerator and freeze until partially frozen. Scrape mixture from sides and bottom of tray and stir until smooth but not melted. Replace in freezing tray until firm, about 2 hours.

Fruit Ice Cream—Omit vanilla and salt; add 1½ cups crushed strawberries, raspberries or drained canned pineapple, and ¼ cup powdered sugar. Follow directions in basic recipe, adding sweetened fruit to water-milk mixture. *Fruit adds Vitamin C to plain ice cream.*

APRICOT MOUSSE
This Recipe Is a Good Source of Vitamin A.

INGREDIENTS:

1 cup apricot pulp

1 teaspoon lemon juice (or more)

4 egg whites

¼ teaspoon salt

¾ tablespoon sugar

½ cup heavy cream, whipped

DIRECTIONS: Force cooked or canned apricots through sieve or ricer to make 1 cup pulp. Add lemon juice. In a large bowl, beat egg whites until they stand in peaks. Gradually add sugar and salt, beating until a light meringue results. Fold in fruit pulp. Taste, and if necessary add a little more sugar. Stir mixture into whipped cream, turn into freezing tray of automatic refrigerator, and freeze until firm, about 2 to 3 hours, depending upon type of refrigerator. Crushed strawberries, cooked prunes, or crushed rhubarb also make excellent mousses.

CITRUS SHERBET
This Recipe Is Very Rich in Vitamin C.

INGREDIENTS:

1½ cups orange juice

2 tablespoons lemon juice

1½ cups canned or fresh grapefruit juice

1 tablespoon granulated gelatin

¼ cup cold water

2 cups water

1 cup sugar

1 tablespoon grated orange rind

4 egg yolks, slightly beaten

DIRECTIONS: Prepare fruit juices. Soften gelatin by soaking in cold water 5 minutes. Combine water, sugar and grated rind in saucepan and bring to boil, stirring constantly. In a mixing bowl, add small amount of sugar syrup to slightly beaten egg yolks, stirring constantly. Return this to remaining syrup and cook over medium heat 1 minute, stirring constantly. Remove from heat and add soaked gelatin. Strain, cool, add fruit juices, and turn into freezing tray of automatic refrigerator. Freeze until firm, about 2 hours, stirring occasionally.

BALANCED MEAL SUGGESTIONS: *Lunch*—Pimiento Coleslaw; Cheese Soufflé; Whole Wheat Rolls; *Orange Ice;* Milk.

Dinner—Mixed Greens Salad; Baked Ham with Fruit, or Roast Stuffed Shoulder of Lamb; Baked Potatoes; Carrots and Peas; *Citrus Sherbet.*

PUDDINGS

This Chart Gives Approximate Food Values for PRUNE PUDDING.
For Vitamin Values of Specific Recipes, See Charts Accompanying Them.

	VITAMINS				MINERALS			ANALYSIS	
	A	B	C	G	CALC.	PHOS.	IRON	CAL.	PROT.
1 PORTION CONTAINS APPROXIMATELY	669 I.U.	31 I.U.	100 I.U.	.3 MGS.	6 MGS.	12 MGS.	1 MGS.	250	5 GMS.
BLACK PART OF COLUMN SHOWS HOW MUCH OF DAILY NEED IS SUPPLIED BY ONE PORTION									
AVERAGE DAILY NEED	5000 I.U.	600 I.U.	1500 I.U.	2.7 MGS.	800 MGS.	1320 MGS.	12 MGS.	2000-3000	70 GMS.

COMMENTS: Puddings made with fruit provide a filling dessert especially good for hearty eaters who are not satisfied with a simple fruit cup. They utilize chiefly the dried fruits, like prunes, raisins, figs and dates, all of which are fairly rich in the Vitamin B complex, iron and important fruit sugars. None of these puddings, however, can be considered a contributor to the Vitamin C intake for the day, as fresh fruit desserts are. Be doubly sure to provide fresh orange or tomato juice and vegetables high in Vitamin C on the days when you serve any of these puddings.

Use puddings as desserts for a light supper or dinner, preferably after a meal that is not rich or filling. Especially good during the winter, rather than summer, since at that time most persons need more food, including the "stick-to-the-ribs" kind of dessert.

PRUNE PUDDING

	1 PORTION CONTAINS APPROXIMATELY	DAILY NEED
A	669	5000 I.U.
B	31	600 I.U.
C	100	1500 I.U.
G	.3	2.7 MGS.

INGREDIENTS:

½ pound dried prunes
3 cups water
1 1-inch stick cinnamon
¾ cup sugar
⅛ teaspoon salt

5 tablespoons cornstarch
½ cup cold water
1 tablespoon lemon juice
½ cup chopped nut meats
(optional)

DIRECTIONS: Wash prunes, cover with 3 cups water and let stand 2 hours. Using same water, cook in covered saucepan until soft, about 20 minutes. Drain, reserving juice, and pit prunes. Return fruit and juice to saucepan, and add cinnamon. In a bowl combine sugar, salt and cornstarch. Mix with ½ cup cold water, stirring until smooth and well blended. Add gradually to fruit. Cook over low heat, stirring constantly until mixture thickens, about 5 minutes. Remove cinnamon, and stir in lemon juice and nut meats. Pour into mold and chill. Serve plain or with whipped cream.

APPLESAUCE-GRAHAM PUDDING

	1 PORTION CONTAINS APPROXIMATELY	DAILY NEED
A	496	5000 I.U.
B	25	600 I.U.
C	76	1500 I.U.
G	.03	2.7 MGS.

INGREDIENTS:

1 cup (¼ pound) Graham
  cracker crumbs
¼ cup chopped walnuts
½ cup brown sugar

½ teaspoon cinnamon
5 tablespoons butter, melted
2 cups (1 No. 2 can) applesauce
2 tablespoons lemon juice

DIRECTIONS: Combine crumbs, walnuts, sugar and cinnamon, and mix well. Melt butter in 9-inch baking dish or deep pie pan. Add crumb mixture and mix thoroughly. Remove ½ cup crumb mixture. Distribute remaining crumbs around sides and bottom of pan. Turn applesauce into crumb-lined baking dish. Sprinkle with lemon juice and then cover applesauce with remaining crumb mixture. Bake in hot oven (400° F.) about 20 to 25 minutes, just until thoroughly heated and delicately browned.

104

DATE AND NUT REFRIGERATOR PUDDING

This Pudding Is a Good Source of Vitamin B₁.

INGREDIENTS:

½ pound Graham crackers   1 cup chopped dates
½ pound marshmallows, cut fine   1 cup thin cream or rich milk
1 cup chopped walnuts

DIRECTIONS: Roll or grind crackers and mix with marshmallows, walnuts and dates. Add cream slowly until the mixture is moist enough to form into a roll. Wrap in waxed paper and place in refrigerator. Chill several hours. Slice and serve with whipped cream or Soft Custard (page 114).

BALANCED MEAL SUGGESTIONS: *Luncheon or Supper*—Green Pepper Coleslaw; New England Clam Chowder; Pumpernickel Toast; *Prune Pudding;* Milk.

PASTRIES

This Chart Gives Approximate Food Values for APPLE PIE.
For Vitamin Values of Specific Recipes, See Charts Accompanying Them.

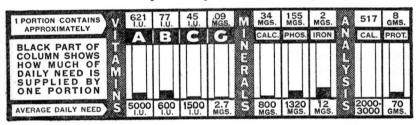

1 PORTION CONTAINS APPROXIMATELY	VITAMINS	A 621 I.U.	B 77 I.U.	C 45 I.U.	G .09 MGS.	MINERALS	CALC. 34 MGS.	PHOS. 155 MGS.	IRON 2 MGS.	ANALYSIS	CAL. 517	PROT. 8 GMS.
BLACK PART OF COLUMN SHOWS HOW MUCH OF DAILY NEED IS SUPPLIED BY ONE PORTION												
AVERAGE DAILY NEED		5000 I.U.	600 I.U.	1500 I.U.	2.7 MGS.		800 MGS.	1320 MGS.	12 MGS.		2000-3000	70 GMS.

COMMENTS: Pastry desserts provide a rich way to serve fruits, in contrast to simple fruit mixtures and ices. Because fruits are cooked, however, vitamin values are greatly lessened. It has been shown, for example, that apple pie contains only one-fifth the Vitamin C of fresh apples. Hence, cooked fillings for pies, tarts, etc., not recommended from vitamin viewpoint, but are, of course, good sources of minerals, fats and carbohydrates.

When made of whole wheat or Graham cracker pastry, pie crusts contain considerable amounts of the Vitamin B complex. From the nutritional viewpoint, therefore, pies made with highly milled flours far less desirable, even though the flour be enriched with Vitamin B₁.

105

Pastries often difficult to digest, because of high fat content. Should not be eaten by the elderly or those with digestive troubles. Often digestibility depends upon balance of rest of meal; hence, planning pastries for dessert in light, unconcentrated meals is of utmost importance. Should never follow a heavy menu made up of concentrated or rich foods.

Deep-dish pies, tarts and other pastries with only one crust preferable to those with both shell and cover for persons with digestive troubles, as fat value is halved. Pastries generally high in calorie content; should not be eaten by reducers. Cream and Custard Pies especially rich; provide a good way to serve eggs and milk to children and the underweight. Iron-Rich Tarts valuable to anyone with nutritional anemia.

Serve chiefly at dinner after a light meal, or for supper. Any pie or tart may be substituted for the ones mentioned in Balanced Meal Suggestions. Best not to serve Custard, Cream or Lemon Pies at meal containing another egg dish.

STANDARD WHOLE WHEAT PASTRY
(Two-Crust Pie)

INGREDIENTS:

2½ cups whole wheat flour
1 teaspoon salt
⅔ cup cold shortening

7 to 9 tablespoons cold water
(approximate)

DIRECTIONS: Mix flour and salt thoroughly. A bland fat, such as a vegetable shortening, is best for pastry. Butter may be used for ½ the required quantity of shortening, but it should be unsalted. Cut in shortening with a pastry blender or 2 knives, until mixture of flour and fat has been cut into pieces the size of navy beans. Do not cut too fine. Add 1 tablespoon cold water and, with a steel fork or 2 knives, cut in (or mix) as much of the flour mixture as the water will take up. Continue adding water, 1 tablespoon at a time, until there are several balls of dough and very little dry mixture left in the bowl.

Press balls together lightly with the fingers. Then, if all the dry mixture is not taken up, add just enough water—a few drops should be sufficient— to take up remaining dry mixture. Do not use any more water than necessary, as dough must not be wet. This is important to insure a flaky, tender crust. Divide dough into 2 portions. Do not handle dough any more than necessary, either in mixing or rolling. Place one portion on very lightly floured board or smooth surface. Dust rolling pin with flour. Roll dough each way from center to edge until pastry is 2 inches larger than pie pan, and about ⅛ inch thick. Roll on one side only. Do not turn dough. Should dough stick to board when being rolled, carefully lift edge of dough with spatula and very lightly sprinkle board with flour only as needed.

When dough is rolled, place pie pan beside it. Fold dough in half, carefully lift it into pan and open it up. Fill with desired pie mixture. Roll remaining portion of dough for upper crust 1 inch larger than pan. Fold and use knife or scissors to cut several slits at fold. This is to permit steam to escape as pie bakes. Moisten edge of lower crust with water or milk. Lift upper crust carefully and unfold over pie filling. Press edges of crusts together, trim, and seal edges by pressing them together with tines of fork. Top crust may be cut in strips and arranged in lattice form, if preferred. This recipe will make 1 2-crust 9-inch pie; 2 pastry shells; or 12 tart shells.

Pastry Shell—Prepare ½ basic recipe. Roll dough lightly to ⅛ inch thickness, and 1 to 1½ inches larger than pie pan. Fold, prick several times with tines of fork, and place in or on pan according to either of following methods: (1) To use when pie filling (such as fruit, custard or pumpkin) is to be baked in unbaked shell—fit into pie pan and trim so that pastry hangs over edge about 1 inch all around. Double pastry edge by folding back overlapping dough to rim of pan. Shape it to stand upright at right angles to plate, and press into fluted shape. (2) To use when cooked pie fillings (such as stirred custard, cream or fruit) are placed in already baked shell—invert pie pan and unfold pastry over back of pan. Hold pan over pastry board and press pastry firmly to rim of pie pan, and with knife or scissors trim pastry evenly with edge of pan. Bake in hot oven (450° F.) about 15 minutes. To remove from pan, cool slightly and invert carefully on serving plate. Chill thoroughly before filling with cooked or fresh fruit.

One-crust pie shell recipe also used to top such pies as deep-dish fruit, vegetable or meat pies. Place unbaked dough over contents of baking dish, then trim the edge of the pastry, turn it under and press it down on moistened edge of dish.

Tart or Patty Shells—Prepare ½ basic recipe. Roll dough lightly to ⅛ inch thickness and cut in 5-inch rounds. Prick all over with tines of fork and fit over backs of 6 tart, muffin or patty pans. Bake in hot oven (450° F.) about 10 minutes, until light brown. Cool slightly. Remove carefully from pans. Cool thoroughly before filling with fresh, preserved, canned, cooked or dried fruit (flavored with whipped cream), or any type of custard or cream mixture. Yield: 6 tarts.

Cheese Bits—Gather together various pieces of unbaked dough trimmed in making pies, tarts, etc. Roll pastry ⅛ inch thick. Sprinkle liberally with grated cheese and paprika; fold and roll again; repeat, folding and rolling several times. Cut into finger lengths. Place on baking sheet and bake in hot oven (450° F.) about 5 to 7 minutes, until delicately browned.

GRAHAM CRACKER PASTRY

INGREDIENTS:

¼ pound Graham crackers (1 cup crumbs)

6 tablespoons butter
3 tablespoons brown sugar

DIRECTIONS: Use rolling pin to crush Graham crackers into fine crumbs. Melt butter in 9-inch pie pan, add sugar and crumbs, and mix thoroughly. Press mixture evenly and firmly around sides and bottom of pan. Chill before adding filling.

APPLE PIE

VITAMINS	1 PORTION CONTAINS APPROXIMATELY	DAILY NEED
A	621	5000 I.U.
B	77	600 I.U.
C	45	1500 I.U.
G	.09	2.7 MGS.

INGREDIENTS:

1 recipe Whole Wheat Pastry (page 106)
1 tablespoon granulated sugar
1 tablespoon flour
4½ cups pared, sliced apples

½ to ¾ cup brown sugar, firmly packed
¼ teaspoon salt
2 tablespoons butter

DIRECTIONS: Line 9-inch pie pan with pastry. Mix 1 tablespoon sugar with flour and sprinkle over pastry to prevent crust from becoming soggy. Mix apples with remaining sugar and salt. Sprinkle apples with a few drops to 1 teaspoon lemon juice for additional flavor, or mix ½ teaspoon cinnamon or ½ teaspoon nutmeg with sugar and salt before mixing with apples. Fill shell with fruit. Dot with butter and cover with pastry. Bake in moderately hot oven (425° F.) 30 to 40 minutes, until apples are soft.

Rhubarb Pie—Replace apples with 4 cups diced rhubarb. Sprinkle pastry with 1 tablespoon sugar mixed with 1 tablespoon flour. If tart pie is desired, use only 1 cup sugar. Mix 3 tablespoons flour with the sugar. Add to fruit.

Rhubarb Pineapple Pie—Replace apples with 3 cups diced rhubarb and 1 cup drained, canned, crushed pineapple. Use about ¾ to 1 cup sugar, depending upon sweetness of pineapple. Mix sugar with 3 tablespoons flour and add to fruit. Proceed as in recipe for Apple Pie.

Fresh Berry Pie—Replace apples with 4 cups washed blackberries, raspberries, blueberries or hulled strawberries. Mix 1 cup granulated sugar with 3 tablespoons flour and add to fruit. Proceed as in recipe for Apple Pie. Be particularly careful to have fruit drained before filling pastry.

Sour Cherry Pie—Replace apples with 3 cups pitted sour cherries. Mix 1½ cups sugar with 3 tablespoons of flour and then with fruit. Proceed as in recipe for Apple Pie.

Fresh Peach Pie—Replace apples with 4 cups peeled, sliced peaches (be sure peaches are juicy). Flavor with a sprinkle of nutmeg or lemon juice. Mix 1 cup sugar with 3 tablespoons flour and then with fruit. Proceed as in recipe for Apple Pie.

Canned or Cooked Fruit Pies—Replace apples with 2 to 2½ cups canned or cooked fruit and ½ cup fruit juice. Use from ¾ to 1 cup sugar, depending upon amount of sugar with which fruit has been prepared. Proceed as in recipe for Apple Pie.

PUMPKIN PIE

INGREDIENTS:

½ recipe Whole Wheat Pastry (page 106)
2 cups canned or cooked, riced pumpkin (page 287)
¾ cup brown sugar, firmly packed
½ teaspoon cinnamon
½ teaspoon mace

½ teaspoon ginger
¼ teaspoon ground cloves (optional)
½ teaspoon salt
2 eggs, slightly beaten
2 cups rich milk

DIRECTIONS: Prepare Pastry Shell (page 107). Do not bake. In a bowl, mix ingredients thoroughly, in the order given. Pour into unbaked shell and bake in a hot oven (450° F.) 10 minutes. Then reduce heat to moderate (375° F.), and bake about 30 minutes longer, or just until the filling is firm in center. Do not overcook. When knife inserted in center comes out clean, pie is done. For a richer filling, add one more egg. This mixture may be baked without pastry, in individual custard cups or ramekins, like Baked Custard (page 113).

CUSTARD PIE

INGREDIENTS:

½ recipe Whole Wheat Pastry
   (page 106)
4 eggs
¾ cup brown sugar,
   firmly packed

½ teaspoon salt
2½ cups scalded milk
1 teaspoon vanilla extract
nutmeg to taste

DIRECTIONS: Prepare Pastry Shell (page 107). Bake shell in hot oven (450° F.) 10 minutes. (This partial baking prevents soggy crust.) Beat eggs slightly and stir in sugar and salt, mixing well. Stir in scalded milk and vanilla extract, beating until sugar is dissolved. Strain into partially baked shell and sprinkle with nutmeg. Reduce heat to moderate (350° F.), and continue baking 30 to 40 minutes, or just until knife inserted in center comes out clean. Do not overcook.

Coconut Custard Pie—Follow basic recipe, but add ½ to 1 cup shredded coconut to custard mixture before baking, and sprinkle top of pie filling with coconut.

CREAM PIE

VITAMINS	1 PORTION CONTAINS APPROXIMATELY	DAILY NEED
A	552	5000 I.U.
B	42	600 I.U.
C	11	1500 I.U.
G	.08	2.7 MGS.

INGREDIENTS:

½ recipe Whole Wheat Pastry
   (page 106)
2 cups milk
5 tablespoons flour

½ cup sugar
¼ teaspoon salt
2 egg yolks, slightly beaten
1 teaspoon vanilla extract

DIRECTIONS: Prepare and bake Pastry Shell (page 107), or Tart Shells. Scald milk in double boiler. In a mixing bowl, combine flour, sugar, and salt, and mix thoroughly. Add gradually to scalded milk, stirring constantly. Continue stirring over hot water until mixture is smooth and thick. Cover and cook 15 minutes, stirring occasionally. Add gradually to slightly beaten egg yolks, stirring constantly, and when well blended, return to double boiler and cook 1 minute longer. Cool, add vanilla extract, and pour into baked pastry shell or tart shells. Cover with Meringue (page 111), and bake in slow oven (325° F.) about 15 minutes, just until lightly browned.

Banana Cream Pie—Follow basic recipe, but slice 2 bananas and arrange in baked pastry shell before adding cream filling. Substitute whipped cream for meringue and do not return to oven.

Berry Cream Pie—Follow basic recipe, but after cream filling has been placed in baked pastry shell, arrange 1 cup prepared sliced strawberries (or other fruit) over filling and garnish, if desired, with whipped cream.

Coconut Cream Pie—Follow basic recipe, but add ½ cup shredded coconut to cream filling before pouring into baked pastry shell, and sprinkle ½ cup coconut on meringue before baking.

	1 PORTION CONTAINS APPROXIMATELY	DAILY NEED
A	714	5000 I.U.
B	54	600 I.U.
C	28	1500 I.U.
G	.13	2.7 MGS.

IRON RICH TARTS

INGREDIENTS:

½ recipe Whole Wheat Pastry (page 106)
½ cup cut raisins
½ cup finely cut dates
½ cup finely cut figs
½ cup chopped nuts
2 tablespoons flour
¼ teaspoon salt
1 cup brown sugar, firmly packed
2 eggs, well beaten

DIRECTIONS: Prepare pastry and bake Tart Shells as directed (page 107). Combine other ingredients in double boiler in order given. Mix well. Cook over hot water about 20 minutes, or until mixture thickens, stirring occasionally. Approximate yield: 2 cups filling.

MERINGUE

INGREDIENTS:

2 egg whites
4 to 6 tablespoons sugar
½ teaspoon vanilla extract

DIRECTIONS: Beat egg whites until stiff but not dry. Add sugar gradually, beating constantly. (Four tablespoons sugar make a less sweet meringue, but it will be high and fluffy.) Add vanilla extract, and pile meringue lightly on filling in baked pastry or tart shell. Bake in slow oven (325° F.) about 15 minutes, just until lightly browned. Never use a high temperature or overcook meringue, whether used for pies or baked as cookies.

LEMON MERINGUE PIE

V A T I M I N S	1 PORTION CONTAINS APPROXIMATELY	DAILY NEED
Ⓐ	594	5000 I.U.
Ⓑ	43	600 I.U.
Ⓒ	160	1500 I.U.
Ⓖ	.13	2.7 MGS.

INGREDIENTS:

½ recipe Whole Wheat Pastry (page 106)
1 cup sugar
3 tablespoons flour
3 tablespoons cornstarch
¼ teaspoon salt

2 cups boiling water
1 tablespoon butter
2 lemon rinds, grated
6 to 8 tablespoons lemon juice
3 egg yolks, slightly beaten

DIRECTIONS: Prepare and bake Pastry Shell (page 107). Cool before filling. Mix sugar, flour, cornstarch and salt in top part of double boiler. Add boiling water gradually, stirring constantly. Stir mixture over direct heat until it boils and thickens. Place over hot water and cook 20 minutes, stirring occasionally. Add butter. In a mixing bowl, add grated lemon rind and lemon juice to slightly beaten egg yolks, then beat into hot mixture, stirring constantly. Cook 1 minute longer and remove from heat. Cool and pour into baked pastry shell. Cover with Meringue (page 111), and bake in slow oven (325° F.) about 15 minutes, just until lightly browned.

BALANCED MEAL SUGGESTIONS: *Lunch or Supper*—Vegetable Juice Cocktail; Fish Salad; *Sour Cherry Pie* or *Berry Cream Pie.*

Dinner—Cabbage and Onion Salad; Veal Loaf; Spinach; Stewed Tomatoes; *Deep-Dish Apple Pie* or *Lemon Meringue Pie.*

CUSTARDS

COMMENTS: Simple custards make excellent desserts for practically everyone, but are especially good for growing children, convalescents or other people on a light diet, and the aged. Consisting chiefly of eggs and milk, they supply important Class A protein, high in quality but not very great in quantity. Excellent sources of all the vitamins except Vitamin C, minerals—particularly iron and copper, needed for building normal blood—and a little carbohydrate. Custards particularly excellent way of getting milk into the diet of those who do not like it but need it for growth and health.

Baked and Boiled Custards the simplest type, and best used for children, convalescents and older persons. The many variations, which involve the addition of fruit, nuts, rice, etc., supply added flavor as well as more nutrients.

Simplest custards medium in calorie content; may be eaten occasionally by reducers if they are especially fond of this type dessert.

Use as dessert for lunch, supper or dinner after almost any meal, except one with other egg or milk dishes in it. Because of creamy, smooth texture, are best served after a meal of crisp foods of more definite character, rather than stews or casserole dishes which have a similar soft texture. The soft custard combined or served with crushed or sliced fruit especially good, from the nutritional standpoint, after a meal low in easily available vitamins, minerals or Class A proteins. Any custard may be substituted for the ones suggested in the Balanced Meal Suggestions.

While we usually suggest some sort of fruit for dessert at almost all luncheon and dinner menus, we find custards an ideal dessert for those meals already containing fruit—fruit salad or fruit canapés, for example.

VITAMINS	1 PORTION CONTAINS APPROXIMATELY	DAILY NEED	
A	528	5000 I.U.	BAKED CUSTARD
B	19	600 I.U.	
C	16	1500 I.U.	
G	32	2.7 MGS.	

INGREDIENTS:

3 eggs
3 tablespoons sugar
1/4 teaspoon salt

3 cups milk
1 teaspoon vanilla extract
1/8 teaspoon nutmeg

DIRECTIONS: Beat eggs enough to mix the yolks and whites thoroughly, and add remaining ingredients, beating until sugar is dissolved. Strain into individual custard cups and set in pan of hot water. If custard is to be removed from cup when served, butter cup before filling with custard. Bake in a moderate oven (375° F.) about 25 to 30 minutes, just until custard is firm in the center. Test by inserting silver knife blade; if knife comes out clean, custard is done. Do not overcook, causing custard to separate and ruining its delicate texture. Set cups in cold water immediately to prevent custard from continuing to cook from heat retained in cups. Chill and serve plain or with whipped cream.

SOFT (OR STIRRED) CUSTARD

INGREDIENTS:

2 cups scalded milk

2 eggs or 4 egg yolks,
slightly beaten

4 tablespoons sugar

¼ teaspoon salt

½ teaspoon vanilla extract
(or sherry to taste)

DIRECTIONS: Scald milk in top part of double boiler. In a mixing bowl, beat eggs or egg yolks with sugar and salt until well mixed. Pour scalded milk gradually into egg mixture, stirring constantly until thoroughly mixed. Return to double boiler and stir constantly over hot water until mixture stops foaming and begins to coat silver spoon, about 2 minutes. Dip silver spoon into custard and take it out. If custard forms a straight line across spoon, mixture should be removed from hot water immediately. If the line is wavy, custard is not quite done. Be very careful not to overcook.

When custard is finished (in about 3 to 5 minutes), remove from heat and set pan in cold water immediately. This will prevent overcooking or curdling, as custard continues cooking after it is removed from the heat unless the pan containing it is cooled at once. Strain, add flavoring, and chill. Serve as simple dessert or as sauce over fruit or simple cake. For a slightly thicker custard and deeper yellow color, use 3 eggs or 6 egg yolks. For a fuller-bodied custard sauce, use 3 egg yolks.

Fruit Custard—Prepare custard according to directions in basic recipe. Place about 3 tablespoons diced or crushed fresh or canned fruit in each of 6 parfait glasses, cover with custard and chill. Serve garnished with diced fruit or whipped cream. *This fruit adds Vitamin C to the custard.*

Banana-Peanut Custard—Prepare custard according to directions in basic recipe. Place thin layer of broken bits of Graham crackers in bottoms of 6 sherbet glasses. Slice ½ banana into each glass and cover with Soft Custard. Chill. Sprinkle each custard with 2 teaspoons chopped salted peanuts (or other nut meats). *This variation adds Vitamin B to the custard.*

BALANCED MEAL SUGGESTIONS: *Lunch*—Spring Consommé; Fruit Salad; Whole Wheat Rolls; *Baked Custard.*

Dinner—Celery and Apple Salad; Beef Patties; Broccoli; Parsley Potatoes; *Banana-Peanut Custard.*

Supper—Pimiento Coleslaw; Vegetable Plate (Spinach, Cauliflower with Cheese Sauce Beets, Carrots); Rye Toast; *Fruit Custard.*

CAKES

This Chart Gives Approximate Food Values for BASIC WHITE CAKE. For Vitamin Values of Specific Recipes, See Charts Accompanying Them.

		A	B	C	G		CALC.	PHOS.	IRON		CAL.	PROT.
1 PORTION CONTAINS APPROXIMATELY	VITAMINS	494 I.U.	32 I.U.	3 I.U.	.17 MGS.	MINERALS	107 MGS.	77 MGS.	.6 MGS.	ANALYSIS	312	5 GMS.
BLACK PART OF COLUMN SHOWS HOW MUCH OF DAILY NEED IS SUPPLIED BY ONE PORTION												
AVERAGE DAILY NEED		5000 I.U.	600 I.U.	1500 I.U.	2.7 MGS.		800 MGS.	1320 MGS.	12 MGS.		2000-3000	70 GMS.

COMMENTS: Cakes contribute chiefly starch and sugar to the diet. If made with molasses and fruits to supply the sugar, they can be a nutritional contribution to the diet, particularly for growing children and those needing to gain weight. Should be eaten only occasionally by reducers.

Since all cakes made with baking powder cannot be considered as sure sources of Vitamin B_1 (baking powder or soda destroys some of this vitamin in cooking), they must be relied upon for other nutritional or taste values. All recipes in this section have vitamin and mineral value either within themselves or in their use as agents for combining with fruits. One exception is Basic Butter Cake, which is included as a "luxury" item for the diet. It cannot be considered a source of vitamins (except for ones contained in eggs), but is merely a sweet for use on special occasions.

The fruit cake and Molasses Ginger Cake supply considerable iron. Latter contains other members of Vitamin B complex not harmed by baking soda, but its Vitamin B_1 is diminished. Fruit cake, of course, can be considered reliable source of whole Vitamin B complex, as it does not require a chemical leavening agent, like soda. Cheese Cake an extremely rich, sweet cake, high in Vitamins A and B_1, iron, fat and carbohydrate. An excellent dish for underweight children and adults.

Always serve cakes at end of a light meal, never as dessert for concentrated, rich meal. In other words, no matter what kind of cake it is, use only after a meal of salad, main protein dish (non-fatty meat, fish or eggs), and vegetables low in calorie content.

BUTTER CAKE
(Basic Cake Recipe)

INGREDIENTS:

2 cups sifted cake flour

3 teaspoons tartrate baking powder

¼ teaspoon salt

½ cup shortening

1 cup sugar

2 eggs, well beaten

¾ cup milk

1 teaspoon vanilla extract

DIRECTIONS: Mix and sift flour, baking powder and salt. In a separate bowl, cream shortening, add sugar gradually, and cream until light and fluffy. Stir in well-beaten eggs and mix thoroughly. Add sifted dry ingredients alternately with milk, stirring well after each addition. Add vanilla extract. Bake in 2 greased 9-inch layer cake pans, or 2 sets greased muffin pans, in moderate oven (375° F.) 25 to 30 minutes, or in greased 8-inch square pan, 40 to 50 minutes. Cool and frost.

One-Egg Cake—Proceed as in basic recipe, using only 1 egg and reducing shortening to ¼ cup.

White Cake—Proceed as in basic recipe. Use 3 stiffly beaten egg whites to replace the 2 whole eggs.

MOLASSES GINGER CAKE

VITAMINS	1 PORTION CONTAINS APPROXIMATELY	DAILY NEED
A	376	5000 I.U.
B	42	600 I.U.
C	4	1500 I.U.
G	.08	2.7 MGS.

INGREDIENTS:

2 cups whole wheat flour

½ cup sugar

1½ teaspoons baking soda

½ teaspoon salt

1 teaspoon ginger

1 teaspoon cinnamon

¼ teaspoon nutmeg

⅔ cup molasses

1 cup sweet or sour milk

1 egg

3 tablespoons shortening, melted

DIRECTIONS: Mix thoroughly all dry ingredients. In a separate bowl, beat together molasses, milk, egg, and cooled melted shortening, until well blended. Add liquid to dry ingredients, beating just until smooth and well mixed. Bake in greased shallow baking pan in moderate oven (350° F.) about 35 minutes. Serve hot or cold, plain or topped with whipped cream.

116

SHORTCAKE

Each portion contains approximately:
Vit. A—93 I.U.; Vit. B₁—38 I.U.; Vit. G—.16 Mgs.

INGREDIENTS:

3 cups sifted flour	1 tablespoon sugar
4½ teaspoons tartrate baking powder	½ cup shortening
	¾ cup milk (approximate)
½ teaspoon salt	2 tablespoons softened butter

DIRECTIONS: To make light, tender shortcakes, do not handle dough any more than necessary. Mix and sift dry ingredients. Cut in shortening with 2 knives or pastry blender until flour-fat globules are the size of pea beans. Stir in milk gradually, using a steel fork, mixing just enough to make a smooth dough.

For individual shortcakes, drop dough from large spoon into 12 2-inch rounds and put rounds together with softened butter. Place on baking sheet to bake. For 1 large shortcake, turn half of dough into an 8-inch layer cake pan, spread with softened butter and then turn out other half to fit on top. Bake in hot oven (450° F.) about 12 to 15 minutes for individual shortcakes; 15 to 20 minutes for large shortcake. To serve, split baked shortcake and spread crushed fruit, sweetened to taste, between layers and over top. Serve shortcake with plain or whipped cream.

ECONOMY ORANGE SPONGE CAKE

INGREDIENTS:

1 cup sifted cake flour	3 eggs
1 teaspoon tartrate baking powder	1 teaspoon grated orange rind
¼ teaspoon salt	¼ cup orange juice
1 cup sugar	

DIRECTIONS: Mix sifted flour, baking powder and salt, and sift twice. Sift sugar. Break eggs into bowl and beat until lemon-colored. Add sifted sugar and beat until very light and fluffy. Add orange rind and juice and beat until well blended. Fold in flour gradually. Bake in small greased muffin pans in moderate oven (350° F.) about 20 minutes, or in greased 8-inch square pan about 35 minutes. Cake will be baked when crust is evenly browned; will not shrink from sides of pan as do butter cakes. When done, remove from oven and place pan on cake cooler to cool. When cool, loosen from pan with spatula or knife. Sponge cakes usually served unfrosted. Serve with fresh or canned fruit or a pudding sauce.

CHEESE CAKE

INGREDIENTS:

4 cups Graham cracker crumbs (or 1 package Zwieback)
2 tablespoons butter
2 tablespoons granulated sugar
½ cup brown sugar, firmly packed
2 tablespoons flour

¼ teaspoon salt
1 pound cream cheese
1 teaspoon vanilla extract
4 egg yolks
1 cup cream (or rich milk)
4 egg whites, stiffly beaten

DIRECTIONS: To make crust: Roll or grind crackers or Zwieback into very fine crumbs. Cream butter and granulated sugar until very smooth. Add crumbs and mix thoroughly. Press mixture evenly around inside of well-buttered 9-inch spring form mold.

To make filling: Mix brown sugar, flour and salt. Soften cheese with wooden spoon, add dry ingredients and cream together thoroughly. Add vanilla extract and unbeaten egg yolks. Beat thoroughly and stir in cream. Fold in stiffly beaten egg whites. Turn cheese mixture on top of crumb mixture. Sprinkle with nutmeg, if desired. Bake in slow oven (325° F.) about 1 hour, until center is firm.

REFRIGERATOR FRUIT CAKE (UNCOOKED)

This Cake Is Exceptionally Rich in All the Vitamins and Minerals

INGREDIENTS:

1 pound seeded raisins
1 10-ounce package pitted dates
1 8-ounce package figs
1 pound walnut meats
1 orange rind, grated
1 lemon rind, grated

⅓ cup brown sugar, firmly packed
1 teaspoon nutmeg
2 teaspoons cinnamon
¼ teaspoon ground ginger
¼ cup orange juice
3 tablespoons lemon juice (or sherry flavoring)

DIRECTIONS: Put fruits and walnuts through meat grinder. Mix sugar and spices, and blend thoroughly with fruit and nut mixture. Add fruit juices and mix well. Press firmly into buttered loaf pan lined with buttered waxed paper. Smooth over top, cover with several thicknesses of waxed

118

paper and keep in refrigerator at least 10 hours before serving. Slice very thin and serve like ordinary fruit cake. If desired, sprinkle with powdered sugar. This cake will keep several weeks. Store in refrigerator.

BALANCED MEAL SUGGESTIONS: *Dinner*—Lettuce Salad; Beef Patties; Spinach; Cauliflower; *Economy Sponge Cake* with Fresh Fruit or *Molasses Ginger Cake.*

Supper—Vegetable Juice Cocktail; Tuna Fish Salad with Tomato Wedges; *Cheese Cake;* Milk.

SMALL CAKES AND COOKIES

COMMENTS: Cookies, like cake, supply chiefly starches and sugars to the diet. Those made with whole wheat flour (Oatmeal Spice Cookies, Honey-Nut Cookies) and baking powder or soda, not good sources of Vitamin B_1, as such agents damage this vitamin. All cookies have other values, however, which recommend them as light sweets for anyone not having to watch his weight. Oatmeal Spice Cookies and Honey-Nut Cookies, for example, have other members of the Vitamin B complex, iron and (especially Honey-Nut Cookies) fat and protein.

Use cookies to top a meal that is neither heavy nor rich. Reducers and those not requiring a large amount of starches and sugars should eat cookies only occasionally after a light meal. Always eat cookies and small cakes when fresh, as they do not keep well.

BROWNIES

INGREDIENTS:

¼ cup butter, melted
1 cup sugar
1 egg
2 squares chocolate, melted

1 teaspoon vanilla extract
½ cup sifted cake flour
½ cup chopped nut meats

DIRECTIONS: Stir melted butter into sugar and blend well. Add unbeaten egg. Stir in melted chocolate and vanilla extract. In a separate bowl, combine nut meats and sifted flour. Add to chocolate mixture and blend well. Bake in greased 8-inch pan in a slow oven (325° F.) 25 to 30 minutes. Cool slightly and cut into small squares.

OATMEAL
SPICE COOKIES

INGREDIENTS:

2 cups whole wheat flour
¾ teaspoon soda
½ teaspoon salt
½ teaspoon cinnamon
　(or more)
½ teaspoon cloves
1 cup shortening

1½ cups brown sugar,
　firmly packed
2 eggs, well beaten
1½ cups rolled oats
1 cup chopped nut meats
1 cup chopped seeded raisins
¼ cup sour milk or buttermilk

DIRECTIONS: Mix thoroughly flour, soda, salt and spices. In a separate bowl, cream shortening, add sugar slowly, and cream until fluffy. Stir in well-beaten eggs. Add rolled oats, nut meats and raisins, and mix well. Stir in sifted dry ingredients alternately with sour milk or buttermilk. Drop by teaspoonfuls about 2 inches apart on greased baking sheet. Let stand a few minutes and flatten dough by pressing with tongs of a fork or by stamping with a glass covered with a damp cloth, if flat cookie is desired. Bake in slow oven (325° F.) 10 to 15 minutes.

NUT MERINGUES

INGREDIENTS:

2 egg whites, stiffly beaten
½ cup brown sugar, firmly packed
¼ teaspoon salt

½ teaspoon almond extract
1 cup ground nut meats

DIRECTIONS: Beat egg whites until they are stiff enough to hold their shape. Fold in sugar and salt carefully. Add almond extract and nut meats. Drop by tablespoonfuls about 2 inches apart on ungreased baking sheet and bake in moderate oven (350° F.) about 15 to 20 minutes. Remove from pans with wet spatula at once.

NUT MACAROONS

INGREDIENTS:

2 egg whites, stiffly beaten
1 cup brown sugar, firmly packed
½ teaspoon vanilla extract

2 cups corn flakes
½ cup chopped nut meats
1 cup shredded coconut

DIRECTIONS: Beat egg whites until they are stiff enough to hold their shape. Fold in sugar gradually. Fold in vanilla extract, corn flakes, nut meats and coconut. Drop by tablespoonfuls, about 2 inches apart, on greased baking sheet and bake in a moderate oven (350° F.) about 15 to 20 minutes. A standard measuring tablespoon which has a round bowl may be used for shaping macaroons. This insures a regular shape and better appearance. Remove sheets from oven, place on a damp towel and remove macaroons immediately with a wet spatula or a sharp knife. If macaroons become hardened on sheet, return to oven for a few minutes.

VITAMINS	1 PORTION CONTAINS APPROXIMATELY	DAILY NEED
A	388	5000 I.U.
B	59	600 I.U.
C	18	1500 I.U.
G	.04	2.7 MGS.

HONEY-NUT COOKIES

INGREDIENTS:

¾ cup whole wheat flour
¼ teaspoon baking soda
¼ teaspoon salt
¼ cup butter
½ cup peanut butter

⅓ cup brown sugar
⅓ cup honey
1 egg, slightly beaten
1 orange rind, grated

DIRECTIONS: Mix thoroughly flour, baking soda and salt. In a separate bowl, cream butter, and stir in peanut butter, sugar and honey. Add dry ingredients. Beat until mixture is smooth and creamy. Stir in beaten egg and orange rind until well blended. Drop by teaspoonfuls, about 2 inches apart, on a lightly buttered baking sheet. Press flat with fork and bake in moderate oven (350° F.) 10 to 13 minutes.

BALANCED MEAL SUGGESTIONS: *Lunch*—Tomato and Lettuce Salad; New England Clam Chowder; Fresh Fruit Cup; *Nut Macaroons.*

Dinner—Combination Salad; Tuna Fish with Cheese; Broccoli; Baked Apples; *Oatmeal Spice Cookies.*

EGGS AND CHEESE

This Chart Gives Approximate Food Values for POACHED EGGS. For Vitamin Values of Specific Recipe See Chart Accompanying It.

	VITAMINS				MINERALS			ANALYSIS	
1 PORTION CONTAINS APPROXIMATELY	750 I.U.	18 I.U.	3 I.U.	.22 MGS.	34 MGS.	112 MGS.	1.3 MGS.	75	7 GMS.
	A	B	C	G	CALC.	PHOS.	IRON	CAL.	PROT.
BLACK PART OF COLUMN SHOWS HOW MUCH OF DAILY NEED IS SUPPLIED BY ONE PORTION									
AVERAGE DAILY NEED	5000 I.U.	600 I.U.	1500 I.U.	2.7 MGS.	800 MGS.	1320 MGS.	12 MGS.	2000-3000	70 GMS.

COMMENTS: Eggs provide Class A protein, and are rich in every vitamin (except C) and all the important minerals. They rank as milk's equal in the human diet, and every child and adult should eat at least four or five eggs per week. People along in years, however, should probably not have more than this amount, as egg yolk is high in cholesterol content and so may help to hasten degenerative processes.

Reducers may eat plain egg dishes freely, but should avoid those made with much butter, cream sauces, mayonnaise, etc., and should omit toast or bacon which often accompany eggs.

Fried eggs are inadvisable for most people, especially children, the elderly and anyone with a weak digestion or gall bladder trouble. Stuffed eggs are also not recommended for small children or adults with digestive difficulties. Coddled and poached eggs are among most easily digested of all forms of eggs. Better suited for soft or convalescent diets than raw eggs.

Fortification of eggs with parsley, milk, pimiento, cheese, etc., always increases protective value of dish. Egg-cheese combinations provide especially good form of protein, and should be used occasionally in place of meat.

Egg white begins to coagulate at 131° F. to 137° F.; becomes jellylike at 140° F.; coagulates completely at 149° F. Egg yolk begins to coagulate at 143° F. to 149° F.; coagulates fully at 158° F.

Because of this coagulation, eggs should always be cooked slowly, without high heat; otherwise, they will be tough, leathery and not easily digested. Thus, water in which eggs are coddled or poached should never boil. Water best at 185° F. Oven temperatures (for baking eggs) may be as high as 300° F. to 350° F. Use cooking thermometer for best results.

POACHED EGGS

INGREDIENTS:

1 quart boiling water	6 eggs
¼ teaspoon lemon juice	6 slices hot buttered toast
2 teaspoons salt	

DIRECTIONS: Heat water to boiling point in large skillet. Add lemon juice and salt. Turn heat very low. Break each egg carefully into a cup or saucer and carefully slip into the water; or place eggs in greased muffin rings or an egg poacher (to help preserve their shape) and place containers in the water. Be sure water covers eggs.

Cook eggs just until whites are set or firm, and a white film forms over the yolks. Do not overcook. While eggs are cooking, prepare toast. Use skimmer to remove eggs as soon as set, and serve at once on hot, buttered toast. Add seasoning and butter to taste. May be served with cheese sauce, if desired.

CODDLED EGGS
(Soft, Medium or Hard-Cooked)

INGREDIENTS:

6 eggs	6 cups boiling water

DIRECTIONS: Use spoon or tongs to slip eggs into boiling water; cover pan and remove it from heat at once. Let stand in warm place 6 to 8 minutes for soft-cooked eggs and about 10 minutes for medium-cooked eggs. For hard-cooked eggs, do not remove pan from heat, but as soon as water boils, reduce heat as low as possible and slip eggs gently into water. Cover pan but do not permit water to boil again. Eggs will be hard-cooked in 20 to 25 minutes. Then remove eggs, place in cold water to cover for a few minutes, and crack shells to permit liberation of sulphur. Placing eggs in cold water makes shell removal easier.

If eggs are to be used as garnish, place them in ice water until thoroughly chilled; this prevents crumbling of yolk or breaking of whites when sliced.

Soft-Cooked Eggs (Double Boiler Method)—Fill lower part of double boiler ⅓ full of boiling water. Fill upper part of double boiler ½ full of boiling water. Place both parts over direct heat and let water boil rapidly. Then place upper part into lower container and turn off heat. Use spoon or tongs to place eggs in upper part. Cover tightly. Eggs will be soft-cooked in 5 minutes. Lift each egg from water and carefully crack shell, removing one-half of it; then, with small spatula, remove egg whole. It will be soft and creamy throughout.

SCRAMBLED EGGS	VITAMINS	1 PORTION CONTAINS APPROXIMATELY		DAILY NEED
		A	914	5000 I.U.
		B₁	23	600 I.U.
		C	5	1500 I.U.
		G	26	2.7 MGS.

INGREDIENTS:

6 eggs
1 teaspoon salt
⅛ teaspoon pepper

½ cup milk
3 tablespoons butter

DIRECTIONS: Break eggs into bowl. Beat slightly, and add seasoning and milk. Melt butter in heavy skillet. Reduce heat and pour in egg mixture. As soon as mixture begins to thicken, stir it with steel fork slowly and constantly over low heat, scraping eggs from bottom of pan as they cook to prevent their becoming dry and hard. A further precaution is to turn off heat (or, if necessary, to remove pan from heat) before eggs are entirely cooked, as pan retains sufficient heat to complete the cooking. Cook just until eggs have a creamy, fluffy consistency. Serve at once.

Continental Scrambled Eggs—Add 2 tablespoons minced parsley, 1 tablespoon minced chives, or ¼ cup minced pimiento to egg-milk mixture before it is cooked, and then proceed as in basic recipe. *Approximate vitamin values per portion: Vit. A—980 I.U.; Vit. B₁—4 I.U.; Vit. C—733 I.U.; Vit. G—.01 Mg.*

Scrambled Eggs with Sautéed Vegetables—Sauté 2 tablespoons chopped onions, 2 tablespoons minced green peppers and ½ cup sliced mushrooms in butter about 3 minutes. Then add egg-milk mixture and proceed as in basic recipe. *Approximate vitamin values per portion: Vit. A—138 I.U.; Vit. B₁—4 I.U.; Vit. C—124 I.U.; Vit. G—.03 Mg.*

	1 PORTION CONTAINS APPROXIMATELY	DAILY NEED
A	779	5000 I.U.
B	19	600 I.U.
C	10	1500 I.U.
G	.22	2.7 MGS.

DEVILED EGGS

INGREDIENTS:

6 hard-cooked eggs
1 teaspoon butter
½ teaspoon salt
⅛ teaspoon pepper
¼ teaspoon dry mustard

2 tablespoons Mayonnaise
(approximate)
few drops lemon juice
(or cider vinegar)
⅛ teaspoon paprika

DIRECTIONS: Prepare hard-cooked eggs as directed on page 123. Cut into halves crosswise or lengthwise. Use a small spoon to remove yolks to a small bowl, being careful not to break the whites. Force yolks through a sieve or ricer. Add butter, seasoning and mayonnaise. Mix until creamy and smooth. Add a few drops of lemon juice or vinegar for a more piquant flavor. Refill whites with yolk mixture and sprinkle lightly with paprika for color. Chill before serving. If desired, mix minced onions, pimiento, parsley, chives or watercress to taste with the mashed egg yolks.

CREAMED EGGS

Each portion contains approximately:
Vit. A—1807 I.U.; Vit. B₁—119 I.U.; Vit. C—57 I.U.; Vit. G—.4 Mg.

INGREDIENTS:

6 hard-cooked eggs
2 cups Cream Sauce (page 217)
1 tablespoon onion juice
or minced onion
3 tablespoons minced parsley

½ teaspoon celery salt (or 1 teaspoon Worcestershire sauce or ½ teaspoon each salt and sauce)
6 slices hot buttered toast

DIRECTIONS: Prepare hard-cooked eggs as directed on page 123. Cut eggs into halves lengthwise. Remove yolks and cut egg whites into long strips or chop coarsely. Add egg whites to Cream Sauce with onion juice, parsley and celery salt. Heat thoroughly, but do not boil.

Arrange toast on hot platter or individual dishes and cover with creamed egg mixture. Force egg yolks through coarse sieve and sprinkle over top (or egg yolks may be stirred into cream mixture just before serving).

Creamed Eggs with Cheese—Add ½ to 1 cup grated or shredded American cheese to Cream Sauce, stirring constantly until cheese melts and is well blended. (Amount of cheese used depends upon how strongly flavored a cheese sauce is desired.) Proceed as directed in basic recipe. *Cheese adds: 368 I.U. of Vitamin A; .1 mg. of Vitamin G, to plain Creamed Eggs.*

Creamed Eggs with Meat—Add ½ to 1 cup minced or diced cooked meat to Cream Sauce. Bacon, ham, tongue or giblets are the more popular suggestions. Proceed as directed in basic recipe. *Meat adds: 67 I.U. of Vitamin B_1; .03 mg. of Vitamin G.*

Creamed Eggs with Pimiento—Add ¼ cup minced pimiento to Cream Sauce. Proceed as directed in basic recipe. *Pimiento adds: 605 I.U. of Vitamin A; 709 I.U. of Vitamin C.*

FOAMY OMELET

VITAMINS	1 PORTION CONTAINS APPROXIMATELY	DAILY NEED
A	843	5000 I.U.
B	19	600 I.U.
C		1500 I.U.
G	.22	2.7 MGS.

INGREDIENTS:

6 eggs, separated
6 tablespoons water
½ teaspoon salt

dash of pepper
2 tablespoons butter

DIRECTIONS: Separate eggs; beat whites until they stand in peaks. Beat yolks with water and seasoning until foamy. Fold in stiffly beaten whites. Melt butter in heavy skillet. Reduce heat, add eggs and cook over low heat, cutting omelet as it cooks. Use spatula to lift edges of omelet as it cooks and gently push cooked eggs to center of pan, letting uncooked egg liquid run to outer edge of pan to cook. When all the egg mixture is partly cooked to a soft consistency and bottom is lightly browned, place about 3 inches from preheated broiler heat, and cook about 1 minute, just until top is dry and delicately browned. Cut part way through center. Fold and serve immediately on hot platter.

If you have a special omelet pan, just butter both halves of it, place egg mixture in one half of pan, cover tightly with remaining half and cook over low heat about 8 to 10 minutes. Do not open cover (thus letting steam escape) for at least 7 minutes. Omelet will be cooked when it has risen to top of cover and is delicately browned. Serve at once.

126

FRENCH OMELET

Each portion contains approximately:
Vit. A—908 I.U.; Vit. B₁—22 I.U.; Vit. G—.25 Mg.

INGREDIENTS:

6 eggs
6 tablespoons milk
½ teaspoon salt

dash of pepper
3 tablespoons butter

DIRECTIONS: Beat eggs slightly; add milk and seasoning. Melt butter in heavy skillet and pour in egg mixture. Cook over low heat about 10 minutes. Cut omelet with a spatula as egg on bottom of pan cooks; this cutting process is to permit uncooked egg liquid to run through cut to bottom of pan to cook. The success of this dish depends upon constant watching, cutting cooked portion and lifting of edges of omelet.

When cooked, omelet should have a delicate crust, and be of a soft, creamy consistency, not dry or tough. To remove, hold a warm platter over omelet and carefully turn pan upside down, keeping plate close to omelet.

Omelet with Creamed Vegetables—Add ½ to 1 cup sautéed mushrooms, cooked or canned buttered peas, lima beans, corn, chopped carrots, or cut asparagus to 1 cup Cream Sauce (page 217). Serve omelet on hot platter with creamed vegetables between or around edges. *Vegetables add: Vit. C—35 I.U.; Vit. G—.01 Mg.*

VITAMINS	1 PORTION CONTAINS APPROXIMATELY	DAILY NEED
A	1215	5000 I.U.
B	19	600 I.U.
C	8	1500 I.U.
G	.46	2.7 MGS.

BAKED CHEESE OMELET

INGREDIENTS:

1½ cups milk
1 teaspoon salt
3 tablespoons yellow cornmeal

2 cups (½ pound) grated or shredded American cheese
3 egg yolks, well beaten
3 egg whites, stiffly beaten

DIRECTIONS: Scald milk in top of double boiler. Add salt and cornmeal, stirring until mixture thickens. Remove from heat, add cheese and stir until well blended. Add slowly, small amounts at a time, to well-beaten egg yolks, stirring constantly. Fold in stiffly beaten egg whites. Pour in buttered 2-quart casserole and bake in moderately hot oven (425° F.) just until firm throughout and delicately browned, about 20 to 25 minutes.

BAKED EGGS, MUSHROOM SAUCE

INGREDIENTS:

1 can cream of mushroom soup
6 eggs
salt and pepper

2 teaspoons butter
6 slices hot buttered toast
3 tablespoons minced parsley

DIRECTIONS: Empty soup into deep pie pan or casserole. Break eggs into a saucer, one at a time, and then slip carefully into soup. Dot yolks with salt, pepper and butter. Bake in a moderate oven (375° F.) about 15 minutes or until eggs begin to set and become firm. Use skimmer to remove eggs; serve on hot toast with soup poured over eggs. Sprinkle with minced parsley.

BAKED EGGS AND CHEESE

INGREDIENTS:

6 eggs
6 teaspoons butter
6 teaspoons grated American cheese

3 teaspoons fine, dry bread crumbs
1 teaspoon salt
⅛ teaspoon pepper
paprika

DIRECTIONS: Melt butter in 6 individual ramekins (or casserole). Break eggs into dishes (or dish), season to taste and sprinkle with the mixed cheese and bread crumbs. Set dishes in a pan containing hot water and bake in a moderate oven (375° F.) until eggs are set and the crumbs brown, about 15 minutes. Just before serving, garnish with paprika.

Baked Pepper Eggs—Melt 4 tablespoons butter in skillet. Add 3 tablespoons chopped green pepper and 3 tablespoons chopped onion, and sauté until onions are yellow, about 3 minutes. Turn into 6 buttered ramekins or a greased shallow baking dish; break 6 eggs into dishes (or dish) and top with ¼ cup bread crumbs mixed with 6 tablespoons grated cheese. Bake in moderate oven (375° F.) about 15 minutes, until eggs are firm.

BASIC SOUFFLÉ

INGREDIENTS:

2 tablespoons butter
2 tablespoons flour
1 cup hot milk
3 egg yolks, well beaten
1 teaspoon salt
⅛ teaspoon pepper

1 cup cooked, strained vegetables
   (or grated American cheese or
   chopped cooked meat)
1 tablespoon minced onion
   (chives, parsley, pimiento, etc.)
3 egg whites, stiffly beaten

DIRECTIONS: Melt butter in heavy skillet, then reduce heat and add flour, stirring constantly until well blended and smooth. Add milk gradually, stirring over low heat until mixture is thick and boils. Add small amount at a time to well-beaten egg yolks, stirring constantly. Add cooked, strained vegetables (mashed or minced), cheese or meat and season to taste. Minced onion, chives, parsley, pimiento, green pepper, etc., may be added for further flavor. Fold in stiffly beaten egg whites. Pour into well-buttered casserole and set in pan of hot water. Bake in moderate oven (350° F.) about 40 minutes until firm in center. Serve at once.

FRENCH CHEESE SOUFFLE

Each portion contains approximately:
Vit. A—793 I.U.; Vit. B₁—13 I.U.; Vit. G—.3 Mg.

INGREDIENTS:

1 cup milk
3 tablespoons quick-cooking
   tapioca
1 teaspoon salt

1 cup grated cheese
½ teaspoon dry mustard
3 egg yolks, well beaten
3 egg whites, stiffly beaten

DIRECTIONS: Combine tapioca and milk in top part of double boiler, and cook over hot water, stirring frequently, until mixture is thick and clear (about 8 to 10 minutes). Remove from heat, add cheese and seasonings, and stir until well blended. Add small amount of tapioca-cheese mixture to well-beaten egg yolks, stirring constantly. Add egg yolk mixture to remaining tapioca mixture, stirring constantly. Fold in stiffly beaten egg whites. Pour into casserole and bake in moderately hot oven (425° F.) about 25 minutes.

CORN AND TOMATO SOUFFLE

Each portion contains approximately:
Vit. A—1626 I.U.; Vit. B₁—33 I.U.; Vit. C—229 I.U.; Vit. G—.35 Mg.

INGREDIENTS:

1 tablespoon butter
1 small onion, minced
4 tablespoons minced pepper
½ cup tomato paste
½ teaspoon salt

1 cup (¼ pound) shredded American cheese
2 cups canned or cooked yellow whole kernel corn
3 eggs, separated

DIRECTIONS: Melt butter in heavy skillet. Add onion and green pepper, and sauté until onions are yellow, about 3 minutes, stirring occasionally. Add salt, tomato paste and cheese. Stir constantly until cheese melts, then stir in corn. Remove from heat and cool slightly. Meanwhile, separate eggs; beat yolks until creamy and beat whites until stiff enough to stand in peaks. Stir yolks into corn mixture and mix thoroughly. Fold in stiffly beaten egg whites. Pour into buttered casserole and set in pan of hot water. Bake in moderate oven (350° F.) about 40 to 50 minutes or until firm in center. Serve at once.

BALANCED MEAL SUGGESTIONS: *Breakfast*—Orange Juice; *Poached* or *Coddled Eggs;* Whole Wheat Toast; Milk (coffee for adults). *Dinner*—Cucumber Salad; *Baked Cheese Omelet* or *Foamy Omelet;* Sweet Potato-Apple Casserole; Spinach; Date-Nut Refrigerator Pudding.

CHEESE

This Chart Gives Approximate Food Values for WELSH RAREBIT.
For Vitamin Values of Specific Recipes, See Charts Accompanying Them.

1 PORTION CONTAINS APPROXIMATELY	VITAMINS	A	B	C	G	MINERALS	CALC.	PHOS.	IRON	ANALYSIS	CAL.	PROT.
		872 I.U.	97 I.U.	10 I.U.	.34 MGS.		415 MGS.	341 MGS.	.9 MGS.		254	13 GMS.
BLACK PART OF COLUMN SHOWS HOW MUCH OF DAILY NEED IS SUPPLIED BY ONE PORTION												
AVERAGE DAILY NEED		5000 I.U.	600 I.U.	1500 I.U.	2.7 MGS.		800 MGS.	1320 MGS.	12 MGS.		2000-3000	70 GMS.

COMMENTS: Cheese is made up of Class A protein—largely casein from milk. When made from whole milk, is rich in Vitamin A, and high in fat content. Cheese made with rennet (a coagulating substance), a fine source of calcium; thus a good food for growing children. Cottage and pot cheese are poor in this mineral because they are coagulated with acid instead of rennet, and most of their calcium escapes into whey.

In general, cheese can be divided into two classes: hard or soft (including in-between types); and ripened or unripened. Hard cheeses familiar to most people are American and English Cheddars, Swiss, Edam, Roquefort, Gruyère and Parmesan. Soft cheeses—cottage, cream, Brie, Camembert, Limburg, Neufchâtel and Stilton—have creamier, almost liquid consistencies. Cottage and Neufchâtel are both unripened and hence perishable. Both must be refrigerated and consumed within a short time after making. Ripened cheeses, which include all Cheddars, are both more flavorful and more digestible after months or even years of ripening. Milk casein is partly digested during ripening process.

Packaged or processed cheese is usually a ripened cheese which has been ground, melted, blended, emulsified and pasteurized.

Cheese a concentrated, high-protein, high-fat food, and should be treated as one. Use as meat substitute, or blend into sauces and add to foods which need its flavor or food value. Of the 400 or so varieties of cheese, some may be difficult to digest and some not. Those highest in fat content are not recommended for anyone with poor digestion. Cottage cheese made of skim milk is very low in fat content—often best for the elderly. Distress most often arises when cheese is unwisely used as between-meal or bedtime snack, or at the end of a rich, heavy meal. Cheese most easily digested when it accompanies salads or other bulky foods or hard crackers which make for thorough chewing. Cheese a highly economical protein food. Penny for penny, supplies better protein, and more calcium, phosphorus, Vitamin A and energy value, than muscle meats.

Cheddar-type cheese best choice for cooking purposes because it is relatively cheap, melts easily and does not readily become stringy. Method of cooking cheese extremely important. Always use a low temperature, and cook only long enough to melt. High temperature or over-long cooking causes hardening and stringiness because heat separates fat and makes a rubbery curd.

Cheeses made solely by lactic acid souring are known as pot cheese and cottage cheese. Pot cheese is original cheese produced from curds of skim milk to which lactic acid has been added (or from sour milk). If sweet cream is added, result is cottage cheese.

WELSH RAREBIT

INGREDIENTS:

1 tablespoon butter

2 tablespoons cornstarch
(or 1 tablespoon flour)

1 cup rich milk

2 cups (½ pound) soft, mild
cheese (American), shredded

½ teaspoon salt

¼ teaspoon mustard

¼ teaspoon paprika

1 teaspoon Worcestershire sauce
(optional)

6 slices unbuttered toast (or
desired amount of crackers)

DIRECTIONS: Melt butter in skillet over low heat. Do not permit butter to bubble or sizzle. Add cornstarch (or flour) and stir constantly until well blended. Add milk gradually, stirring constantly, and cook 2 minutes. Add cheese and seasoning and stir over *medium* (not high) heat until cheese is melted. Success of rarebit depends upon not too high heat and constant stirring while cooking as much as upon the quality of cheese. Serve on toast or on crackers. Serve at once and eat directly it is served.

Rarebit should be smooth and creamy, never stringy. Should it become stringy, remove from heat immediately and stir in 1 slightly beaten egg. If cheese has not been overcooked, this often restores proper texture.

Fish Rarebit—Reduce cheese in basic recipe to 1 cup (¼ pound), add 1 to 1½ cups canned or cooked shrimp or tuna, 1 tablespoon minced onion, 3 tablespoons minced green pepper and 4 tablespoons minced pimiento with the cheese, and proceed as in basic recipe. *This variation adds: Vit. A—422 I.U.; Vit. B₁—12 I.U.; Vit. C—886 I.U.; Vit. G—.02 Mg.*

TOMATO RAREBIT

Each portion contains approximately:
Vit. A—1562 I.U.; Vit. B₁—98 I.U.; Vit. C—94 I.U.; Vit. G—.27 Mg.

INGREDIENTS:

1 tablespoon minced onion

1 tablespoon butter

½ teaspoon dry mustard
(optional)

1 can condensed tomato soup

1 to 2 cups (¼ to ½ pound)
shredded American cheese

½ teaspoon salt

6 slices unbuttered toast (or
2½ cups boiled brown rice)

DIRECTIONS: Sauté onion in butter until yellow, about 2 minutes. Stir in mustard, if desired. Add soup and heat just until it comes to a boil. Add cheese and salt, stirring constantly until cheese is melted. Serve at once on toast or boiled rice.

CORN-CHEESE CASSEROLE

INGREDIENTS:

3 tablespoons butter
3 tablespoons flour
1 teaspoon salt
1 tablespoon sugar
1¼ cups milk

2 cups canned cream-style corn
1 cup (¼ pound) grated American cheese
2 eggs, well beaten

DIRECTIONS: Melt butter in small saucepan; stir in flour, salt and sugar. Add milk gradually, stirring constantly over low heat until mixture thickens and boils. Stir in corn and cheese. Fold in well-beaten eggs. Pour into greased casserole and set in pan of hot water. Bake in moderate oven (375° F.) about 40 minutes, until firm in center and delicately browned.

CHEESE FONDUE

INGREDIENTS:

1 cup milk
1 cup soft bread crumbs
1 tablespoon butter
2 cups (½ pound) grated American cheese

1 teaspoon salt
¼ teaspoon paprika
3 egg yolks, unbeaten
3 egg whites, stiffly beaten

DIRECTIONS: Scald milk with bread crumbs and butter over low heat, stirring constantly with a fork until mixture is smooth and bubbles. Do not boil. Remove from heat, add cheese and seasoning, and stir until well mixed. Separate eggs and add yolks one at a time, mixing well after each addition. Beat egg whites until they stand in peaks; fold into cheese mixture. Pour into casserole and bake in moderate oven (375° F.) about 20 minutes.

BALANCED MEAL SUGGESTIONS: *Lunch* or *Supper*—Green Pepper Coleslaw; *Welsh Rarebit* or *Tomato Rarebit;* Fresh Pineapple; Milk.

133

FISH

This Chart Gives Approximate Food Values for BROILED FISH (HALIBUT).
For Vitamin Values of Specific Recipes, See Charts Accompanying Them.

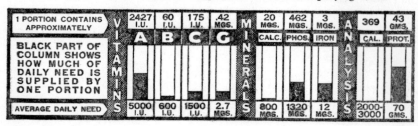

1 PORTION CONTAINS APPROXIMATELY	VITAMINS	2427 I.U.	60 I.U.	175 I.U.	.42 MGS.	MINERALS	20 MGS.	462 MGS.	3 MGS.	ANALYSIS	369	43 GMS.
BLACK PART OF COLUMN SHOWS HOW MUCH OF DAILY NEED IS SUPPLIED BY ONE PORTION		A	B	C	G		CALC.	PHOS.	IRON		CAL.	PROT.
AVERAGE DAILY NEED		5000 I.U.	600 I.U.	1500 I.U.	2.7 MGS.		800 MGS.	1320 MGS.	12 MGS.		2000-3000	70 GMS.

COMMENTS: Fish are flesh (protein) food consisting of two broad groups: those with scales (fish), and those without (shellfish). There are more than 140 edible fish available in the United States, although the average person is familiar with perhaps only ten varieties. The leading types common to most markets may be classified as lean or fat fish.

	Lean Fish		*Fat Fish*
black fish	king fish	bonito	salmon
bluefish	perch	butterfish	sardines
cod	pickerel	herring	shad
flounder	smelt	swordfish	tuna
haddock	trout	mackerel	whitefish
halibut	weakfish	pompano	

Lean fish have about 2 per cent fat; medium-fat fish up to 5 per cent; very fat fish, such as salmon, butterfish, etc., contain as much as 15 to 20 per cent fat. All fish have a high mineral content and are apt to be richer in certain of the vitamins than meats.

Fish oils and livers (cod liver, halibut liver, tuna or salmon oil) exceptional sources of Vitamin A and also Vitamin D (one of few food sources of sunshine vitamin). Do not rely on flesh of fish to supply these vitamins, however. Fish—especially salt water fish—is our most important source of iodine, needed for proper functioning of glands. Today everyone, even though he lives far inland, can obtain fish, and should eat it once a week at least for its iodine content, if for no other reason.

Freshness of fish is primary consideration. Flesh should be firm; eyes bright and unsunken; scales tight. Flesh should not leave a dent when pressed with the finger. Fresh fish never has a strong (tainted) odor.

Fish spoils quickly, but can be kept for a short time if packed in ice. If stored in refrigerator, place in coldest part and be sure fish is cleaned, salted, and wrapped in waxed paper to protect other foods in refrigerator.

Fish has tender flesh requiring careful handling and cooking to keep shape and texture. Fish is cooked just until it flakes (separates easily). Different types of fish must be cooked to suit their characteristics. Generally speaking, fat fish should be broiled or baked; lean fish, poached or broiled. Fillets are small strips of boned and skinned fish. In broiling fillets, use the broiler rack if it has a fairly fine mesh; use broiler pan otherwise. Brush lean fish with butter or oil before cooking.

Simplest ways to cook fish usually the best ways. Use almost any fillet (halibut, haddock, cod, perch, fluke, etc.) for baking or broiling; use large fish (bluefish, bonito, etc.) for stuffing. Use leftover or canned fish for flaked fish salad, casserole dishes, etc.

Fish lends itself well to garnishing with high-vitamin foods, like parsley and lemon. Lean fish usually calls for rich dressing, like Lemon or Parsley Butter (pages 222-223) or Tomato Sauce (page 221). Where possible, incorporate garnish in dish (sprinkle minced parsley on top of fish, rather than serve sprigs as decoration), so that it has added Vitamin C value, which fish lacks. Always serve fish on hot platter, as it cools rapidly.

Fish prices vary greatly, according to catches and demand. Fish in season always cheapest. Buy when bargain. Quick-frozen fish from reliable packer, excellent value. Should be used same day as purchased. Tradition of serving fish on Fridays makes fish most expensive at end of week. Economy-wise homemakers will buy fish on Mondays, when supply usually is greatest and demand lowest. Cheap fish generally has best flavor, as it is at height of season when the price is lowest.

Waste in fish is high, averaging 50 per cent. Some parts can be used to make fish "pot liquor," useful in poaching fish. Such pot liquor is an ideal base for fish sauces, chowders or stews.

BROILED FISH

INGREDIENTS:

1 3- to 4-pound fish   1 teaspoon paprika
(or 6 small fish)   ¼ cup melted butter (or salad oil)
1 teaspoon salt   Lemon Butter (page 222)

DIRECTIONS: Have dealer split and clean whole fish. Wash thoroughly and blot with paper towel or cloth. Be sure fish is dry before cooking. Mix salt and paprika with melted butter or salad oil and brush over fish. Place fish, skin-side down, on well-greased broiler pan (or rack, if fish is fatty). Broil 2 inches from moderate heat about 10 to 15 minutes, until fish is brown and flakes when tried with a fork. Small fish or thick fillets may be turned to brown both sides. Serve on hot platter with Lemon Butter.

FILLETS BAKED IN MILK

INGREDIENTS:

2 pounds fish fillets   3 tablespoons butter
1 cup milk (or sour cream)   2 tablespoons minced parsley
1 teaspoon salt   (or chives)
⅛ teaspoon pepper

DIRECTIONS: Wash fillets, cut into pieces for serving and arrange in greased baking dish. Pour over just enough milk or sour cream to cover. Sprinkle with salt and pepper and dot with butter. Bake in moderate oven (375° F.) about 15 minutes, or until fish flakes when tested with fork. Serve garnished with minced parsley or chives.

If desired, soak fillets in milk to cover, then dip in fine crumbs or cornmeal and place in shallow greased baking pan. Dot with butter and bake in hot oven (500° F.) about 10 minutes, or until well browned.

BAKED FISH

INGREDIENTS:

1 3- to 4-pound fish
1 teaspoon salt
1 teaspoon paprika
1 teaspoon onion juice

¼ cup melted butter (or salad oil)
6 lemon quarters
watercress
Parsley Butter (page 223)

DIRECTIONS: Have fish split and cleaned at dealer's. Wash thoroughly. Place in greased shallow baking pan. Mix salt, paprika and onion juice with butter or salad oil, and brush over fish. Bake, skin-side down, in a moderately hot oven (425° F.) 30 to 40 minutes, until fish is well browned and flakes from bone when tried with a fork. Garnish with quartered lemon and watercress, and serve with Parsley Butter. If you have a plank or oven-proof platter, arrange fish in center of plank and bake as directed. After fish has baked 25 minutes, surround with 12 halves buttered, quick-cooked carrots, 12 buttered mushroom caps, 6 halves of fresh tomatoes and 3 cups mashed potatoes (for border). Continue baking about 5 to 10 minutes longer.

	1 PORTION CONTAINS APPROXIMATELY	DAILY NEED	
A	1188	5000 I.U.	
B	115	600 I.U.	**STUFFED**
C	638	1500 I.U.	**BAKED FISH**
G	.47	2.7 MGS.	

VITAMINS

STUFFED BAKED FISH

INGREDIENTS:

1 3- to 4-pound fish
1 teaspoon salt
2 tablespoons flour
⅛ teaspoon pepper
¼ cup melted butter (or salad oil)

1 cup Fish Stuffing (page 226)
6 lemon quarters
2 tablespoons minced parsley
watercress
tomato wedges

DIRECTIONS: Have fish cleaned and prepared for baking at dealer's. Wash thoroughly, drain and sprinkle inside and out with salt. Fill opening with stuffing and sew or tie securely. Place in buttered baking pan, sprinkle with pepper and flour, and dot with butter. Bake in hot oven (450° F.) about 30 to 40 minutes, or just until fish is well browned.

If fish is not fatty, baste occasionally with ¼ cup butter melted in ¼ cup boiling water. Add more water if pan becomes dry. Do not baste any fatty fish, like mackerel, and do not add water to pan. Serve on hot platter garnished with minced parsley, watercress, tomato wedges and lemon quarters.

POACHED FISH

INGREDIENTS:

3 pounds fish
2 quarts boiling water
2 tablespoons vinegar
  (or lemon juice)
½ cup chopped celery and leaves
¼ cup chopped carrot
¼ cup chopped onion

4 peppercorns
2 cloves
1 bay leaf
2 teaspoons salt
1½ cups Fish Cream Sauce
  (page 218)

DIRECTIONS: Fish must be absolutely fresh, without slightest touch of strong odor. Dry-meated fish preferable, as flesh remains firm (fresh cod, halibut, haddock, tuna or salmon are those most commonly used). Wash fish, cut in pieces for serving and tie securely in cheesecloth or a clean sugar bag (or use regular fish kettle with rack if you have one). Place in water with vinegar or lemon juice (to keep fish from breaking), vegetables and seasonings. Cover utensil and simmer about 20 to 25 minutes, until fish flakes when tried with fork. *Do not boil,* but keep water always at simmering stage (about 180° F.). Drain and remove from cheesecloth. Serve on hot platter with Fish Cream Sauce, made with fish liquor.

FISH ROE

Each portion contains approximately:
Vit. A—7018 I.U.; Vit. B₁—98 I.U.; Vit. C—354 I.U.; Vit. G—.03 Mg.

INGREDIENTS:

2 pounds shad roe
1 tablespoon lemon juice
  (or vinegar)

1 quart boiling water
6 slices lemon
Parsley Butter (page 223)

DIRECTIONS: Although other roe may be used, it is not generally so firm as shad. Simmer (do not boil) roe in water and lemon juice about 8 minutes. Drain and chill in cold water just long enough so roe can be handled. Dry and broil or sauté. Serve with Parsley Butter, and garnish with sliced lemons. If desired, cut roe into small pieces after poaching and combine with Cream Sauce (page 217). Season to taste.

BALANCED MEAL SUGGESTIONS: *Lunch*—Pimiento Coleslaw; *Broiled Fish;* Bran Muffins; Citrus Cup; Milk.

Dinner—Mixed Greens Salad; *Fillets Baked in Milk;* Parsley Potatoes; Carrots and Peas; Open-Faced Apple Pie.

SALMON AND TUNA FISH

This Chart Gives Approximate Food Values for SALMON-PEA CASSEROLE.

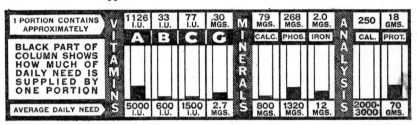

		A	B	C	G		CALC.	PHOS.	IRON		CAL.	PROT.
1 PORTION CONTAINS APPROXIMATELY	VITAMINS	1126 I.U.	33 I.U.	77 I.U.	.30 MGS.	MINERALS	79 MGS.	268 MGS.	2.0 MGS.	ANALYSIS	250	18 GMS.
BLACK PART OF COLUMN SHOWS HOW MUCH OF DAILY NEED IS SUPPLIED BY ONE PORTION												
AVERAGE DAILY NEED		5000 I.U.	600 I.U.	1500 I.U.	2.7 MGS.		800 MGS.	1320 MGS.	12 MGS.		2000-3000	70 GMS.

COMMENTS: Salmon and tuna fish differ from other fish in high fat content. Flavor and texture of these two very distinctive; also most commonly used canned fish. Have, generally, same nutritional value and uses as other fish (page 134), although salmon supplies a little more Vitamin A than any other fish, and salmon and tuna both supply Vitamin D. Both salmon and tuna fairly high in calorie content.

SALMON-PEA CASSEROLE

INGREDIENTS:

2 cups canned or cooked flaked salmon (or tuna)
2 cups canned or cooked peas
1 tablespoon minced onion
2 tablespoons minced parsley
3 tablespoons butter

3 tablespoons flour
1½ cups milk and liquid from salmon and peas
4 tablespoons bread or cracker crumbs
2 tablespoons butter

DIRECTIONS: Drain salmon and peas, reserving liquid. Combine liquid with enough milk to make 1½ cups altogether. Melt butter in heavy skillet, and stir in flour over low heat until well blended. Add to liquid gradually, stirring constantly until mixture boils and thickens. Stir in salmon, peas and seasoning, and turn into buttered 2-quart casserole or shallow baking dish. Sprinkle with bread crumbs and dot with butter. Bake in hot oven (450° F.) about 10 minutes, just until crumbs are browned.

SALMON LOAF

INGREDIENTS:

2 cups cooked or canned salmon
½ teaspoon salt
¼ teaspoon pepper
1 tablespoon minced onion
1½ cups soft bread crumbs

1 egg, slightly beaten
1 cup milk
1 tablespoon lemon juice
2 tablespoons minced parsley

DIRECTIONS: Turn salmon and salmon liquid into bowl, add seasoning and bread crumbs and mix thoroughly. Combine beaten egg and milk and add to salmon mixture. Stir in lemon juice and place in buttered loaf pan. Dot with butter and bake in moderately hot oven (400° F.) 25 to 30 minutes, or until delicately brown. Serve plain, garnished with minced parsley or Tomato Sauce (page 221).

TUNA-TOMATO CASSEROLE

INGREDIENTS:

1 cup cooked or 1 7-ounce can tuna fish
3 tablespoons butter
3 tablespoons flour
2 cups tomato juice
½ teaspoon salt

⅛ teaspoon pepper
¼ teaspoon sugar
1½ cups cut or canned corn (whole kernel)
1 cup soft bread crumbs
4 tablespoons buttered crumbs

DIRECTIONS: Flake tuna fish. Melt butter in skillet and add flour, stirring constantly over low heat until smooth and well blended. Add tomato juice, salt, pepper and sugar, and stir constantly until mixture boils and thickens. Combine sauce, tuna fish, corn and soft bread crumbs, and pour into buttered casserole. Cover top with buttered bread crumbs and bake in moderately hot oven (425° F.) 15 to 20 minutes, until delicately browned.

1 PORTION CONTAINS APPROXIMATELY	DAILY NEED
Ⓐ 1128	5000 I.U.
Ⓑ 18	600 I.U.
Ⓒ 312	1500 I.U.
Ⓖ .32	2.7 MGS.

VITAMINS

TUNA FISH
WITH CHEESE

INGREDIENTS:

1 cup cooked or 1 7-ounce can
  tuna fish
3 tablespoons butter
3 tablespoons flour
¾ teaspoon salt
⅛ teaspoon pepper

1½ cups milk
¾ teaspoon Worcestershire sauce
  (optional)
1 cup grated cheese
3 tablespoons minced pimiento

DIRECTIONS: Flake tuna. Melt butter in skillet, add flour, salt and pepper, and stir over low heat until smooth and well blended. Add milk slowly, stirring constantly until mixture boils and thickens. Stir in Worcestershire sauce. Add cheese and stir until cheese melts. Add pimientos and flaked tuna fish. Mix well, pour in greased baking dish and bake in moderately hot oven (425° F.) about 15 minutes, until top is delicately browned. Serve with buttered noodles.

Mixture may be served as a creamed fish on toast or combined with boiled noodles, and need not be baked. If not baked, after adding fish to cheese sauce, just stir gently over medium heat about 5 minutes, until fish is thoroughly heated and all flavors are well blended.

BALANCED MEAL SUGGESTIONS: *Supper*—Carrot Salad; *Salmon-Pea Casserole* or *Tuna Fish with Cheese;* Pineapple; Milk.

Dinner—Mixed Salad; *Tuna-Tomato Casserole* or *Salmon Loaf;* Baked Potatoes; Spinach; Fresh Fruit Plate.

SHELLFISH

This Chart Gives Approximate Food Values for STEAMED CLAMS.
For Vitamin Values of Specific Recipes, See Charts Accompanying Them.

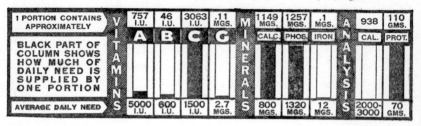

1 PORTION CONTAINS APPROXIMATELY	VITAMINS	757 I.U.	46 I.U.	3063 I.U.	.11 MGS.	MINERALS	1149 MGS.	1257 MGS.	.1 MGS.	ANALYSIS	938	110 GMS.
		A	B	C	G		CALC.	PHOS.	IRON		CAL.	PROT.
BLACK PART OF COLUMN SHOWS HOW MUCH OF DAILY NEED IS SUPPLIED BY ONE PORTION												
AVERAGE DAILY NEED		5000 I.U.	600 I.U.	1500 I.U.	2.7 MGS.		800 MGS.	1320 MGS.	12 MGS.		2000-3000	70 GMS.

COMMENTS: Shellfish fall into two groups: mollusks and crustaceans. Mollusks are of soft structure, and include clams, oysters and scallops. Perhaps above all other fish and shellfish, these are superior vitamin foods. Classed as protein (like meats and fish), they actually supply more protective vitamins and minerals than they do of proteins. As charts indicate, clams an excellent source of Vitamin C, containing about two-thirds as much (weight for weight) as orange juice. Oysters and scallops, too, yield large amount of Vitamin C. Since both clams and oysters often eaten raw, are thus a highly important source of the vitamin that protects gums and blood vessels. Clams, oysters and scallops also contain large quantities of iron, as well as the all-important iodine, which is not supplied to diet in appreciable quantities from any other source but seafood.

Clams, oysters and scallops, as long as they are absolutely fresh and correctly prepared, very easily digested. Like vegetables, are low in calorie content and fairly high in water content, which makes them excellent foods for balancing otherwise heavy or concentrated meal. Their character in these respects very unusual for a protein food, and should be taken advantage of by reducers and persons with digestive difficulties (but no allergies).

Use just as you would any fish, as main dish for dinner or supper. Clams and oysters both lend themselves to making into broths and chowders (page 232), and as such are excellent lunch or supper main-dish soups. Usual method of preparing oysters or scallops is to dip in flour or crumbs and fry. Such a cooking procedure adds indigestible material, which explains many cases of digestive distress attributed to shellfish themselves.

Like other shellfish, the crustacean group which include shrimp, crabs and lobster are excellent protective foods, containing surprisingly large amounts of Vitamins C and G. Are, in addition, our most important source of iodine, the chemical needed for normal functioning of the glandular system.

Low in calorie content, very easy to digest (if fresh and cooked properly), crabs, lobster and shrimp are good for reducers and those needing non-concentrated foods (in contrast to fatty meats, fowl, cheese, etc.), which may produce digestive distress.

Shrimp especially valuable and tasteful if mixed with such vegetables as green peppers, onions or pimientos, as in Shrimp Creole. Fish is made doubly protective by vegetable additions.

Lobster fairly expensive in many localities, but in others when in season, very cheap. Has no special virtues over and above any other shellfish, so need not be bought if too dear.

VITAMINS	1 PORTION CONTAINS APPROXIMATELY	DAILY NEED	STEAMED CLAMS
A	757	5000 I.U.	
B	46	600 I.U.	
C	3063	1500 I.U.	
G	.11	2.7 MGS.	

INGREDIENTS:

4 quarts (½ peck) unshelled clams

1 cup boiling water

¾ cup melted butter

2 tablespoons lemon juice

DIRECTIONS: Be certain clams are absolutely fresh and alive when purchased. If they are alive, shells will be tightly closed. If shells happen to be open, should snap closed when touched. If they do not close, clams are no longer alive and should not be purchased.

Wash and scrub clams well. Put into a large kettle with water, cover kettle and steam just until shells open, about 10 to 15 minutes. Do not overcook, as long cooking will make clams tough. Serve with individual dishes of butter seasoned with lemon juice or celery salt. Strain clam broth remaining in kettle, season with celery salt and minced parsley, and serve hot with clams, or chill and use cold as clam juice cocktail. Mixing equal parts clam juice and tomato juice provides good variation.

BAKED OYSTERS

	1 PORTION CONTAINS APPROXIMATELY	DAILY NEED
A	853	5000 I.U.
B	50	600 I.U.
C	212	1500 I.U.
G	.56	2.7 MGS.

INGREDIENTS:

36 oysters in shells
1 small green pepper, finely minced
1 small onion, finely minced
2 tablespoons lemon juice
3 tablespoons butter

DIRECTIONS: Be certain oysters are absolutely fresh when purchased. If bought in shells, should be alive, which is indicated by tightly closed shells. If shells happen to be open, should snap closed when touched. If they do not snap, oysters are no longer alive and should not be purchased. Have dealer open oysters and give you half the shells. Arrange oysters on half-shells in baking pan. Sprinkle tops with green pepper, onion and lemon juice, and dot with butter. Bake in hot oven (450° F.) about 10 minutes, or just until oysters puff up.

CREAMED OYSTERS AND CELERY

	1 PORTION CONTAINS APPROXIMATELY	DAILY NEED
A	1218	5000 I.U.
B	63	600 I.U.
C	281	1500 I.U.
G	.64	2.7 MGS.

INGREDIENTS:

1½ pints shelled oysters
3 tablespoons butter
1 cup diced celery
3 tablespoons flour
½ teaspoon salt
⅛ teaspoon pepper
2 cups oyster liquor and milk
1 pimiento, minced
2 tablespoons minced parsley (or watercress)

DIRECTIONS: Be certain oysters are absolutely fresh when purchased. Pick over oysters, remove bits of shell, drain and reserve liquor. Strain liquid, if necessary, to remove any bits of shell. Melt butter in large skillet, and sauté celery about 3 minutes. Stir in flour, salt and pepper, and when well blended, add reserved oyster liquor and milk slowly, stirring constantly over low heat until mixture boils and thickens. Add oysters and pimiento, and cook over low heat about 3 minutes longer, just until oysters are thoroughly heated. Serve at once on toast, garnished with parsley or watercress.

BROILED SCALLOPS

INGREDIENTS:

1 quart small scallops
1 egg, slightly beaten
2 tablespoons water
1 teaspoon salt
¼ teaspoon pepper

1½ cups fine, dry bread or cracker crumbs
1 lemon, sliced
2 tablespoons minced parsley

DIRECTIONS: Be certain scallops are absolutely fresh when purchased. Wash scallops, drain and dry. Dip in slightly beaten egg diluted with water, and roll in seasoned crumbs. Place scallops on buttered broiler pan, or on buttered heat-proof platter, dot with butter and broil 3 inches from moderate heat about 15 minutes, turning once during cooking. Serve with sliced lemon and garnish with minced parsley.

BALANCED MEAL SUGGESTIONS: *Supper*—Mixed Greens Salad; *Broiled Scallops or Baked Oysters;* Stewed Tomatoes; Pumpkin Pie.

BOILED SHRIMPS

Each portion contains approximately:
Vit. B$_1$—29 I.U.; Vit. C—110 I.U.; Vit. G—.23 Mg.

INGREDIENTS:

1½ pounds fresh shrimps
  (2¾ cups boiled)
2 teaspoons salt

1 quart water
2 slices lemon

DIRECTIONS: Be certain shrimps are absolutely fresh (or properly refrigerated during shipping) when purchased. Drop shrimps into boiling salted water. Add lemon slices to water. Boil 10 to 15 minutes, just until shrimps turn pink. Drain to serve hot, or let cool in cooking water to use cold. Remove shells and black intestinal vein running along back.

Serve hot with tartar sauce or any Butter Sauce (page 222), or combine with Cream or Cheese Sauce (page 217 or 218). To use cold, chill in fish stock, drain and clean before serving in salad.

SHRIMP CREOLE

VITAMINS	1 PORTION CONTAINS APPROXIMATELY	DAILY NEED
A	1323	5000 I.U.
B₁	32	600 I.U.
C	761	1500 I.U.
G	.24	2.7 MGS.

INGREDIENTS:

½ medium-sized onion, chopped
1 green pepper, chopped
2 tablespoons butter
2 tablespoons flour
2 cups (1 can) condensed
    mushroom soup
½ teaspoon salt

⅛ teaspoon pepper
¼ teaspoon thyme
1 small bay leaf
2 tablespoons chopped pimiento
2 cups cooked or canned shrimps
3 tablespoons minced parsley

DIRECTIONS: Sauté onion and green peppers in butter 3 minutes, stirring occasionally. Stir in flour until smooth and well blended, then add soup gradually and cook until thick, stirring constantly. Add seasonings and shrimps and cook about 5 minutes, just until shrimps are heated. Remove bay leaf. Serve on toast or boiled rice, and garnish with minced parsley.

BOILED HARD-SHELLED CRABS

Each portion contains approximately:
Vit. A—1558 I.U.; Vit. B₁—28 I.U.; Vit. C—99 I.U.; Vit. G—.32 Mg.

INGREDIENTS:

12 live hard-shelled crabs
boiling water

salt (to measure)

DIRECTIONS: Be certain crabs are still alive when purchased, as indicated by movement of claws and feelers. Wash crabs under running water until free from sand. Fill large kettle ¾ full of boiling water. Add 2 tablespoons salt for each quart water. Handle live crabs with tongs, or hold firmly just behind claws, and plunge head first into water. Cover and boil rapidly about 20 to 25 minutes. Remove from kettle and plunge into cold water after cooking to cool before removing meat. Break off claws and apron, or tail. Open and fold back shells at tail end, and remove spongy substance (gills, stomach and intestine) between two halves of body and between sides of top shell and body. Remove meat, flake and pick over carefully to remove bits of cartilage. Crack claws with nut cracker or hammer and remove meat. Serve hot in shell with melted butter, or use meat cold for salad.

VITAMINS	1 PORTION CONTAINS APPROXIMATELY	DAILY NEED
A	2109	5000 I.U.
B₁	27	600 I.U.
C	82	1500 I.U.
G	.37	2.7 MGS.

DEVILED CRABS

INGREDIENTS:

1 pound (2 cups) cooked or canned crabmeat
6 crab shells
4 tablespoons butter
2 tablespoons flour
½ teaspoon salt
½ teaspoon dry mustard
½ teaspoon paprika
1 cup milk
2 tablespoons chopped parsley
1 tablespoon lemon juice
1 cup bread crumbs
2 tablespoons melted butter

DIRECTIONS: Pick over crabmeat to remove cartilage, and flake. In a large saucepan, melt butter, stir in flour, salt, mustard and paprika. When well blended, add milk slowly, stirring constantly over low heat until mixture thickens and boils. Stir in parsley, lemon juice and crabmeat. Fill crab shells or place in greased 1½-quart baking dish. Top with bread crumbs and melted butter. Bake in a moderate oven (375° F.) about 10 minutes.

BROILED LIVE LOBSTER

Each portion contains approximately:
Vit. A—370 I.U.; Vit. B₁—44 I.U.; Vit. C—70 I.U.; Vit. G—.16 Mg.

INGREDIENTS:

6 small or 3 large lobsters
melted butter (or salad oil)
salt and pepper

DIRECTIONS: Be certain lobster is alive when purchased, as indicated by movement of claws and feelers. Make sure that wooden plugs remain in claws. Place live lobster on its back on a board, and hold body between claws and tail. Then with large sharp knife, split from head to tip of tail. Remove sac near head, and intestinal vein. Crack large claws with hammer. Put lobster on greased broiler, brush meat with melted butter or salad oil, and sprinkle with salt and pepper. Broil shell-side down 2 inches from heat about 5 minutes, until lobster turns pink. Serve with melted butter.

BALANCED MEAL SUGGESTIONS: *Supper* — Carrot and Raisin Salad; *Shrimp Rarebit* or *Deviled Crabs;* Asparagus; Lemon Tarts.

147

MUSCLE MEATS

BEEF

This Chart Gives Approximate Food Values for ROAST BEEF.
For Vitamin Values of Specific Recipes, See Charts Accompanying Them.

	VITAMINS				MINERALS			ANALYSIS	
	A	B	C	G	CALC.	PHOS.	IRON	CAL.	PROT.
1 PORTION CONTAINS APPROXIMATELY	103 I.U.	45 I.U.	33 I.U.	.5 MGS.	32 MGS.	506 MGS.	MGS.	655	40 GMS.
BLACK PART OF COLUMN SHOWS HOW MUCH OF DAILY NEED IS SUPPLIED BY ONE PORTION									
AVERAGE DAILY NEED	5000 I.U.	600 I.U.	1500 I.U.	2.7 MGS.	800 MGS.	1320 MGS.	12 MGS.	2000-3000	70 GMS.

COMMENTS: Like all muscle meats, beef is an excellent source of proteins —the building blocks of the body. Plain broiled or roasted meats are easiest to digest. Those prepared rare or medium retain more of the Vitamin B complex than long-cooked meat. Thus, tender and well-hung—or ground— meats, which can be cooked in a shorter time than tougher cuts, really provide more Vitamin B complex to the user. A high quality, quickly cooked meat like Broiled Steak is perhaps the most vitamin-rich of all beef cuts. However, tender, quick-cooking cuts are more expensive so the wise house- wife who must watch her food dollar will add vitamin-rich vegetables, eggs, milk, etc., to cheaper cuts of meat requiring longer cooking times.

With the exception of the roast and steak, all of these beef dishes are economical because they use cheaper cuts of meat and fortify them with vegetables, eggs, milks, cheese, etc., to raise their vitamin and mineral contents. Follow the recipes closely, as it is essential that these important additions should not be overcooked and their vitamins thus wasted.

As a further economy note, be sure to reserve the liquids from any canned or cooked vegetables mentioned in the recipes. Sometimes only the vegetable is put into the dish, but the pot liquors should be saved and used later. Extra meat juice should be also saved for the soup stock pot, etc.

Liver is an excellent Vitamin A fortifier of economy beef dishes. Beef

Patties and Beef Meat Loaf have their vitamin and mineral values greatly increased when ground liver or bone marrow is substituted for part of the ground beef. The Grade B protein values of muscle meats are really given Grade A protein properties by addition of liver and other organ meats. Such fortified dishes are especially valuable for people with nutritional anemia, or growing children, because of high iron content of liver.

In general, patties an ideal way to use meats, for many reasons: short cooking time, ease of digestion, economy, etc. For the aged, convalescent or dyspeptic, they are a preferred meat dish.

Fatty or fried meats are apt to be indigestible, and are taboo for reducers as well as those with impaired digestive powers. Meats are acid-ash; low in roughage. Leftover combinations of meat sometimes are less digestible than freshly prepared dishes, and are not recommended for small children or anyone with a weak digestion unless fat content is reduced. Note that none of the dishes (especially the Beef Stew) is thickened with flour. This is unnecessary, as thickening is no help to digestion.

Some of these beef recipes are really one-dish meals (Beef Stew), and need only a salad and a dessert to round them out. A recipe which already contains one starchy ingredient, such as potatoes or rice, should be served with vegetables which are less concentrated—leafy vegetables, carrots, etc. Never serve potatoes with a rice dish.

Reducers should choose meat dishes which do not contain large amounts of potatoes, butter or other foods high in calorie content. Simple broiled or roast beef, or beef dishes containing vegetables low in calorie content like tomatoes, etc., are recommended for anyone who has to watch his weight.

Use of internal thermometer in roasting meat is strongly recommended as the old minutes-per-pound timing is too variable. The initial expense of the thermometer will be justified many times over by tender, juicier meats and —in many cases—fuel savings. Be sure that the thermometer does not touch bone or fat when inserted. (See individual recipes for correct use of thermometer on different kinds of meats.)

Broiling time for steaks can only be approximated because of varying tenderness of different cuts, varying degrees of thickness, actual amount of heat, and personal preference. Generally speaking, if a family likes well-done meat, it is best to buy 1-inch steaks to cut cooking time. Those who like rare meat may choose thick steaks.

149

ROAST PRIME RIBS OF BEEF

	1 PORTION CONTAINS: APPROXIMATELY	DAILY NEED
A	103	5000 I.U.
B	.45	600 I.U.
C	33	1500 I.U.
G	.5	2.7 MGS.

INGREDIENTS:

3 ribs of beef (about 4 to 5 pounds)   salt and pepper to taste

DIRECTIONS: Place standing roast fat side up in an open roasting pan. The choicest cut is from the 12th rib end, although any from the 6th to 12th ribs may be used. Season with salt and pepper. Roast in a slow oven (300° F.), allowing 18 minutes per pound for rare roast (internal thermometer temperature should be 140° F.) ; 22 minutes per pound for medium (internal temperature should be 150° F.) ; 30 minutes per pound for well done (internal temperature should be 160° F.). If roast weighs less than 5 pounds, add about 3 minutes per pound for each degree of doneness respectively.

During the roasting, baste meat occasionally with fat in pan, turning meat to have it evenly cooked. Allow ½ pound of meat for each person. In large cuts of meat, economical to buy more than is needed, and use leftovers next day. (This applies to pot roasts, whole hams, legs of lamb, loins of pork, etc. All vitamin charts are computed, however, on the basis of one portion.)

Degree of "doneness" of roast beef depends upon coagulation of red part of the blood of the beef (oxyhemoglobin). Red color of meat begins to turn pink at 145° F., and then grayish brown at 147° F.

Only way to determine accurately just when interior of roast has reached proper degree of heat is to use meat thermometer. With sharp knife or skewer, puncture meat to insert thermometer in fat side of thickest portion of roast so that thermometer bulb reaches center of largest muscle, but does not touch bone or fat.

Cooking by minutes-per-pound calculation is very inaccurate because pieces of meat of the same weight vary in thickness, as well as in proportion of bone or fat to meat. Standing rib roast cooks in less time than more compact boned and rolled rib roast. Have butcher fold roasts flat (shallow in depth) to saving cooking time.

BALANCED MEAL SUGGESTIONS: *Dinner*—Asparagus Salad; *Prime Ribs of Beef,* Pan Gravy; Baked Potatoes; Mixed Greens; Fruit Cup.

BROILED
BEEF PATTIES

INGREDIENTS:

1½ pounds chopped round, chuck, brisket or shank
1 clove garlic, peeled and minced (or 1 small onion, minced)

1½ teaspoons salt
¼ teaspoon pepper
1 egg, slightly beaten
2 tablespoons minced parsley

DIRECTIONS: Preheat broiling oven 5 to 10 minutes and grease broiler pan. Combine ingredients and mix thoroughly. Shape meat into patties and place in the pan about 2½ inches below moderate heat (350° F.). Broil ¾-inch patties approximately 5 minutes per side for rare meat; 8 minutes per side for medium; 10 minutes per side for well done. Cooking time will vary with thickness of patty. If family likes well-done meat, reduce thickness of patty to ½ inch to save cooking time. Dot with butter and sprinkle with minced parsley just before serving.

BALANCED MEAL SUGGESTIONS: *Dinner*—Pimiento Coleslaw; *Broiled Beef Patties;* Creamed Carrots; Kale; Iron-Rich Tarts.

VITAMINS	1 PORTION CONTAINS APPROXIMATELY	DAILY NEED
Ⓐ	103	5000 I.U.
Ⓑ	55	600 I.U.
Ⓒ	58	1500 I.U.
Ⓖ	.49	2.7 MGS.

BROILED STEAK

INGREDIENTS:

3 pounds porterhouse, tenderloin or "choice cut" chuck steak (or 4 pounds sirloin steak)

salt and pepper to taste
butter (optional)

DIRECTIONS: Preheat broiling oven 5 to 10 minutes and grease broiler rack. Wipe steak with cloth and cut fat edge in several places to prevent curling. Place on rack and broil about 3 inches below moderate heat (350° F.). Leave door of oven open, unless directions for use of range state otherwise. Best results are obtained if a moderate temperature is maintained throughout broiling period, and steak has to be turned only once to cook evenly. Turn meat when upper side is nicely browned.

Broil 1½-inch steaks approximately 13 minutes per side for rare meat; 15 minutes per side for medium; 18 minutes per side for well done. When done, sprinkle steak with salt and pepper, and spread with butter, if desired. For steaks over 1½ inches thick, allow 3 to 5 minutes longer cooking time for each side. Chuck steaks require 5 minutes longer cooking time for each side than porterhouse or sirloin. A 1½-inch club steak weighs about 1¼ pounds; a porterhouse, about 2½ pounds; a sirloin steak, 4½ pounds. Naturally, cooking time increases with thicker cuts of steak.

BALANCED MEAL SUGGESTIONS: *Dinner*—Lettuce and Tomato Salad; *Broiled Steak;* Corn with Green Pepper; Parsley Potatoes; Sour Cherry Pie.

BEEF STEW

VITAMINS	1 PORTION CONTAINS APPROXIMATELY	DAILY NEED
A	1270	5000 I.U.
B	59	600 I.U.
C	288	1500 I.U.
G	.45	2.7 MGS.

INGREDIENTS:

- 2 pounds chuck, rump or round
- 1 tablespoon butter or fat
- 4 cups boiling water
- ¼ cup celery leaves
- 2 sprigs parsley
- 1 bay leaf
- 1 teaspoon salt
- ¼ teaspoon pepper
- 6 small onions, peeled
- 4 small potatoes, peeled and quartered
- 4 small carrots, cut into strips
- 1 cup fresh or canned peas
- 3 tablespoons minced parsley

DIRECTIONS: Have beef cut into 1-inch pieces for stewing. Melt fat in large heavy kettle, and sauté beef until brown on all sides. Add water, celery leaves, herbs and seasonings, and simmer over low heat for 1½ hours. Add potatoes and onions and simmer 15 minutes longer. Then add peas and carrots and simmer another 15 minutes. (If peas are canned or quick-frozen, they need not be added until last 7 minutes of cooking time.) In complete cooking time of 2 hours, all ingredients will be done. Sprinkle with minced parsley before serving.

BALANCED MEAL SUGGESTIONS: *Dinner*—Lettuce and Tomato Salad; *Beef Stew;* One-Crust Apple Pie.

152

	1 PORTION CONTAINS APPROXIMATELY	DAILY NEED	
A	1580	5000 I.U.	
B	113	600 I.U.	**BEEF MEAT LOAF**
C	274	1500 I.U.	
G	.41	2.7 MGS.	

INGREDIENTS:

½ cup milk
1 cup dry bread crumbs
1½ pounds chopped round, chuck, brisket or shank
2 eggs, slightly beaten
1 medium-sized onion, minced

½ green pepper, minced
1 tablespoon salt
¼ teaspoon pepper
3 tablespoons butter, melted
½ cup chili sauce
3 tablespoons minced parsley

DIRECTIONS: Add bread crumbs to milk in large mixing bowl. When milk is absorbed, add meat, slightly beaten eggs, onion, green pepper, seasonings and melted butter. Mix together thoroughly and turn into greased 8"x4" loaf pan. Cover loaf with chili sauce. Bake in moderate oven (350° F.) about 45 minutes, just until loaf shrinks from sides of pan. Garnish with minced parsley sprinkled over loaf.

	1 PORTION CONTAINS APPROXIMATELY	DAILY NEED	
A	10,635	5000 I.U.	
B	129	600 I.U.	**BEEF-LIVER LOAF**
C	369	1500 I.U.	
G	1.4	2.7 MGS.	

To add considerable Vitamin A to the regular meat loaf, use ground liver to replace part of the beef in basic recipe above. Chart indicates how vitamin value of loaf is increased when ½ pound liver is used.

Beef-Veal Loaf—Replace ½ pound ground beef with ½ pound ground veal. Follow directions in basic recipe.

Beef-Marrow Loaf—To give blood-building value, replace butter with 3 tablespoons chopped beef marrow. Follow directions in basic recipe.

BALANCED MEAL SUGGESTIONS: *Dinner*—Cabbage and Carrot Salad; *Beef Meat Loaf;* Baked Potatoes; String Beans; Citrus Fruit Cup.

Supper: Vegetable Soup; Cold Sliced *Beef-Veal Loaf;* Potato Salad; Sliced Tomatoes; Baked Apples.

BEEF
RICE CASSEROLE

VITAMINS	1 PORTION CONTAINS APPROXIMATELY		DAILY NEED
A	1574		5000 I.U.
B	92		600 I.U.
C		761	1500 I.U.
G	.39		2.7 MGS.

INGREDIENTS:

1½ pounds ground beef (or 2 cups chopped leftover meat)
2 teaspoons salt
¼ teaspoon pepper
2 tablespoons minced parsley
1 medium-sized onion, minced

1 green pepper, minced
2 tablespoons butter (or fat)
2 cans condensed tomato soup
1½ cups cooked Brown Rice (page 289)

DIRECTIONS: Prepare rice. Combine meat with seasonings and parsley. Mince onion and green pepper and sauté in fat in heavy skillet until onions are light yellow, about 2 minutes. Add meat to skillet and stir with steel fork until crumbly and brown, about 4 minutes. Add soup and stir well. Place hot rice in buttered casserole or baking dish. Pour meat-tomato mixture over rice, and bake in moderate oven (375° F.) about 10 minutes. Serve garnished with parsley; if desired, sprinkle with grated Parmesan cheese.

SPANISH STEAK

Each Portion Contains Approximately:
Vit. A—868 I. U.; Vit. B₁—50 I. U.; Vit. C—332 I. U.; Vit. G—.47 I. U.

INGREDIENTS:

2½ pounds chuck, flank or round steak, cut 1 inch thick
1 cup boiling water
3 medium-sized onions, sliced
½ cup chili sauce

2 tablespoons butter
1 medium-sized green pepper, chopped
6 mushrooms, sliced
1 cup canned tomatoes

DIRECTIONS: Place steak in 2-quart casserole or deep baking dish. Add water, onions and chili sauce. Cover pan and bake in moderate oven (350° F.), about 1 hour, until almost tender. In a skillet, sauté chopped pepper and mushrooms in butter about 3 minutes, stirring occasionally to prevent burning. Add with tomatoes to meat. Cook 20 minutes or until meat is tender. Cooking time will depend upon tenderness and thickness of steak.

BALANCED MEAL SUGGESTIONS: *Dinner*—Lettuce Salad; *Spanish Steak;* Green Lima Beans; Parsley Carrots; Peach Shortcake.

VEAL

This Chart Gives Approximate Food Values for ROAST LEG OF VEAL.
For Vitamin Values of Specific Recipes, See Charts Accompanying Them.

	VITAMINS				MINERALS			ANALYSIS	
1 PORTION CONTAINS APPROXIMATELY	79 I.U.	89 I.U.	15 I.U.	.56 MGS.	70 MGS.	1027 MGS.	12 MGS.	633	98 GMS.
	A	B	C	G	CALC.	PHOS.	IRON	CAL.	PROT.
BLACK PART OF COLUMN SHOWS HOW MUCH OF DAILY NEED IS SUPPLIED BY ONE PORTION									
AVERAGE DAILY NEED	5000 I.U.	600 I.U.	1500 I.U.	2.7 MGS.	800 MGS.	1320 MGS.	12 MGS.	2000-3000	70 GMS.

COMMENTS: Shoulder or breast cuts of veal are not suitable for dry-heat roasting because all veal requires moist-heat cooking. Because of lack of fat, veal does not broil well, and roasts require larding because of deficiency of fat. Also, veal has great deal of connective tissue which can be tenderized only by moist cooking. Instead of water, sour cream or tomato juice may be used as the liquid. The sour cream adds fat, which veal needs, and the acid of both sour cream and tomatoes helps to make meat more tender and flavorful.

Roast veal easy to digest and comparatively low in calorie content. Good choice for reducers if served plain or with Tomato Sauce (page 221). Reputation veal has unfortunately gained as being "hard to digest" is result of poor cooking methods, such as breading and frying.

Veal rather bland in taste; combination dishes such as stews, loaves, etc., preferred by many people. A simple Tomato Sauce adds needed flavor.

ROAST VEAL

INGREDIENTS:

6 pounds leg, loin or shoulder of veal

salt and pepper to taste

6 strips bacon (or 4 tablespoons butter)

1 cup boiling water

DIRECTIONS: Wipe meat with cloth, rub with salt and pepper and place on rack skin-side up in uncovered shallow roasting pan. Lay strips of bacon over top of meat, or dot meat with butter. Roast in slow oven (300° F.)

about 3 hours, allowing 25 minutes per pound for leg, and about 30 minutes per pound for other cuts (internal thermometer temperature, 168° F.). Baste occasionally, adding more water if necessary. Serve plain or with a sharp sauce, like Tomato Sauce (page 221).

Stuffed Veal Shoulder—Have bone of shoulder or leg removed or have dealer prepare pocket in breast. Fill cavity with Prune-Apple Stuffing (page 227). Sew or skewer opening. Rub pan or meat with clove of garlic for additional flavor. Proceed as in basic recipe.

BALANCED MEAL SUGGESTIONS: *Dinner*—Lettuce Salad with Roquefort Cheese Dressing; *Roast Veal;* Candied Sweet Potatoes; Brussels Sprouts; Ice Cream with Fruit Sauce.

BRAISED VEAL CUTLETS

VITAMINS	1 PORTION CONTAINS APPROXIMATELY	DAILY NEED
A	190	5000 I.U.
B	71	600 I.U.
C	18	1500 I.U.
G	.37	2.7 MGS.

INGREDIENTS:

2 pounds veal cutlet or 6 loin veal chops

3 tablespoons butter (or bacon fat)
1 cup water

DIRECTIONS: Melt fat in heavy skillet. Sear cutlet or chops over high heat until lightly browned on both sides. Add water. Reduce heat and cover skillet. Simmer slowly at 180° F. until tender, about 45 minutes, depending upon thickness of meat. Season and serve with Tomato Sauce (page 221).

Veal Paprika—Have dealer cut veal cutlet into 2-inch pieces, then cook as directed in basic recipe above. Add 1 small peeled clove of garlic to veal while cooking, if desired. When meat is tender, remove garlic if used and stir in ¾ cup sour or sweet cream and 1 teaspoon paprika. Just heat cream; do not boil. Season and garnish with minced parsley.

Veal with Mushrooms—Cook as directed in basic recipe. After meat has cooked 30 minutes, add 1 cup (¼ pound) sliced mushrooms. Cover and continue cooking about 15 minutes longer, until meat is tender. Just before serving, add ½ cup rich milk or sour cream and simmer for 1 minute. Do not boil. Garnish with minced parsley. ***This variation of Braised Veal Cutlets supplies 838 I.U. of Vitamin A per portion.***

156

VEAL LOAF

Each Portion Contains Approximately:
Vit. A—701 I. U.; Vit. B₁—197 I. U.; Vit. C—176 I. U.; Vit. G—.46 Mg.

INGREDIENTS:

1 pound ground veal
½ pound ground lean pork
1 cup cracker (or bread) crumbs
1 onion, minced
4 tablespoons minced green
   pepper

1 cup sliced mushrooms (¼ pound
   fresh or 1 7-ounce can)
2 teaspoons salt
¼ teaspoon pepper
2 eggs, slightly beaten
4 tablespoons ketchup (or milk)

DIRECTIONS: Mix all ingredients together in order given in large mixing bowl. Turn into greased 8"x4" loaf pan and bake in moderate oven (375° F.) about 1 hour, until loaf shrinks from sides of pan. Sprinkle with minced parsley, and garnish with slices of tomato and hard-cooked eggs, if desired. Loaf may be more highly flavored by substituting ¼ pound ground cured ham for ¼ pound of the ground veal. Vitamins may be added by substituting ¼ pound ground, sautéed (or otherwise precooked) liver for part veal.

VITAMINS	1 PORTION CONTAINS APPROXIMATELY	DAILY NEED
A	1457	5000 I.U.
B	91	600 I.U.
C	243	1500 I.U.
G	.50	2.7 MGS.

VEAL STEW

INGREDIENTS:

2 pounds stewing veal, cut into
   1-inch pieces
1 quart boiling water
⅛ teaspoon thyme
1 bay leaf
2 teaspoons salt
¼ teaspoon pepper

12 small onions
3 medium-sized carrots, diced
3 medium-sized potatoes, diced
2 tablespoons lemon juice
2 egg yolks, slightly beaten
3 tablespoons minced parsley

DIRECTIONS: Wash veal and cover with boiling water. Add seasonings and onions. Cover pot and simmer 40 minutes. Add carrots and potatoes and cook about 20 minutes longer, just until meat and vegetables are tender. Add lemon juice to slightly beaten egg yolks. Stir in a little of the hot sauce and then return to remaining hot mixture, stirring constantly just until well blended. Do not boil. Add parsley and serve.

LAMB

This Chart Gives Approximate Food Values for ROAST LEG OF LAMB.
For Vitamin Values of Specific Recipes, See Charts Accompanying Them.

1 PORTION CONTAINS APPROXIMATELY	VITAMINS	.5 I.U. A	121 I.U. B	72 I.U. C	.76 MGS. G	MINERALS	26 MGS. CALC.	488 MGS. PHOS.	3.9 MGS. IRON	ANALYSIS	525 CAL.	45 GMS. PROT.
BLACK PART OF COLUMN SHOWS HOW MUCH OF DAILY NEED IS SUPPLIED BY ONE PORTION												
AVERAGE DAILY NEED		5000 I.U.	600 I.U.	1500 I.U.	2.7 MGS.		800 MGS.	1320 MGS.	12 MGS.		2000-3000	70 GMS.

COMMENTS: Lamb formerly thought to be more easily digested than "red" meats, such as beef. This is not true. In fact, many cuts of lamb higher in fat content than beef, and so take longer to digest. Reducers and others watching their weight will do well to choose mutton rather than lamb (mutton is lower in fat content), and to trim carefully all types of lamb used.

Many people like distinctive flavors of lamb and mutton, but those who find them less agreeable will welcome "combination" dishes—stews, casseroles, etc. Lamb and mutton probably higher in Vitamin B complex than beef.

Legs of lamb are tender enough for dry-heat roasting. Neck, shoulder, breast and shanks require moist heat (page 37) for best results in texture and flavor. Organ parts have similar value to those of beef.

For best flavor and nutritional value, leg of mutton may be tenderized by marinating. To marinate meat weighing 5 or 6 pounds, use following recipe:

MARINATING PROCESS

INGREDIENTS:

5 tablespoons lemon juice or lime juice or cider vinegar

1 teaspoon chopped parsley

1 small onion, chopped

2 teaspoons chopped celery leaves

½ crushed garlic clove (optional)

DIRECTIONS: Mix ingredients and rub into meat six to eight hours before using. Dilute slightly, if necessary, with more lemon juice or water to stretch amount.

Acid of this mixture will tenderize meat by breaking down tough meat fibers, thus cutting cooking time considerably. Can be further seasoned with 1 bay leaf and sprig of thyme. If meat is lean, 2 tablespoons vegetable oil may be added to improve flavor and modify dryness. Probably best to marinate all tough cuts of meat.

For complete general discussion of muscle meats, see Comments on Beef.

ROAST LEG OF LAMB

INGREDIENTS:

1 6-pound leg of lamb   garlic clove (optional)
salt and pepper to taste

DIRECTIONS: Wipe meat with cloth. Do not remove thin skin. Rub with salt and pepper (and garlic, if desired). Place fat-side up in uncovered roaster. Insert meat thermometer in thickest portion of meat, not touching bone, and roast in slow oven (300° F.). For a medium-done roast, allow 30 minutes per pound (internal thermometer temperature, 156° F.). For a well-done roast, allow 40 minutes per pound (internal thermometer temperature, 168° F.). For an extremely well-done roast (as some prefer lamb), allow 45 minutes per pound (internal thermometer temperature, 180° F.).

ROAST STUFFED SHOULDER OF LAMB

Each Portion Contains Approximately:
Vit. A—1521 I. U.; Vit. B₁—279 I. U.; Vit. C—60 I. U.; Vit. G—.9 Mg.

INGREDIENTS:

4 pounds shoulder of lamb   2½ cups Bread Stuffing with
salt and pepper to taste   Watercress (page 225)
12 apricot halves   ½ cup water (optional)

DIRECTIONS: Have bone removed from meat, wipe meat with cloth and sprinkle outside and in with salt and pepper. Fill cavity with stuffing, and sew or fasten ends with skewers. Roll or leave flat, as desired. Place in roasting pan and add water. Bake uncovered in moderate oven (350° F.) about 2 hours (allowing 30 to 35 minutes per pound). Turn meat during baking and baste occasionally. Add apricots during last 15 minutes.

BALANCED MEAL SUGGESTIONS: *Dinner*—Pineapple Salad; *Roast Stuffed Shoulder of Lamb;* Baked Sweet Potatoes; String Beans with Onion; Berries.

BROILED LAMB CHOPS

	1 PORTION CONTAINS APPROXIMATELY	DAILY NEED
A		5000 I.U.
B	147	600 I.U.
C	54	1500 I.U.
G	.76	2.7 MGS.

VITAMINS

INGREDIENTS:

12 rib (or 6 loin or shoulder) lamb chops

salt and pepper to taste

DIRECTIONS: Have chops cut ¾ to 1 inch thick. Remove part of fat. Preheat broiling oven 10 minutes. Place chops on greased broiler rack, about 3 inches below moderate heat. When lightly browned on upper side, turn to cook other side. For 1-inch chops, allow about 6 minutes for each side; for 1½- to 2-inch chops, allow about 9 to 11 minutes for each side. Place on hot platter and sprinkle with salt and pepper.

Thick loin chops (often called English chops) are 2 to 3 inches thick and require about 12 to 15 minutes for each side. Rib chops with meat removed from rib ends often called French chops.

If desired, pan-broil lamb chops in hot skillet. Rub surface of sizzling pan with piece of fat cut from chop. Sear chops on both sides, then reduce heat and continue cooking, turning occasionally. Pour off excess fat as it accumulates so that chops will broil and not fry. Pan-broil approximately the same length of time as above.

Lamb-Fruit Grill—Broil chops as directed in basic recipe. During last 5 minutes of cooking, place 6 slices canned pineapple or 6 thick slices peeled orange alongside chops on broiler rack. Dot fruit with small amount of butter before placing under heat. *By including fruit in this recipe, the vitamin values of the dish become approximately: Vit. A—90 I.U.; Vit. B₁—153 I.U.; Vit. C—121 I.U.; Vit. G—.76 Mg.*

Lamb-Tomato Grill—Broil chops as directed in basic recipe. Place alongside chops 12 mushroom caps, and broil as directed on page 274. During last 5 minutes of cooking, place 6 thick slices of tomato on rack with chops and mushrooms. Dot tomatoes with small amount of butter before placing under heat.

BALANCED MEAL SUGGESTIONS: *Dinner*—Pimiento Coleslaw; *Broiled Lamb-Fruit Grill;* Green Lima Beans; Cauliflower; Fruit Ice Cream.

BROILED LAMB-LIVER PATTIES

Each Portion Contains Approximately:
Vit. A—2534 I. U.; Vit. B₁—104 I. U.; Vit. C—408 I. U.; Vit. G—1.2 Mg.

INGREDIENTS:

½ pound lamb liver, sliced ½ inch thick

2 tablespoons butter

1 pound lean lamb (neck, shoulder or shank), ground

1 teaspoon salt

¼ teaspoon pepper

6 slices bacon (optional)

6 slices (about 2 medium-sized) tomatoes

DIRECTIONS: Sauté liver in butter about 1 minute on each side. Turn as soon as it changes color. Cool and grind or chop very fine. Combine lamb, liver and seasonings. Shape into patties about 1 inch thick. Wrap a strip of bacon around each, if desired, and fasten with small skewer or toothpicks. Preheat broiling oven at moderate temperature 5 to 10 minutes and grease broiler pan. Place patties in pan about 2½ inches below heat, and broil about 8 minutes on each side, using medium heat. Then top each patty with a slice of tomato, dot with butter and continue broiling until tomato is slightly browned, about 3 minutes longer. Stewed, canned or fresh apricot or peach halves, or canned pineapple may be substituted for tomato.

BALANCED MEAL SUGGESTIONS: *Dinner*—Carrot-Raisin Salad; *Broiled Lamb-Liver Patties;* Corn and Green Pepper; Candied Sweet Potatoes; Fruit Gelatin.

BRAISED MUTTON CHOPS WITH KIDNEYS

INGREDIENTS:

6 mutton chops with kidneys

1 teaspoon salt

½ teaspoon pepper

12 small potatoes

12 very small carrots

6 small onions

1 cup canned tomatoes

3 tablespoons minced parsley

DIRECTIONS: Have mutton chops boned and rolled around kidneys. Wipe meat and sear on both sides in hot skillet. Place in 2-quart casserole, sprinkle with salt and pepper and cover with vegetables (except parsley). Bake in moderate oven (375° F.) about 40 minutes, just until meat and vegetables are tender. Sprinkle with minced parsley just before serving.

BALANCED MEAL SUGGESTIONS: *Dinner*—Mixed Greens Salad; *Braised Mutton Chops with Kidneys;* Citrus Fruit Cup.

PORK

1 PORTION CONTAINS APPROXIMATELY	VITAMINS	I.U.	481 I.U.	33 I.U.	.60 MGS.	MINERALS	28 MGS.	504 MGS.	3.5 MGS.	ANALYSIS	455	44 GMS.
		A	B	C	G		CALC.	PHOS.	IRON		CAL.	PROT.
BLACK PART OF COLUMN SHOWS HOW MUCH OF DAILY NEED IS SUPPLIED BY ONE PORTION												
AVERAGE DAILY NEED		5000 I.U.	600 I.U.	1500 I.U.	2.7 MGS.		800 MGS.	1320 MGS.	12 MGS.		2000-3000	70 GMS.

COMMENTS: Pork generally divided into two classifications: fresh pork and cured or smoked pork (ham, bacon, etc.). Because fresh pork often infested with trichinae (microscopic worms), thorough cooking is necessary. Cured pork probably free from this danger, as it is subjected to high heat and long periods of smoking. If you buy graded, inspected pork or ham, and cook according to directions given in each recipe, you need have no fears. Good quality pork grayish-pink in color and fine grained. Characteristic flavor due to fat imbedded in cells. Cured bacon and tenderized ham, ribs and loin chops suitable for broiling (well done). All cuts suitable for braising (moist-heat cooking). Pan-broil bacon very slowly, turning frequently, until crisp. Drain off fat as it accumulates. Badly broiled (often burned) bacon results when heat is too high.

Cheapest of all muscle meats, and eaten in largest quantities in this country. According to analyses of raw meats, richest of all muscle meats in Vitamin B complex, but long cooking necessary (for fresh pork) destroys at least half of Vitamin B value.

Highest in fat content of all muscle meats. For this reason, takes longest to digest, and not recommended for anyone with weak digestion, or for young children. Cured pork or ham (including broiled, crisp bacon) preferable in many cases. All forms of pork questionable for reducers. Should be served with fruits and vegetables of high water content to offset concentrated meat.

FRESH ROAST PORK

INGREDIENTS:

4 pounds tenderloin, loin or   salt and pepper to taste
shoulder of pork

DIRECTIONS: Wipe meat with cloth, and rub with salt and pepper. Place fat-side up in uncovered roaster. Insert meat thermometer so that bulb reaches center of thickest muscle. Place in moderate oven (350° F.), allowing about 45 minutes per pound (large roasts require only 35 to 40 minutes per pound). Cook until thermometer reaches 185° F. For additional flavor, sprinkle meat before baking with 1/4 teaspoon thyme, and arrange 2 apples (sliced) on top of meat. Serve with applesauce, cranberries or spiced fruit.

BALANCED MEAL SUGGESTIONS: *Dinner*—Mixed Greens Salad; *Roast Pork* with Applesauce; Cauliflower; Spinach; Grapefruit Cup.

Supper: Tomato Juice; *Cold Roast Pork;* Mixed Greens Salad; Potato Salad; Fruit Cup with Cranberry Sauce.

VITAMINS	1 PORTION CONTAINS APPROXIMATELY		DAILY NEED
A			5000 I.U.
B		769	600 I.U.
C	57		1500 I.U.
G	.60		2.7 MGS.

BROILED PORK CHOPS

INGREDIENTS:

6 pork chops, 1 inch thick   salt and pepper to taste

DIRECTIONS: Wipe meat with cloth and sprinkle with salt and pepper. Preheat broiler 10 minutes. Place chops on broiler rack and broil 3 inches below moderate heat. Broil about 15 minutes on each side, just until tender. Overcooking makes meat dry, but be sure not to undercook.

Pan-Broiled Pork Chops—Do not grease skillet, as pork chops can be pan-broiled in their own fat. Sprinkle salt into sizzling skillet and put in chops. Sear on both sides until lightly browned. Reduce heat, cover pan and cook about 30 minutes, just until tender, turning once to cook evenly. Pour off excess fat as chops cook so they will broil and not fry. Do not overcook.

BALANCED MEAL SUGGESTIONS: *Dinner*—Cucumber Salad; *Broiled Pork Chops;* Mashed Potatoes; String Beans; Citrus Sherbet.

ROAST SPARERIBS

	1 PORTION CONTAINS APPROXIMATELY	DAILY NEED
A		5000 I.U.
B	481	600 I.U.
C	39	1500 I.U.
G	.60	2.7 MGS.

VITAMINS

INGREDIENTS:

4 pounds fresh spareribs
salt and pepper to taste

¼ cup chopped onion

DIRECTIONS: Wipe meat with cloth and cut into serving pieces if desired. Rub with salt and pepper and place in large baking pan. Sprinkle with onion. For additional flavor, sprinkle with ¼ teaspoon thyme and bake 2 apples, sliced, with the meat. Cover and bake in hot oven (450° F.) about 45 minutes, until tender. Turn meat once during baking. Remove cover during last 15 minutes to brown meat.

BALANCED MEAL SUGGESTIONS: *Dinner*—Lettuce and Tomato Salad; *Roast Spareribs;* Mashed Potatoes; Sauerkraut; Citrus Fruit Cup.

BAKED HAM WITH FRUIT

	1 PORTION CONTAINS APPROXIMATELY	DAILY NEED
A	116	5000 I.U.
B	504	600 I.U.
C	17	1500 I.U.
G	.6	2.7 MGS.

VITAMINS

INGREDIENTS:

1 whole ham, 12 to 14 pounds
whole cloves
1 cup firmly packed brown sugar
7 slices canned pineapple
7 large cooked prunes

½ cup syrup from canned
pineapple
½ cup honey
watercress, chicory or parsley

DIRECTIONS: Cook ham, following packer's directions on label. If purchasing half a ham, be sure to note cooking instructions before ham is cut. Allow ½ pound per serving. Tender or tenderized ham does not require soaking before baking. Bake skin-side up in open roaster, allowing whatever minutes per pound packer specifies. Hams are usually baked in slow oven (300° F.). Time varies from 18 to 30 minutes per pound.

Thirty minutes before ham is done, remove rind and score fat with sharp knife, crisscross fashion, to form 1-inch diamonds. Stud ham with whole clove in center of each diamond. Remove fat drippings from baking pan. Blend sugar, pineapple syrup and honey and pour half this mixture over ham. Return to hot oven (450° F.), and bake for 15 minutes.

Take pan from oven, pour remaining sugar-honey mixture over ham and arrange prunes in center of pineapple slices around ham. Return to oven and continue to bake about 15 minutes longer, until ham is deep, golden brown. Serve on hot platter, surrounded by fruit and garnished with watercress, chicory or sprigs of parsley.

Although large ham is more than is needed for one meal, economical to purchase it and use in leftover dishes. For variation, unpeeled apple slices, canned apricot halves or unpeeled fresh or canned peach halves may replace pineapple.

BALANCED MEAL SUGGESTIONS: *Dinner*—Green Pepper Coleslaw; *Baked Ham with Fruit;* Baked Sweet Potatoes; String Beans with Onion; Cantaloupe or Canned Apricots.

VITAMINS	1 PORTION CONTAINS APPROXIMATELY	DAILY NEED
A	1133	5000 I.U.
B₁	190	600 I.U.
C	45	1500 I.U.
G	.43	2.7 MGS.

HAM AND CHEESE CASSEROLE

INGREDIENTS:

1 cup diced, cooked carrots
1 cup diced, cooked potatoes
1½ cups coarsely chopped boiled or leftover baked ham
1 tablespoon minced onion
1 cup Cream Sauce (page 217)
⅛ teaspoon paprika
¼ cup grated American cheese

DIRECTIONS: Arrange carrots, potatoes, ham and onion in greased 8-inch casserole. Prepare Cream Sauce, omitting salt and adding paprika for additional seasoning, and using pot liquor as part of liquid if vegetables are freshly prepared. Sprinkle with cheese. Bake in hot oven (425° F.) about 15 minutes, just until cheese melts and is golden brown.

BALANCED MEAL SUGGESTIONS: *Dinner*—Citrus Salad; *Ham and Cheese Casserole;* Asparagus; Deep-Dish Peach Pie.

CHINESE CHOP SUEY

	1 PORTION CONTAINS APPROXIMATELY	DAILY NEED
A	1475	5000 I.U.
B	302	600 I.U.
C	1102	1500 I.U.
G	.7	2.7 MGS.

INGREDIENTS:

1 pound fresh pork tenderloin, veal cutlet or round steak
3 tablespoons salad oil
1 teaspoon salt
2 medium-sized onions, sliced
1 cup shredded green pepper
1 cup (¼ pound) sliced mushrooms
1 cup shredded celery
1 cup shredded Chinese cabbage
4 cups stock (or 4 bouillon cubes dissolved in 4 cups boiling water)
1 No. 2 can bean sprouts
2 tablespoons cornstarch
1 tablespoon cold water
2 tablespoons soy sauce
1 tablespoon sugar

DIRECTIONS: Have meat cut into 1-inch cubes. Heat oil in heavy skillet, add salt, and blend well. Add onions, green pepper, mushrooms, celery and meat, and sauté until meat is lightly browned on all sides. Add Chinese cabbage and stock. Cover and simmer slowly about 45 minutes. Add drained bean sprouts. Add water gradually to cornstarch, mixing to a smooth paste. Slowly add to meat, stirring constantly until well blended and thick, about 5 minutes. Add soy sauce and sugar, and stir until sugar is dissolved. Serve with Boiled Brown Rice (page 289).

BALANCED MEAL SUGGESTIONS: *Dinner*—Tomato Juice or Clear Consommé; *Chinese Chop Suey* with Rice; Orange or Grapefruit Cup; Nut Macaroons.

ORGAN MEATS

BRAINS

This Chart Gives Approximate Food Values for COOKED BRAINS.

	VITAMINS				MINERALS			ANALYSIS	
1 PORTION CONTAINS APPROXIMATELY	421 I.U.	107 I.U.	289 I.U.	.6 MGS.	24 MGS.	881 MGS.	5 MGS.	276	22 GMS.
	A	B	C	G	CALC.	PHOS.	IRON	CAL.	PROT.
BLACK PART OF COLUMN SHOWS HOW MUCH OF DAILY NEED IS SUPPLIED BY ONE PORTION									
AVERAGE DAILY NEED	5000 I.U.	600 I.U.	1500 I.U.	2.7 MGS.	800 MGS.	1320 MGS.	12 MGS.	2000-3000	70 GMS.

COMMENTS: Brains are an organ meat, containing Class A complete protein, and rich in the Vitamin B complex. Elderly persons and those with a tendency to liver disorders or hardening of the arteries should eat brains rarely, as this meat is high in cholesterol (a fat which tends to accelerate such degenerative processes).

Lemon juice incorporated in recipes adds welcome tart flavor, but to add Vitamin C to brains dishes, serve them with lemon wedges as garnish. The juice added during cooking does not contribute Vitamin C because heat destroys most of this nutrient. Brains almost always require a sauce served with them, but even so, a garnish of lemon wedges provides a needed tartness.

Careful preparation is necessary in cooking this tender meat (it is of extremely soft texture) to prevent its falling apart. Proper cooking methods are important to make it attractive and palatable, as well as digestible. Brains must always be soaked and cooked (simmered, not boiled) in acidulated water before serving in any manner whatever. This preparation keeps them white and firm.

Cooked or Broiled brains with a simple tomato sauce preferred to Sautéed Brains; use of flour as well as fat in sautéing make dish heavier and less easy to digest. If brains are to be sautéed, use as little fat as possible.

167

Scrambled Eggs and Brains best choice nutritionally because of substantial vitamin additions. Especially good for anemic persons. Combination of cooked brains with diced cooked chicken (or veal), or cooked or canned peas, in a cream sauce is a popular dish. Compared with other meats, brains medium in calorie content; may be used by reducers as main dinner dish.

COOKED BRAINS

INGREDIENTS:

6 pairs calf, pig or lamb brains
2 tablespoons lemon juice (or 1
1 quart water
2 teaspoons salt

tablespoon cider vinegar)
1 cup Tomato (page 221) or Mock
Hollandaise (page 220) Sauce

DIRECTIONS: Be certain brains are absolutely fresh when purchased, as they are a perishable food. Soak in cold salted water (1 teaspoon salt to 1 quart water) about 30 minutes. Drain carefully with sieve and remove membrane, being careful not to break tender tissue.

In saucepan, boil just enough water to cover meat, and add lemon juice and 1 teaspoon salt. (Acid helps keep brains white.) Use skimmer to slip gently into boiling water. Reduce heat and simmer about 15 or 20 minutes, just until tender enough to be pierced with a fork. Avoid cooking brains in rapidly boiling water, as it will make them tough, and do not overcook, as brains are very soft in texture and easily fall apart. Carefully remove from water, using skimmer or sieve, and immediately place in enough cold water to cover to keep brains firm. Drain, slice and combine with hot Tomato or Mock Hollandaise Sauce or combine with diced cooked or canned chicken or veal in Cream Sauce (page 217).

Sautéed Brains—Prepare brains, cook and place in cold water as directed in basic recipe. Drain and place under a weight to prevent curling. Dip in seasoned flour (or dip in 1 egg beaten with 1 tablespoon water, then roll in ½ cup seasoned bread or cracker crumbs). Melt small amount butter in large skillet and sauté brains over medium heat just until golden brown on both sides. Sprinkle with minced parsley and serve with lemon wedges.

Broiled Brains—Prepare brains, cook and place in cold water as directed in basic recipe. Drain, and dip in melted butter or salad oil. Place in greased shallow baking pan and broil about 3 inches from high heat. Cook just until delicately browned, about 3 minutes on each side. Serve with Lemon Butter (page 222) and sprinkle with minced parsley.

VITAMINS	1 PORTION CONTAINS APPROXIMATELY	DAILY NEED
A	867	5000 I.U.
B	66	600 I.U.
C	315	1500 I.U.
G	.47	2.7 MGS.

SCRAMBLED EGGS AND BRAINS

INGREDIENTS:

3 pairs calf, pig or lamb brains
4 eggs
½ cup milk
½ teaspoon Worcestershire sauce
  (or 1 tablespoon ketchup)
1 teaspoon salt

½ teaspoon pepper
2 tablespoons butter
1 tablespoon minced green pepper
  (or minced onion)
1 tablespoon minced parsley

DIRECTIONS: Prepare and cook brains as directed in basic recipe for cooked brains. Drain and dice. Beat eggs with milk, salt, pepper and Worcestershire sauce or ketchup. Melt butter in large skillet and sauté minced green pepper or onion in the butter about 2 minutes. Add brains and sauté about 1 minute. Add egg mixture and proceed as directed in recipe for Scrambled Eggs (page 124). Serve garnished with minced parsley.

BALANCED MEAL SUGGESTIONS: *Lunch*—Lettuce-Tomato Salad; *Scrambled Eggs and Brains;* Stewed Apricots; Milk.

Dinner—Pimiento Coleslaw; *Broiled Brains;* Potatoes and Chard; Fruit Cup or Deep-Dish Peach Pie.

HEART

This Chart Gives Approximate Food Values for COOKED HEART.

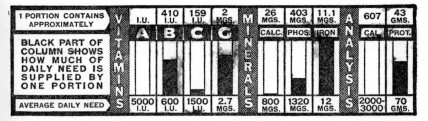

1 PORTION CONTAINS APPROXIMATELY	VITAMINS	A	B	C	G	MINERALS	CALC.	PHOS.	IRON	ANALYSIS	CAL.	PROT.
		410 I.U.	159 I.U.	2 MGS.			26 MGS.	403 MGS.	11.1 MGS.		607	43 GMS.
BLACK PART OF COLUMN SHOWS HOW MUCH OF DAILY NEED IS SUPPLIED BY ONE PORTION												
AVERAGE DAILY NEED		5000 I.U.	600 I.U.	1500 I.U.	2.7 MGS.		800 MGS.	1320 MGS.	12 MGS.		2000-3000	70 GMS.

COMMENTS: Heart is a Class A complete protein, rich in the Vitamin B complex, with extra quantities of Vitamin G. Rather high in cholesterol content, which limits use for elderly persons. Shortened cooking time, achieved through cutting into smaller portions, helps retain Vitamin B values.

Substantial portions of ground heart can be incorporated in meat loaves, patties, etc. This way of using heart most satisfactory, especially if some members of the family do not like heart by itself. Plain cooked heart fairly high in calorie content; reducers should eat it sparingly.

Serving heart with liver or kidneys superb nutritionally. Because of richness in iron and phosphorus, excellent for persons with anemia to vary plain liver diet, which may become monotonous.

In Baked Stuffed Heart, protective qualities are supplemented by Vitamin Stuffing. Tomato Sauce for basting adds additional Vitamin C, as long as it is eaten with heart as gravy. High in calorie content; if reducers wish to eat dish occasionally, should use Vitamin rather than Bread Stuffing.

COOKED HEART

INGREDIENTS:

1 beef heart (or 3 calf or 6 lamb hearts)	1 bay leaf
4 peppercorns	½ cup shredded celery leaves (or 1 teaspoon celery salt)
2 whole cloves	2 medium-sized onions, sliced

DIRECTIONS: Be certain hearts are absolutely fresh when purchased. Wash hearts thoroughly in cold water and remove arteries, fat and veins (or have dealer do this). Cut into halves or small pieces. In saucepan, boil enough water to cover meat. Then add heart, peppercorns, cloves, bay leaf, celery leaves and onion slices. Cover and simmer ½ hour. Add salt (1 teaspoon per pound) and continue simmering until tender. Cooking time will be about ¾ to 1 hour for calf and lamb heart, and about 1 to 1½ hours or longer for beef heart, depending upon age and size. Drain and trim, removing all remaining fat and gristle—only lean meat should be served. Slice crosswise to serve.

Sliced Cold Heart—Prepare heart and cook until tender as directed in basic recipe. Then remove fat and gristle, strain stock in which heart has been cooked and return heart to stock to cool. So that heart will retain flavor and juices, allow to remain in stock and store covered in refrigerator until served. Drain, slice and serve with tart jelly, horseradish or mustard.

170

Broiled Heart—Prepare heart as directed in basic recipe for Cooked Heart, then cut into ½-inch slices. Dip slices in salad oil or melted butter and, if desired, in seasoned bread crumbs. Place on shallow broiling pan about 3 inches under high heat; broil about 3 minutes on each side. Do not overcook.

Sautéed Heart—Prepare heart as directed in recipe for Broiled Heart. Melt 2 tablespoons butter in skillet and place heart slices in it. Cook about 3 minutes on each side, depending upon thickness of slices. Do not overcook.

VITAMINS	1 PORTION CONTAINS APPROXIMATELY	DAILY NEED	
A	1921	5000 I.U.	BAKED STUFFED HEART
B	380	600 I.U.	
C	380	1500 I.U.	
G	2.8	2.7 MGS.	

INGREDIENTS:

1 beef heart (or 3 calf or 6 lamb hearts)
2 cups Vitamin or Bread Stuffing (page 225)
2 cups canned tomatoes
1 tablespoon minced onion
1 bay leaf
½ cup chopped celery
2 tablespoons butter (or 3 bacon strips)

DIRECTIONS: Prepare heart as directed in basic recipe for Cooked Heart. Cover with boiling water, reduce heat, and precook, simmering slowly, about 20 minutes. Drain and dry. Slit one side of heart, fill with stuffing and sew or skewer edges of opening securely. Place heart in small buttered roasting pan. Add tomatoes, onion, bay leaf and celery. Dot with butter, or fasten bacon strips to heart with skewers or toothpicks. Cover pan and bake in a slow oven (300° F.) until heart is tender, about 2 hours for beef heart, about 1½ hours for calf or lamb hearts, depending upon size and kind of heart. Baste occasionally. As tomato juice cooks away, add hot water as needed. Uncover pan during last 15 minutes of baking. Carve heart crosswise in ½-inch slices. Remove bay leaf from tomato sauce and serve with heart.

BALANCED MEAL SUGGESTIONS: *Lunch*—Celery-Apple Salad; *Cold Sliced Heart;* Cold Potato Salad; Canned Cherries; Milk.

Dinner—Combination Salad; *Baked Stuffed Heart;* Corn and Green Peppers; Fruit Gelatin.

KIDNEYS

This Chart Gives Approximate Food Values for BROILED KIDNEYS.
For Vitamin Values of Specific Recipes, See Charts Accompanying Them.

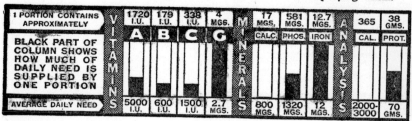

1 PORTION CONTAINS APPROXIMATELY	VITAMINS	1720 I.U.	179 I.U.	338 I.U.	4 MGS.	MINERALS	17 MGS.	581 MGS.	12.7 MGS.	ANALYSIS	365	38 GMS.
		A	B	C	G		CALC.	PHOS.	IRON		CAL.	PROT.
BLACK PART OF COLUMN SHOWS HOW MUCH OF DAILY NEED IS SUPPLIED BY ONE PORTION												
AVERAGE DAILY NEED		5000 I.U.	600 I.U.	1500 I.U.	2.7 MGS.		800 MGS.	1320 MGS.	12 MGS.		2000-3000	70 GMS.

COMMENTS: Kidneys are an excellent Class A complete protein. Contain goodly amounts of the Vitamin B complex (especially Vitamin G). Elderly persons should eat kidneys infrequently, as they are high in cholesterol content. Rich in iron; can be substituted occasionally for liver by persons suffering from anemia. Garnishes of minced parsley and watercress add flavor as well as vitamin values. Kidneys are medium to high in calorie content; reducers should eat them sparingly.

Kidneys may also be ground or chopped and added to meat loaves or patties to supplement the vitamin values of these combination dishes. For serving with eggs, Broiled Kidneys may replace bacon or ham to give that familiar type of dish more vitamins, better proteins and fewer calories.

Proper preparation very important to make kidneys palatable.

BROILED KIDNEYS

INGREDIENTS:

2 beef, 4 veal or 12 lamb kidneys
1 teaspoon salt
1 tablespoon cider vinegar

1 quart water
3 tablespoons salad oil
   (or melted butter)

DIRECTIONS: Be certain kidneys are absolutely fresh when purchased. Wash and cut in halves lengthwise, remove white fatty centers, gristle and

172

tubes. Soak in cold water, to which salt and vinegar have been added. Lamb and veal kidneys require 10 to 15 minutes soaking; beef kidneys, about 30 minutes, depending upon freshness of meat. During soaking, change water several times as it becomes cloudy and develops strong odor. At end of soaking time, drain, rinse under cold running water and dry thoroughly.

Precooking is not necessary. Dip kidneys in seasoned salad oil or melted butter. Place on greased broiler pan or baking sheet and broil about 3 inches from medium heat, turning to cook brown on both sides. Lamb kidneys broil in about 6 to 9 minutes, veal kidneys in about 10 to 12, beef kidneys in about 12 to 15. Always test by cutting into thickest part of kidney. If meat is still raw (showing any signs of blood), broil longer, but do not overcook. Place on hot platter, dot with butter and garnish with minced parsley, watercress or lemon wedges.

Sautéed Kidneys—Prepare and soak kidneys as directed in basic recipe for Broiled Kidneys. Drain, rinse and dry. Cut into thin slices. Melt butter in heavy skillet, add kidneys and cook over medium heat 7 to 10 minutes for lamb kidneys, 10 to 15 minutes for beef or veal kidneys. Stir occasionally to brown kidneys on all sides, adding more butter only as needed. Do not overcook kidneys, and do not cook at too high heat. If desired, sauté ½ pound sliced mushrooms with kidneys. Season to taste before serving.

Kidneys may also be rolled in seasoned flour before sautéing. Just before serving, stir into pan enough cold water or pot liquor (¼ to ½ cup) to make rich gravy, adding a small amount at a time. Stir constantly until mixture is smooth and thick. Sprinkle with minced parsley.

QUICK KIDNEY STEW

INGREDIENTS:

1 beef, 3 veal or 9 lamb kidneys
4 tablespoons butter
3 medium-sized onions, sliced thin
1 teaspoon salt
¼ teaspoon pepper
1 can condensed mock turtle soup
1 tablespoon lemon juice (or vinegar)

DIRECTIONS: Prepare and soak kidneys as directed in recipe for Broiled Kidneys. Drain, dry and slice thin. Melt butter in large skillet, add kidneys and onions, and sauté over a medium heat about 5 minutes, stirring occasionally. Add seasoning and soup, and simmer about 7 to 10 minutes, just until kidneys are tender and soup is thoroughly heated. Stir in lemon juice or vinegar just before serving. Serve on toast or with boiled rice.

BEEF AND KIDNEY STEW

	1 PORTION CONTAINS APPROXIMATELY	DAILY NEED
Ⓐ	2340	5000 I.U.
Ⓑ	176	600 I.U.
Ⓒ	1537	1500 I.U.
Ⓖ	2.4	2.7 MGS.

INGREDIENTS:

6 lamb or 2 veal kidneys
1 pound round steak, cut in cubes
1 pound lean veal or pork, cut in cubes
4 tablespoons bacon fat or butter
1 medium-sized onion, minced

4 tablespoons minced green pepper
1½ cups canned tomatoes
1 teaspoon salt
⅛ teaspoon pepper
4 potatoes, scraped and diced
3 tablespoons minced parsley

DIRECTIONS: Have dealer split kidneys and cut meat in 1-inch pieces. Prepare and soak kidneys as directed in recipe for Broiled Kidneys. Drain, rinse in cold water, and slice. Heat fat in heavy skillet, and add kidneys, meat, onion and green pepper, and sauté until meat is brown, about 5 minutes, stirring occasionally. Add tomatoes and seasoning; cover and simmer gently 30 minutes. Add potatoes, cover, and cook until potatoes are tender, about 15 minutes or longer. During latter part of cooking, add a little more water or tomato juice if necessary. Serve on heated platter and sprinkle with minced parsley.

BALANCED MEAL SUGGESTIONS: *Lunch*—Sliced Tomatoes; *Quick Kidney Stew;* Canned Cherries; Milk.

LIVER

This Chart Gives Approximate Food Values for BROILED LIVER.

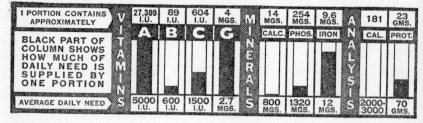

1 PORTION CONTAINS APPROXIMATELY	VITAMINS	A 27,309 I.U.	B 89 I.U.	C 604 I.U.	G 4 MGS.	MINERALS	CALC. 14 MGS.	PHOS. 254 MGS.	IRON 9.6 MGS.	ANALYSIS	CAL. 181	PROT. 23 GMS.
BLACK PART OF COLUMN SHOWS HOW MUCH OF DAILY NEED IS SUPPLIED BY ONE PORTION												
AVERAGE DAILY NEED		5000 I.U.	600 I.U.	1500 I.U.	2.7 MGS.		800 MGS.	1320 MGS.	12 MGS.		2000-3000	70 GMS.

COMMENTS: Liver contains special chemical which, plus liver's richness in iron and copper, makes this meat extremely valuable in the prevention and

174

treatment of nutritional anemia. A Class A complete protein. Beef and calf liver similar in nutritive value; calf liver more expensive because of greater tenderness and more delicate flavor. Fairly low in calorie content.

Remember that an ounce or two of liver can be used to fortify numerous dishes with Vitamin A. For people who object to the flavor of plain liver, we recommend such combinations as Liver and Beef Loaf.

Liver and Spaghetti is another combination especially good for incorporating this meat into the diet of anyone who might not like plain liver. Dish is practically a meal in itself, and addition of liver makes a superb vitamin protective food out of low-cost spaghetti. Excellent for children—particularly those needing to gain weight. Protective nutrients plus high calorie content help to add pounds. Not for reducers.

Chicken livers relatively expensive; considered a delicacy. Often used merely for special occasion luncheon or Sunday morning breakfast.

BROILED LIVER

INGREDIENTS:

1½ pounds beef or calf liver
2 tablespoons melted butter (or salad oil)
1 teaspoon salt
½ teaspoon pepper
2 tablespoons minced parsley (or watercress)

DIRECTIONS: Be certain liver is absolutely fresh when purchased. Have dealer cut liver into ½-inch slices. Wash, and dry thoroughly by blotting with paper towel. Dip slices in melted butter or salad oil, sprinkle with salt and pepper, and place on greased broiler pan or baking sheet. Broil about 3 inches below medium heat, turning once to cook and brown on both sides. Cook from 3 to 5 minutes on each side. Test by cutting through thickest part of slice; there will be no sign of blood when meat is done. Do not overcook, and do not broil under a high heat. Place on hot platter, dot with butter and serve garnished with minced parsley or watercress.

Sautéed Liver—Prepare liver as directed in basic recipe. Melt butter or bacon fat in large skillet, and sauté liver over high heat about 5 minutes. Turn occasionally to brown on both sides. Add more fat as needed. If desired, after liver is cooked, add sour cream to cover (or as much as is available), and reduce heat. Simmer just until cream bubbles; *do not boil.* Serve at once, garnished with minced chives or parsley.

175

Creamed Liver—Dice broiled or sautéed liver and combine with 1 cup Cream Sauce (page 217), to which 1 tablespoon grated onion and 4 table-spoons minced parsley have been added.

Ground Liver Put broiled or sautéed liver through meat grinder, using finest blade (or chop very fine). Season with salt, pepper and minced onion.

COOKED LIVER

INGREDIENTS:

1½ pounds beef or calf liver   1 teaspoon salt (optional)

DIRECTIONS: Have liver cut into ½-inch slices. Wash under cold running water and put in saucepan with hot water to cover. Bring to boil, reduce heat to medium, cover and simmer just until tender. Do not overcook. Add salt, if desired, before removing from heat. Beef liver requires about 7 to 10 minutes to cook through; calf liver about 5 minutes, depending on actual thickness of slice. Drain, and use for Scraped Liver or any desired use.

Scraped Liver—Prepare and cook as in basic recipe for Cooked Liver. When liver is tender, drain and scrape with a sharp knife or put through meat grinder, using finest blade. Season with salt, pepper and a little grated onion. Garnish with minced chives or parsley and sieved hard-cooked eggs.

LIVER-BEEF LOAF

VITAMINS	1 PORTION CONTAINS APPROXIMATELY	DAILY NEED
A	19,949	5000 I.U.
B	82	600 I.U.
C	453	1500 I.U.
G	2.72	2.7 MGS.

INGREDIENTS:

1 pound beef liver (or 1 beef, 2 veal, or 9 lamb kidneys)
3 tablespoons butter
½ cup minced onion
¼ cup diced celery
4 tablespoons finely chopped green pepper
1 pound ground beef

1½ cups chopped carrots
1 tablespoon minced celery leaves
2 tablespoons minced parsley
1 teaspoon salt
¼ teaspoon pepper
2 eggs

DIRECTIONS: Prepare liver as directed in basic recipe for Broiled Liver and cut into ½-inch slices. Or prepare kidneys as directed for Broiled Kidneys (page 172).

176

Melt butter in large skillet and sauté liver or kidneys about 3 minutes. Remove meat from pan and chop fine or put through meat grinder, using the finest blade. Add onion, celery and green pepper to hot skillet (adding more butter if necessary), and sauté about 3 minutes, until onion is yellow. Combine all ingredients and mix thoroughly. Place in buttered baking dish or casserole, cover and bake 30 minutes in moderate oven (375° F.). Uncover and bake about 15 minutes longer, until top is browned.

Serve on hot platter, garnished with parsley or watercress, or put in refrigerator to chill, and serve cold, sliced thin and garnished with crisp celery curls, radish roses, watercress and cucumber or carrot strips.

VITAMINS	1 PORTION CONTAINS APPROXIMATELY	DAILY NEED		
A	19,435	5000 I.U.	**LIVER-BEEF**	
B	109	600 I.U.	**SPAGHETTI**	
C	1406	1500 I.U.		
G	2.5	2.7 MGS.		

INGREDIENTS:

½ pound beef liver, sliced thin
1 pound ground beef
3 tablespoons butter
3 medium-sized onions, chopped
1 green pepper, chopped
2 cups canned tomatoes
1 6-ounce can tomato paste

1 cup boiling water
¼ teaspoon pepper
½ teaspoon salt
1 teaspoon sugar
1 pound spaghetti
¼ cup grated Parmesan cheese

DIRECTIONS: In a large saucepan, cook spaghetti until tender in rapidly boiling, salted water to cover. (If packaged spaghetti is used, note cooking time in directions on label.)

While spaghetti is cooking, wash liver, dry and broil (page 175) or sauté (page 175). Melt butter in skillet and sauté onions and pepper until onions are yellow, about 2 minutes. Add ground beef and sauté until brown, about 3 minutes, stirring occasionally so meat will be crumbled. Add tomatoes, tomato paste, boiling water and seasonings. Cover and simmer over medium heat about 15 minutes. Chop liver very fine or put through food chopper, and add to tomato-meat sauce. Simmer 5 minutes longer, just enough to reheat liver.

Drain spaghetti, and place on hot platter. Serve liver-beef sauce over or around spaghetti, sprinkling with cheese if desired.

CHICKEN LIVERS WITH MUSHROOMS

	1 PORTION CONTAINS APPROXIMATELY	DAILY NEED
A	14,442	5000 I.U.
B	73	600 I.U.
C	171	1500 I.U.
G	3.42	2.7 MGS.

VITAMINS

INGREDIENTS:

12 to 15 chicken livers
4 tablespoons butter
2 cups (½ pound) sliced mushrooms

2 tablespoons minced onion
½ teaspoon salt
⅛ teaspoon pepper (or paprika)

DIRECTIONS: Be certain livers are absolutely fresh when purchased. Wash, rinse and cut livers into small pieces. Melt butter in large skillet and add remaining ingredients. Sauté over low heat, stirring occasionally, about 5 minutes, just until mushrooms and livers are cooked. Serve on toast or boiled rice, or in the fold of an omelet.

Scrambled Eggs and Chicken Livers—Prepare livers and mushrooms as directed in basic recipe but reduce amounts of livers and mushrooms to half. Beat 4 eggs with ½ cup milk. Sauté livers and mushrooms about 5 minutes, add egg mixture and proceed as in recipe for Scrambled Eggs (page 124).

BALANCED MEAL SUGGESTIONS: *Lunch*—Lettuce Salad; *Broiled Liver* and Onions; Broiled Tomatoes; Canned Pears; Cookies; Milk.

SWEETBREADS

This Chart Gives Approximate Food Values for COOKED SWEETBREADS.

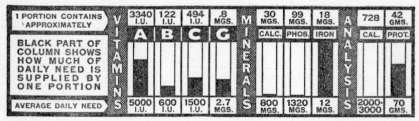

1 PORTION CONTAINS APPROXIMATELY	A	B	C	G		CALC.	PHOS.	IRON		CAL.	PROT.
	3340 I.U.	122 I.U.	494 I.U.	.8 MGS.		30 MGS.	99 MGS.	18 MGS.		728	42 GMS.
BLACK PART OF COLUMN SHOWS HOW MUCH OF DAILY NEED IS SUPPLIED BY ONE PORTION					MINERALS				ANALYSIS		
AVERAGE DAILY NEED	5000 I.U.	600 I.U.	1500 I.U.	2.7 MGS.		800 MGS.	1320 MGS.	12 MGS.		2000-3000	70 GMS.

COMMENTS: An excellent Class A complete protein, particularly rich in iron. Should be eaten sparingly by elderly persons, as extremely high in cholesterol. Reducers should note that sweetbreads are higher in calorie content than most meats of this type. Sweetbreads, like brains, require particularly careful preparation to prevent this delicate meat of soft texture from falling apart. Similar care is necessary in cooking them so they will be palatable as well as digestible. Always soak and cook before broiling, sautéing or combining with a cream sauce. Plain cooked or broiled sweetbreads preferred to sautéed, as cooking in fat makes meat less easily digested. All three are benefited nutritionally as well as in flavor and appearance by minced parsley garnish, Lemon Butter or Hollandaise Sauce. High water content of Sweetbreads and Mushrooms dish makes it lighter and less rich than plain sweetbreads. Pimiento and lemon juice give flavor and protective value. Reducers should omit flour and milk, thus merely sautéing other ingredients. Bland taste and soft texture of sweetbreads call for crispness and brightness in accompanying foods at meals.

COOKED SWEETBREADS

INGREDIENTS:

3 pairs sweetbreads	tablespoon cider vinegar)
boiling water	1 cup Hollandaise Sauce
1 tablespoon salt	(page 220)
2 tablespoons lemon juice (or 1	2 tablespoons minced parsley

DIRECTIONS: Be certain sweetbreads are absolutely fresh when purchased; prepare as soon as possible because they are very perishable. Soak in cold salted water (1 teaspoon salt to 1 quart water) about $\frac{1}{2}$ hour or leave in water if not cooked at once. In saucepan, boil just enough water to cover meat and add salt and lemon juice (acid helps keep meat white). Use skimmer to slip meat gently into boiling water. Cover pan and simmer gently over low heat about 15 minutes, just until tender enough to be pierced with fork. Drain and place in cold water immediately, to keep flesh firm. Carefully remove tubes and membranes. Split or dice and serve or combine with Hollandaise Sauce. Garnish with minced parsley.

Sautéed Sweetbreads—Cook, prepare and split sweetbreads as directed in basic recipe. Sprinkle with salt and pepper. Melt 3 tablespoons butter in skillet and sauté sweetbreads about 3 minutes on each side until golden brown. Sprinkle with parsley. Serve with lemon slices or Lemon Butter. For a very filling, rich dish, serve with Hollandaise Sauce (page 220).

Broiled Sweetbreads—Cook, prepare and split sweetbreads as directed in basic recipe. Preheat broiler 10 minutes. Dip meat in melted butter or salad oil, sprinkle with salt and pepper, and place in greased, shallow broiler pan or baking sheet. Broil 3 inches from high heat about 5 minutes on each side.

SWEETBREADS AND MUSHROOMS

VITAMINS	1 PORTION CONTAINS APPROXIMATELY	DAILY NEED
A	346	5000 I.U.
B	73	600 I.U.
C	84	1500 I.U.
G	.22	2.7 MGS.

INGREDIENTS:

2 pairs sweetbreads	1 teaspoon salt
¼ cup butter	⅛ teaspoon pepper
1 tablespoon minced onion	2 cups rich milk
1 cup (¼ pound) sliced mushrooms	1 pimiento, diced
3 tablespoons flour	1 tablespoon lemon juice
	2 tablespoons minced parsley

DIRECTIONS: Cook, prepare and dice sweetbreads as directed in basic recipe for Cooked Sweetbreads. Melt butter in large skillet and sauté onion and mushrooms over low heat about 3 minutes, stirring occasionally. Stir in flour and seasoning and when well blended, add milk gradually, stirring constantly until mixture boils and thickens. Stir in sweetbreads, pimiento and lemon juice, and just reheat. Sprinkle with minced parsley.

BALANCED MEAL SUGGESTIONS: *Lunch*—Cucumber Salad; *Broiled Sweetbreads;* String Beans; Grapefruit or Berries; Milk.

TONGUE

This Chart Gives Approximate Food Values for BOILED TONGUE.

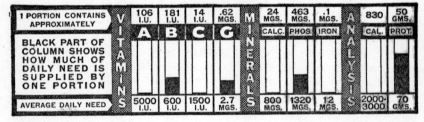

1 PORTION CONTAINS APPROXIMATELY	VITAMINS				MINERALS			ANALYSIS	
	A 106 I.U.	B 181 I.U.	C 14 I.U.	G .62 MGS.	CALC. 24 MGS.	PHOS. 463 MGS.	IRON .1 MGS.	CAL. 830	PROT. 50 GMS.
BLACK PART OF COLUMN SHOWS HOW MUCH OF DAILY NEED IS SUPPLIED BY ONE PORTION									
AVERAGE DAILY NEED	5000 I.U.	600 I.U.	1500 I.U.	2.7 MGS.	800 MGS.	1320 MGS.	12 MGS.	2000-3000	70 GMS.

COMMENTS: A Class A complete protein. Exceptionally rich in phosphorus. Tongue high in calorie content so should be eaten by reducers only occasionally. Tongue Creole, because of vegetables, less fattening. Leftover tongue may be put through meat grinder, using finest blade, and seasoned with a little ketchup or chili sauce for use as a canapé spread.

Tongue, like heart, is a meat that has received considerable exercise and therefore requires long cooking time to become tender and palatable. Whenever possible, purchase lamb tongues for shortest cooking time.

BOILED TONGUE

INGREDIENTS:

1 fresh or smoked beef tongue
(or 6 lamb or 2 calf tongues)
4 peppercorns
2 cloves
1 bay leaf
1 carrot, quartered
1 medium-sized onion, sliced
¼ cup shredded celery leaves

DIRECTIONS: Be certain tongue is absolutely fresh when purchased, unless smoked variety is bought. Scrub tongue with brush and wash thoroughly. Place in large saucepan and cover with boiling water. Add seasonings and vegetables. When water has come to a full boil, cover and simmer until tender.

If tongue comes wrapped in cellophane, cook according to directions on label. All cooking times depend on size and texture of tongue. Beef tongue usually requires about 2 to 3 hours; calf, about 1½ to 2 hours; lamb, about 40 minutes to 1 hour. Remove skin and fat while tongue is hot. Plunging tongue into cold water after cooking helps loosen skin. Serve sliced or whole on hot platter. Garnish with parsley or watercress.

If tongue is to be served cold, remove skin and fat while still hot; strain stock in which meat has been cooked, and return tongue to stock to cool. Tongue, to retain juices and flavor, should remain in stock until served. Store covered in refrigerator until used.

Tongue with Chard and Cauliflower—Simmer and prepare tongue as in basic recipe for Boiled Tongue. Quick-cook separately chard leaves (page 262) and cauliflower (page 260). Place hot tongue in center of hot platter, surround tongue with chopped chard and arrange cauliflowerets on chard. Serve with Lemon Butter (page 222), if desired. *Serving chard with tongue adds considerable Vitamin A to this recipe, as chard is one of the best sources of this vitamin among vegetables.*

181

TONGUE CREOLE

	1 PORTION CONTAINS APPROXIMATELY	DAILY NEED
A	689	5000 I.U.
B	56	600 I.U.
C	361	1500 I.U.
G	.18	2.7 MGS.

VITAMINS

INGREDIENTS:

2 cups diced cooked or canned tongue

½ green pepper, diced

2 medium-sized onions, diced

4 tablespoons melted butter (or salad oil)

1 cup diced fresh (or canned) tomatoes

DIRECTIONS: Melt butter or heat oil in skillet and sauté onions and pepper until onions are yellow, about 3 minutes, stirring occasionally. Add tomatoes and diced tongue. Cover and simmer about 10 minutes, just until tongue is thoroughly heated. Serve plain or on toast or boiled rice.

BALANCED MEAL SUGGESTIONS: *Lunch*—Apple Coleslaw; *Tongue Creole;* Fruit Cup; Milk.

TRIPE

This Chart Gives Approximate Food Values for BOILED TRIPE.

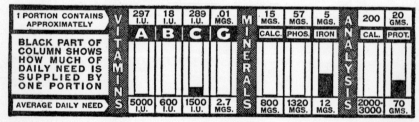

1 PORTION CONTAINS APPROXIMATELY		297 I.U.	18 I.U.	289 I.U.	.01 MGS.		15 MGS.	57 MGS.	5 MGS.		200	20 GMS.
	V I T A M I N S	A	B	C	G	M I N E R A L S	CALC.	PHOS.	IRON	A N A L Y S I S	CAL.	PROT.
BLACK PART OF COLUMN SHOWS HOW MUCH OF DAILY NEED IS SUPPLIED BY ONE PORTION												
AVERAGE DAILY NEED		5000 I.U.	600 I.U.	1500 I.U.	2.7 MGS.		800 MGS.	1320 MGS.	12 MGS.		2000-3000	70 GMS.

COMMENTS: A Class A complete protein, high in vitamin and mineral contents. Especially rich in iron. It is particularly important to buy only the freshest tripe, as it deteriorates rapidly. Combining with vegetables, as in Tripe Creole, makes a dish rich in all vitamins and important minerals, and gives tripe the extra flavor it needs. Preferred way to serve, as tripe is always best accompanied by a well-seasoned sauce. Fairly low in calorie content and high in water content; excellent for reducers. Tripe, like brains and sweetbreads, must be cooked (simmered) until tender before using.

COOKED TRIPE

INGREDIENTS:

1½ pounds honeycomb tripe   2 cups Tomato Sauce (page 221)
1 teaspoon salt

DIRECTIONS: Wash tripe thoroughly and dice (to shorten cooking time). Cover with cold water in large saucepan and bring to a boil. Drain, cover with fresh boiling water, cover pan and simmer until tender. Add salt after cooking ½ hour. When tender, drain, and combine with Tomato Sauce. Length of cooking time depends upon thickness and texture of individual piece of tripe. Honeycomb tripe from young beef considered the choicest; becomes tender in about 40 minutes to 1 hour. Tripe from an older animal may require 1½ to 4 hours to become soft. Unless honeycomb tripe is available, it is often wise to cook tripe day before it is to be used (because of long and uncertain time required for cooking). In that case, leave in liquid after cooking and cool uncovered. Then cover and store in refrigerator.

TRIPE CREOLE

Each Portion Contains Approximately:
Vit. A—1180 I.U.; Vit. B₁—35 I.U.; Vit. C—693 I.U.; Vit. G—.07 Mg.

INGREDIENTS:

1½ pounds cooked honeycomb
  tripe
2 tablespoons butter
2 tablespoons minced onion
1 green pepper, minced
½ cup chopped celery
1 tablespoon flour

salt and pepper to taste
1 cup tripe liquid
  (cooking water)
1 cup condensed tomato paste
  (or 2 cups canned or fresh
  tomatoes)
2 tablespoons minced parsley

DIRECTIONS: Prepare and cook tripe as directed in basic recipe. Drain, reserving 1 cup cooking liquid. Melt butter in large skillet and sauté onion, green pepper and celery about 3 minutes. Reduce heat, add flour and seasonings, and stir until well blended. Gradually stir in tripe liquid and tomato paste (or tomatoes); stir constantly until sauce is smooth and thick. Add tripe, cover and simmer over low heat about 10 minutes, just until tripe is thoroughly heated. Add minced parsley. Serve on toast or with boiled rice.

BALANCED MEAL SUGGESTIONS: *Dinner*—Mixed Vegetable Salad; *Tripe Creole;* Parsley Potatoes; String Beans; Fresh Sliced Peaches.

183

POULTRY

This Chart Gives Approximate Food Values for ROAST CHICKEN. For Vitamin Values of Specific Recipes, See Charts Accompanying Them.

1 PORTION CONTAINS APPROXIMATELY	VITAMINS	691 I.U.	192 I.U.	11 I.U.	.21 MGS.	MINERALS	114 MGS.	356 MGS.	2 MGS.	ANALYSIS	403	38 GMS.
		A	B	C	G		CALC.	PHOS.	IRON		CAL.	PROT.
BLACK PART OF COLUMN SHOWS HOW MUCH OF DAILY NEED IS SUPPLIED BY ONE PORTION												
AVERAGE DAILY NEED		5000 I.U.	600 I.U.	1500 I.U.	2.7 MGS.		800 MGS.	1320 MGS.	12 MGS.		2000-3000	70 GMS.

COMMENTS: Popularity of this form of meat, and share it demands of food budget, merit careful buying and concern for quality. Tremendous amount of inferior poultry is foisted upon the unwary.

Selection—Buy quality birds of a size suitable for needs and intended method of preparation. Always purchase from reliable dealer. Quick-frozen poultry of reliable packers usually quality birds, ready for whatever use desired. Young birds generally more tender. Five-pound fowl will yield 6 servings, or 3 cups diced cooked meat. Capons usually weigh 7 to 8 pounds, and although the most costly, are considered choice buys for roasting.

To be meaty, all chickens should be plump in appearance. Lower end of breastbone should be flexible, not hard. Creamy color indicates presence of fat. Skin should be smooth, moist and free of any discolorations.

Dressing and Drawing—Most poultry is already dressed and will be drawn, at your request, when purchased. Upon selection, dealer will not only remove feet and clean bird, but will split it for broiling or cut it into whatever sized pieces desired. Should poultry be fresh-killed, dress at once, and let hang for at least 6 hours before cooking. (To hang, tie chicken legs with strong cord and let bird drip over large kettle.)

In dressing fresh-killed poultry, remember that birds should be **dry-picked** for best flavor. That is, plucking feathers from dry bird is preferable **to wet**

184

or scalding method—plunging bird for a few moments into sufficient boiling water to cover, and then plucking. Although latter method is quicker and the one commonly used, it is not so good as dry method, because the boiling water injures delicate flavor of fowl.

All poultry should be dressed and drawn (cleaned thoroughly inside and out) as soon as purchased. If prepared at market, examine carefully to be sure bird has been properly cleaned. There should be no trace of kidneys in hollow near end of backbone, nor of red, spongy substance on each side of backbone between ribs. If there is, remove completely.

Refrigeration—If poultry is not cooked directly after purchasing, wash thoroughly, dry, and wrap bird and giblets separately in moisture-proof paper or clean cloth. Keep in refrigerator until cooked. Use as soon as possible.

Preparation (Drawing, Washing and Singeing of Poultry)—To draw: Dry-pick bird at once, if fresh-killed. Use sharp knife or cleaver to cut off head. Remove feet by cutting skin about 1½ inches below leg joints, being careful not to cut tendons; place leg at cut over edge of board and press downward to snap the bone; hold bird firmly and pull off each foot (with the tendon). A pair of poultry shears is convenient for cutting up fowl. Cut around vent at end of tailbone, making hole as small as possible and cut away oil bag. From tailbone, slit skin up to lower end of breastbone. Use hand to reach inside and pull out all organs, including red, spongy lungs between ribs and kidneys in hollow near end of backbone. Be careful in removing liver not to break gall bladder, which is a little green sac attached to liver. Liquid (bile) it contains is very bitter and would give unpleasant taste to any part it touched. Discard all organs but gizzard, heart and liver. (These are giblets and can be cooked as ingredients of stuffings, gravies, soups and egg dishes. Directions for cleaning follow later.)

Feel under skin at neck and pull out windpipe and crop, which are close to breast. If bird is to be roasted, pull neck out taut, and slit loose skin of neck down back of bird to where neck joins body. Pull skin aside and cut off neck at this point; save to cook with giblets. Loose skin at neck will be used to fold over neck opening (whether stuffed or not), and will be sewed or fastened to back of bird with skewers or toothpicks. If bird is not to be roasted, cut off loose skin with neck.

To wash: Wash bird thoroughly inside and out. Hold opening in bird under cold running water. Rinse thoroughly by running water over every bit of surface of bird both inside and outside. Place hand in opening and feel around inside of bird, particularly between ribs, to be sure it is absolutely clean. Make certain there are no traces of lungs or kidneys still clinging to bird. Dry inside and out with cloth or paper towels.

To singe poultry: Although poultry will probably be dressed (plucked) before you select it, many small pinfeathers and traces of down are not entirely removed. To remove by singeing, hold bird over direct flame (gas or candle), spread out wings to expose entire surface, and turn bird constantly and slowly so that every possible trace of hair and down will be burned off. Remove any remaining pinfeathers with pointed knife or kitchen tweezers. Although it is customary to singe bird before drawing, it is easier to handle during singeing after it has been drawn (cleaned), especially if it is large.

CHICKEN

COMMENTS: Chicken high in muscle protein (slightly higher than most meats); comparatively low in fat. Old idea that convalescents or those warned to avoid "red" meats should eat chicken (especially white meat), entirely fallacious, as fowl contains on the whole same properties as muscle meats. Often tenderer and more easily digested, however, than meats high in fat. Slightly lower in calorie content than meat; hence good as main dish for reducers.

Shorter cooking time means that broiled chicken is preferable to roast chicken. Greater ease of digestion makes it overwhelmingly preferred to fried chicken. Broiled chicken is the best choice for reducers.

Broilers a practical dish for one or two persons or small family, where large chicken needed for roasting is out of the question. Should weigh no more than 2 to 2½ pounds for best flavor and tenderness. Especially good when broiled as Southerners like it with thin strips of bacon wrapped around legs and body, or when brushed with garlic.

Combination chicken dishes (Chicken à la King, etc.) offer excellent ways of using high-vitamin foods with chicken—pimientos, leftover vegetables, sweetbreads or other organ meats, etc. Despite the small amounts of flour, cream or milk used in Chicken and Sweetbreads à la King, Chicken Fricassée, etc., calorie content not too high for reducers to eat small portions, if desired. Combination dishes excellent for "stretching" a chicken to fill family's needs.

Use chicken often at seasons when cheap (frequently cheaper than meats). Substitute for meat in dinner menus.

ROAST CHICKEN

Each Portion Contains Approximately:
Vit. A—691 I.U.; Vit. B₁—192 I.U.; Vit. C—11 I.U.; Vit. G—.21 Mg.

INGREDIENTS:

1 4½- to 5-pound chicken
   (or 7- to 8-pound capon)
¼ cup melted butter
   (or bacon fat)

salt and pepper
4 cups Giblet stuffing
   (page 225)

PREPARATION: Have chicken dressed, drawn, singed and washed (page 184). Do not disjoint. To stuff: Sprinkle inside of bird lightly with salt. Use spoon or hand to fill body and neck cavities with desired stuffing, and stuff lightly. Never pack stuffing, as it will expand while cooking and burst skin, thereby spoiling appearance of bird and drying out itself. Use darning needle and heavy thread or white string to sew edges of cavities together. (Skin may also be fastened with special skewers available at dealers for this purpose, and then string interlaced around the ends of the skewers.)

To truss: To have bird keep its shape while roasting, trussing is recommended. Place bird breast up, and fold wings back and under body so that they press against back. Fasten in this position by inserting large steel skewer through wing, body, and wing on opposite side. (Dealer will supply skewer upon request.) Cross ends of legs and fasten to tail by using center of long piece of string to tie them together securely. Turn bird on breast, bring loose string ends to back, cross them, and tie each string securely to each end of skewer. Remember, string is tied across *back* of bird. To keep shape of birds that are not stuffed, place legs through incisions cut in body under bones near tail. Dealer, upon request, will do this for you.

DIRECTIONS: After chicken is trussed, rub outside with melted butter and sprinkle with salt and pepper. Place in baking pan, on trivet, if available, breast-side down or on its side. Bake uncovered in moderate oven (350° F.) until tender, allowing 22 to 25 minutes per pound, depending upon tenderness of bird. Baste occasionally with fat in pan. Half an hour before chicken is done, turn breast-side up or on other side to have it evenly cooked and flavored. To test if chicken is done, pierce joints and thickest part of breast with steel fork. If no blood shows and meat is tender, it is ready to be served.

BALANCED MEAL SUGGESTIONS: *Dinner*—Combination Salad; *Roast Chicken;* Carrots and Peas; Baked Potatoes; Pan Gravy; Pineapple with Mint.

BROILED CHICKEN

INGREDIENTS:

3 (2- to 2½-pound) broilers
salt and pepper

3 tablespoons melted butter, bacon
fat or salad oil (approximate)

PREPARATION: Have chickens dressed, drawn, singed and washed (page 184). Cut through backbone from neck to tail and break joints so that chickens will be flat while broiling. Be sure they are thoroughly clean. If desired, cut out rib bones and remove breastbones. Rinse thoroughly under cold running water and dry.

DIRECTIONS: Preheat broiler necessary time. (Gas ovens require about 10 minutes; electric broilers all differ in preheating time. Note instructions accompanying them.) Brush birds with melted fat or oil and sprinkle with salt and pepper. Arrange on greased broiler rack, skin-side down, and broil 3 to 4 inches below low heat, until tender, about 30 to 45 minutes. Turn birds several times and baste frequently with fat in pan or additional fat.

BALANCED MEAL SUGGESTIONS: *Dinner* — Cucumber Salad; *Broiled Chicken* with Bacon (optional); Chopped Spinach; Baked Sweet Potatoes; Deep-Dish Apple Pie.

STEAMED (BOILED) CHICKEN

Each Portion Contains Approximately:
Vit. A—1417 I.U.; Vit. B₁—56 I.U.; Vit. C—133 I.U.; Vit. G—.21 Mg.

INGREDIENTS:

1 (5-pound) fowl
6 cups boiling water
¼ cup chopped carrots
3 sprigs parsley
1 onion, sliced

3 stalks celery and leaves
6 peppercorns
4 cloves (optional)
1 bay leaf (optional)
1 tablespoon salt

DIRECTIONS: Have chicken dressed, drawn, singed and washed (page 184). Cut into desired pieces for serving. Place in kettle with remaining ingredients, except salt. Let come to a boil, cover tightly, reduce heat, and simmer until tender, about 1½ to 2 hours, depending upon tenderness of fowl. *Do not boil;* rapid cooking causes strong, unpleasant flavor to develop. Even older fowl will eventually become tender if steamed long enough.

Add salt after first hour of cooking. When tender, strain broth. If chicken is not used at once, return to strained broth and let cool, uncovered. For later use, store chicken (boned or not, as desired) in stock, tightly covered, in refrigerator. When ready to use, remove chicken fat which has solidified on top of stock. Use Steamed Chicken for any dish that calls for cooked chicken.

BAKED CHICKEN CASSEROLE

Each Portion Contains Approximately:
Vit. A—995 I.U.; Vit. B₁—51 I.U.; Vit. C—22 I.U.; Vit. G—.23 Mg.

INGREDIENTS:

1 (4-pound) chicken	1 cup diced carrots
2 teaspoons salt	1 cup diced celery
¼ teaspoon paprika	3 tablespoons minced onion
6 tablespoons flour (approximate)	1 cup water
6 tablespoons butter	

PREPARATION: Have chicken dressed, drawn, singed and washed (page 184). Cut into pieces for serving. Make incision in skin between legs and body, close to body; pull or bend back legs, breaking ligaments; cut through flesh, and separate legs from body at joint. Cut through knee joint to separate upper part of legs (thighs) from "drumsticks" (lower part of legs). Cut through skin and flesh around wings (wing joints being close to body), and separate wings from body. Cut through skin on both sides of body about 2 inches below breastbone, extending cut between small ribs to collarbone, to separate back from breast. Then split back and breast in halves, cutting crosswise. Rinse all pieces thoroughly under cold running water, particularly back.

DIRECTIONS: Mix seasoning with flour. Roll each piece of chicken in seasoned flour. Melt butter in skillet and sauté chicken over low heat until lightly browned on all sides. Place in 2-quart casserole or small roaster. Add prepared vegetables to fat left in skillet, and stir over low heat just 2 minutes. Place vegetables in casserole with chicken. Add water, cover, and bake in moderate oven (350° F.) until tender, about 45 to 60 minutes. Baste occasionally by turning pieces of chicken, and add more water as needed.

BALANCED MEAL SUGGESTIONS: *Dinner*—Lettuce and Tomato Salad; *Baked Chicken Casserole;* String Beans; Mashed Potatoes; Cherry Cobbler.

189

CHICKEN FRICASSEE

VITAMINS	1 PORTION CONTAINS APPROXIMATELY	DAILY NEED
A	1273	5000 I.U.
B	63	600 I.U.
C	8	1500 I.U.
G	.21	2.7 MGS.

INGREDIENTS:

1 Steamed (Boiled) Chicken
3 tablespoons chicken fat
(or butter)
4 tablespoons flour
2 cups chicken stock

1 egg yolk, slightly beaten
½ cup cream
1 teaspoon lemon juice (or more)
salt and pepper to taste
3 tablespoons minced parsley

DIRECTIONS: Prepare chicken and cook until tender. Keep chicken hot while preparing sauce. Melt fat in skillet, reduce heat, add flour, and stir until smooth and well blended. Add chicken stock slowly, stirring constantly over low heat until mixture thickens and boils. In a bowl, add cream to slightly beaten egg yolk, and mix well. Add to sauce gradually, stirring constantly for about 1 minute. Just reheat, do not boil. Add lemon juice, salt and pepper and parsley just before serving. Arrange chicken on hot platter, pour sauce over it, and garnish with parsley sprigs.

BALANCED MEAL SUGGESTIONS: *Dinner*—Mixed Vegetable Salad; *Chicken Fricassée;* Boiled Brown Rice; Chopped Spinach; Fruit Cup.

CHICKEN AND SWEETBREADS Á LA KING

Each Portion Contains Approximately:
Vit. A—1189 I.U.; Vit. B₁—46 I.U.; Vit. C—707 I.U.; Vit. G—.25 Mg.

INGREDIENTS:

1 cup cooked (page 188) or
canned chicken
1 pair cooked sweetbreads
(page 179)
4 tablespoons butter
1 cup (¼ pound) sliced
mushrooms
1 green pepper, minced

3 tablespoons flour
½ teaspoon salt
½ teaspoon paprika
1¾ cups milk
2 pimientos, minced
¼ cup cream
2 egg yolks, slightly beaten
1 tablespoon lemon juice

DIRECTIONS: Cut cooked chicken into small cubes, and chop cooked sweetbreads. Melt butter in large skillet, add mushrooms, green pepper and sweetbreads, and sauté over medium heat 5 minutes, stirring occasionally.

Reduce heat, stir in flour, salt, and paprika. When smooth and well blended, add milk gradually, stirring constantly until mixture thickens and boils. Add chicken and pimientos.

In a bowl, add cream to slightly beaten egg yolks, and mix well. Add to sauce gradually, stirring constantly until well blended. Do not boil; just reheat. Add lemon juice and serve immediately. Recipe can be made without sweetbreads, although it will not be so high in nutritional value. Use 1 additional cup chicken to replace sweetbreads.

BALANCED MEAL SUGGESTIONS: *Lunch*—Combination Salad; *Chicken and Sweetbreads à la King;* Rye Toast; Stewed Rhubarb.

	1 PORTION CONTAINS APPROXIMATELY	DAILY NEED	
A	1450	5000 I.U.	**BRUNSWICK STEW**
B	111	600 I.U.	
C	754	1500 I.U.	
G	.45	2.7 MGS.	

INGREDIENTS:

1 (4- to 5-pound) chicken
1 cracked veal shank
5 cups boiling water
1/4 teaspoon pepper
2 medium-sized onions, minced
4 tablespoons minced green pepper

2 cups sliced okra
1 1/2 cups green lima beans
1 1/2 cups fresh cut or canned whole kernel corn
2 cups fresh or canned tomatoes
2 tablespoons butter
2 tablespoons flour

DIRECTIONS: Have chicken dressed, drawn, singed and washed (page 184). Cut into desired pieces for serving. Place in large kettle with veal shank and water. Add onions and pepper, bring to boil, cover tightly, reduce heat, and simmer until almost tender, about 1 hour. Remove veal shank. Add peppers, okra and beans, and cook about 30 minutes, just until vegetables are almost tender. Add corn and tomatoes and cook 10 minutes longer, or until chicken and vegetables are tender. If canned vegetables are used, do not add to chicken until it has practically finished cooking. In small bowl, cream butter with flour until smooth and well blended, and stir slowly into stew. Cook over low heat 2 minutes, until mixture thickens and boils.

BALANCED MEAL SUGGESTIONS: *Dinner*—Pimiento Coleslaw; *Brunswick Stew;* Fruit Gelatin.

COOKED GIBLETS

INGREDIENTS:

giblets from any fowl
(gizzard, heart, liver)

1 tablespoon minced onion

¼ cup shredded celery leaves
salt to taste

PREPARATION: Gizzard, heart and liver known as giblets. After fowl is cleaned, remove fat and membrane from gizzard, then carefully make a gash in thickest part of gizzard, cutting just to—but definitely not through—inner tough lining. Pull outer skin away from inner sac, and discard sac. Should sac be punctured, remove contents thoroughly by washing under running water, and then separate tough inner lining from outer skin by pulling them apart. Cut away arteries and veins from top of heart and remove any clot of blood. If gall bladder has not been separated from liver, carefully cut away, including any part of liver that has greenish color. Rinse giblets thoroughly in cold water, and cook as soon as possible, even if rest of chicken is to be kept for later use.

DIRECTIONS: Place gizzard (and neck, if reserved) in cold water to cover. Add onion and celery leaves. Cover and simmer over low heat about 20 minutes. Add heart, liver and a pinch of salt, and cook until heart is tender, about 10 minutes longer. When giblets are tender, drain, reserve stock for gravy, and chop giblets very fine, discarding tough or fibrous portions.

Giblets should never be thrown away or given to just one member of family who happens to like them. Chopped cooked giblets may be added to stuffings and gravies, incorporated in loaves and soups, or made into sandwich spread. Excellent when combined with Scrambled Eggs or Omelet.

TURKEY

COMMENTS: Nutritional values practically same as those of chicken. When purchasing turkey, allow ¾ pound per serving. Recently, breeders have been producing at all seasons of the year small turkeys that are not priced exorbitantly. In fact, occasionally turkey is cheaper per pound than chicken; a wise "buy" at those times. Leftover cooked turkey may be used in any recipes which call for cooked or canned chicken, as well as many others. Roast turkey trimmings and bones may be used for making Turkey Bone Soup (page 231).

ROAST TURKEY

INGREDIENTS:

1 (10- to 16-pound) turkey   8 to 12 cups Bread Stuffing
salt and pepper   (page 224)
¼ cup melted butter

DIRECTIONS: Prepare, stuff and truss turkey as directed for chicken (page 184). Rub bird with butter and dredge (cover with thin coating) with seasoned flour. Place bird breast-side down or on its side in large roasting pan. Bake, uncovered, in moderate oven (350° F.) until tender, allowing 20 to 24 minutes per pound, depending upon tenderness of bird. Baste every 30 minutes with fat in pan or, if necessary, with additional butter and hot water. Turn bird breast-side up or on other side 30 minutes before it has finished cooking so it will be evenly cooked and flavored. If quick-frozen or graded "fancy" poultry is used, follow cooking directions accompanying it.

BALANCED MEAL SUGGESTIONS: *Dinner*—Mixed Greens Salad; *Roast Turkey;* Parsley Carrots; Mashed Potatoes; Fresh Fruit Bowl.

DUCK

COMMENTS: Protein of duck similar to that of chicken. Persons with digestive difficulties should eat chicken or turkey rather than duck or goose, because the latter have higher fat contents.

Best stuffings for duck are those with tart addition, such as orange, apple, apricot, cranberry, etc. If duck is not stuffed, will have better flavor if 2 halved apples, oranges or onions are baked inside bird during roasting. Remove before serving.

ROAST DUCK

INGREDIENTS:

1 (4- to 6-pound) duck   4 cups Orange Stuffing (page 226)
salt and pepper

DIRECTIONS: Prepare, stuff and truss duck as directed for chicken (page 184). Place duck in roasting pan on trivet or rack, breast-side down or on its side. Roast, uncovered, in moderate oven (350° F.) until tender, allowing 25 to 30 minutes per pound, depending upon tenderness of duck. (Graded "fancy" poultry may have special cooking directions accompanying it. In this case, follow them exactly for best results.) If duck is very fat, basting may be omitted; if not, baste occasionally with orange juice, water or currant jelly during roasting. Turn duck breast-side up or on other side 30 minutes before it has finished cooking so it will be evenly cooked and flavored.

BALANCED MEAL SUGGESTIONS: *Dinner*—Fruit Cup; *Roast Duck;* Sweet Potatoes; String Beans; Sponge Cake with Sliced Peaches.

GOOSE

COMMENTS: Since goose has such a high fat content, should be avoided by persons with digestive troubles or those advanced in years, except on rare occasions. Always use tart stuffing for goose, as for duck, to cut excessively fatty texture and flavor of fowl.

ROAST GOOSE

INGREDIENTS:

1 (8- to 10-pound) goose
salt and pepper

6 to 7 cups Orange Stuffing
(page 226)

DIRECTIONS: Prepare, stuff and truss goose as directed for chicken (page 184). Place goose breast-side down or on its side in roasting pan on trivet or rack. Bake, uncovered, in slow oven (325° F.) until tender, allowing 20 to 25 minutes per pound, depending upon tenderness of goose. Prick skin with fork to allow excess fat to run out. Turn goose breast-side up or on other side 30 minutes before it has finished cooking so it will be evenly cooked and flavored.

BALANCED MEAL SUGGESTIONS: *Dinner*—Pineapple Salad; *Roast Goose;* Beets and Greens; Parsley Potatoes; Stewed Apples and Raisins.

SALADS

This Chart Gives Approximate Food Values for COMBINATION SALAD. For Vitamin Values of Specific Recipes, See Charts Accompanying Them.

1 PORTION CONTAINS APPROXIMATELY	VITAMINS	1739 I.U.	30 I.U.	466 I.U.	.17 MGS.	MINERALS	30 MGS.	48 MGS.	2 MGS.	ANALYSIS	69	1 GMS.
		A	B	C	G		CALC.	PHOS.	IRON		CAL.	PROT.
BLACK PART OF COLUMN SHOWS HOW MUCH OF DAILY NEED IS SUPPLIED BY ONE PORTION												
AVERAGE DAILY NEED		5000 I.U.	600 I.U.	1500 I.U.	2.7 MGS.		800 MGS.	1320 MGS.	12 MGS.		2000-3000	70 GMS.

COMMENTS: Raw vegetable salads serve the serious purpose of introducing some of the richest vitamin foods into the diet in a delicious form, free from any of the hazards of cooking. They satisfy the wholesome instinct for fresh foods and help to fulfill the dictate of nutrition science: Eat some raw foods each day.

We recommend that the salad be served first, as an appetizing introduction to the meal. Both luncheon and dinner should be graced by a salad, for this dish is the most dependable source of protective vitamin and mineral food factors. If a salad is to be the main dish of a lunch or supper, it may be of the more filling type, and portions should be larger.

Simple salads are often the most flavorful. A few ingredients may be quickly prepared, easily crisped and chilled. There is no need to prepare complicated salads with many different vegetables or fruits intricately arranged.

Many people are allergic to or unable to tolerate comfortably any great variety of leafy vegetables. The more complicated the salad, the greater the chance for digestive upsets.

In most instances, it is important to serve the salad as soon as possible after the vegetables have been shredded to avoid oxidation of Vitamin C. Hence, do not prepare salad early in the day, but wait until the very last minute to do the cutting and shredding.

LEAFY SALADS

Green leafy salad ingredients are prepared by shredding, cutting into thin strips with a sharp knife, or cutting into small pieces with scissors. Tender, crisp vegetables like green cabbage leaves, escarole or chicory, green lettuce, watercress, are suitable salad greens. Serve them singly or combined.

Sharp-flavored and less tender greens, such as beet greens, dandelion greens, spinach, etc., are best when used as cooked greens, since they may cause digestive upsets if eaten raw. Suggestions for combining these greens, and directions for cooking them, are given on page 266.

Shredded leaves of suitable salad greens often used as basis or bed for simple fruit salads.

General rules for the use of green salad leaves:

1. Separate leaves (with the exception of green cabbage) and wash thoroughly. Save stems and coarse leaves for stock pot. Drain and dry before placing in tightly covered refrigerator pan (hydrator) or cellophane bag.

2. Place in refrigerator to chill and crisp. Be certain greens are thoroughly dried, else they will become limp as soon as they are removed from refrigerator.

3. Tear lettuce leaves into bits with fingers, cut others into thin strips with scissors or knife. To prepare cabbage for coleslaw, use sharp knife or shredder to cut cabbage as fine as possible. Shake shredded leaves in pan of cold water, drain thoroughly. Such tearing or shredding makes salad easier to eat, and insures proper coating of leaves with dressing.

4. Mix in large wooden salad bowl.

5. Sprinkle dressing on leaves and toss lightly with wooden spoon and fork to coat leaves evenly. Best to add dressing at table just before serving, so greens will not wilt.

MIXED SALADS

Green leaves of suitable salad greens may also be shredded and used either as an ingredient or as a bed for service of "mixed" or garden vegetable salads. Mixed salads may be made from a choice of any or all of the following raw vegetables:

Avocados, carrots, celery, cucumbers, red and green peppers, radishes, scallions, tomatoes.

COOKED VEGETABLE SALADS

Raw cauliflower, turnips, beets, etc., are sometimes used in raw vegetable salads, but too many people are unable to digest comfortably these vegetables which have a rather high cellulose content. It is best to quick-cook and chill the following vegetables before using them as salad ingredients: Asparagus, beets, cauliflower.

Cooked vegetable salads offer splendid opportunities to serve protective vegetables in attractive, flavorful ways, particularly during summer months. However, such salads are substantial—they should not be served with heavy meats. Use them as main luncheon or supper dishes. Such cooked vegetable salad ingredients include: Kidney beans, lima beans, string beans, carrots, peas, potatoes, etc.

SALAD SEASONINGS

Strongly flavored or colorful vegetables which may be chopped, minced or grated, and incorporated in any vegetable salad to suit the taste and improve the salad's protective value are: Chives, garlic, leeks, olives, onions, parsley, pimientos, scallions.

Fresh herbs such as tarragon, sorrel, dill, chervil, etc., if available, add interest to any mixed vegetable salad. A really spicy flavor is obtained if the main ingredients of a salad are marinated in French dressing or lemon juice.

With these basic principles in mind, you can prepare dozens of delicious and delightful vegetable salads to suit your taste, purse, convenience and vitamin needs.

COMBINATION SALAD

INGREDIENTS:

1 cucumber, diced
6 scallions (or 1 small onion), minced
6 radishes, thinly sliced (optional)
2 tablespoons minced parsley
2 medium-sized tomatoes, coarsely chopped
2 cups shredded or chopped green lettuce (or cabbage)
¼ cup French Dressing (page 214)

DIRECTIONS: Combine thoroughly chilled ingredients with dressing, and toss together lightly until evenly coated.

197

ASPARAGUS SALAD

Each Portion Contains Approximately:
Vit. A—1434 I.U.; Vit. B₁—23 I.U.; Vit. C—837 I.U.; Vit. G—.2 Mg.

INGREDIENTS:

18 cooked (or 1 can) asparagus
   tips
6 to 12 lettuce leaves

2 pimientos, cut into strips
¼ cup French Dressing
   (page 214)

DIRECTIONS: Marinate asparagus, arrange on shredded salad greens and garnish with pimiento strips.

CARROT-RAISIN SALAD

VITAMINS	1 PORTION CONTAINS APPROXIMATELY	DAILY NEED
A	1977	5000 I.U.
B	30	600 I.U.
C	309	1500 I.U.
G	.2	2.7 MGS.

INGREDIENTS:

1½ cups shredded carrots
½ cup seedless (or seeded)
   raisins
4 tablespoons lemon juice

6 to 12 lettuce leaves (or 1½
   cups shredded cabbage)
¼ cup Mayonnaise (page 211)

DIRECTIONS: Shred carrots. Soak raisins in lemon juice. Combine ingredients, mix with dressing, and serve in lettuce cups or on shredded cabbage.

COLESLAW (CABBAGE)

VITAMINS	1 PORTION CONTAINS APPROXIMATELY	DAILY NEED
A	285	5000 I.U.
B	27	600 I.U.
C	883	1500 I.U.
G	.17	2.7 MGS.

INGREDIENTS:

3 cups finely shredded cabbage
1 tablespoon minced onion

¾ cup dressing

DIRECTIONS: Select young, tender, green head. Remove wilted or coarse leaves. Cut in wedges and slice (or shred) very fine with slaw cutter or sharp knife. Wash thoroughly by shaking shredded cabbage in pan of cold water (ice water preferred). Drain until almost dry and place in refrigerator to chill and crisp. Cooked Salad Dressing (page 213), Sour Cream Dressing (page 212), French Dressing (page 214), or Mayonnaise (page 211) may be used. Any dressing will be refreshed by addition of 1 tablespoon lemon juice just before using. Combine cabbage, onion and dressing, and garnish with pimiento or green pepper strips, if desired.

Apple Coleslaw—Reduce shredded cabbage of basic recipe to 2 cups. Shred or chop fine 2 medium-sized apples, and drop into dressing as prepared. Mince 2 pimientos. Combine and serve.

Cucumber Coleslaw—Reduce shredded cabbage of basic recipe to 2 cups. Chop coarsely 1 medium-sized cucumber and proceed as in basic recipe.

Parsley Coleslaw—Add ¼ cup minced parsley to basic recipe. *Parsley adds large amount of Vitamin A to Coleslaw.*

Green Pepper Coleslaw—Mince 1 green pepper and add to ingredients in basic recipe. *Green pepper makes Coleslaw exceptionally rich in Vitamins A and C.*

Pimiento Coleslaw—Mince 3 canned pimientos and add to ingredients in basic recipe. *Pimientos add considerable Vitamins A and C to Coleslaw.*

Pineapple Coleslaw—Reduce shredded cabbage of basic recipe to 2 cups. Omit onion. Add 1 cup drained, crushed pineapple. Combine all ingredients with ¾ cup Cooked Fruit Juice Dressing (page 213) or Cooked Salad Dressing (page 213).

	1 PORTION CONTAINS APPROXIMATELY	DAILY NEED	
A	1382	5000 I.U.	
B	26	600 I.U.	**SLICED**
C	176	1500 I.U.	**CUCUMBER SALAD**
G	.17	2.7 MGS.	

VITAMINS

INGREDIENTS:

2 medium-sized cucumbers, sliced thin

6 to 12 lettuce leaves (or 1½ cups shredded cabbage)

2 tablespoons minced parsley, chives, or watercress

¼ cup French Dressing (page 214)

DIRECTIONS: Slice cucumbers on salad greens. Garnish with minced parsley, chives or watercress. Serve dressing separately. If Mayonnaise is used, thin with lemon juice.

199

Cucumbers in Sour Cream—Replace suggested dressings in basic recipe with Sour Cream Dressing (page 212). Drop sliced (or shredded) cucumbers into jar or bowl containing dressing. Cover and shake well. Chill thoroughly. Serve with or without salad greens.

MIXED GREENS SALAD

	1 PORTION CONTAINS APPROXIMATELY	DAILY NEED
A	3342	5000 I.U.
B	33	600 I.U.
C	1108	1500 I.U.
G	.2	2.7 MGS.

INGREDIENTS:

2 cups shredded or chopped lettuce (escarole, chicory or cabbage)
1 bunch watercress, shredded
½ cup minced parsley
½ cup chopped celery
1 green pepper, minced
2 tomatoes, cut in eighths
¼ cup French Dressing (page 214)

DIRECTIONS: Combine thoroughly chilled ingredients with dressing, and toss together lightly until evenly coated.

POTATO SALAD

	1 PORTION CONTAINS APPROXIMATELY	DAILY NEED
A	881	5000 I.U.
B	31	600 I.U.
C	809	1500 I.U.
G	.17	2.7 MGS.

INGREDIENTS:

4 cups diced, boiled potatoes
½ cup diced celery
¼ cup minced or chopped onion
2 pimientos, minced
2 tablespoons minced parsley
½ cup diced cucumber (optional)
¼ cup French Dressing (page 214)
1 cup Mayonnaise or Cooked Salad Dressing (pages 211, 213)

DIRECTIONS: Combine ingredients, except Mayonnaise and cucumbers, and use steel fork to toss together lightly. Place in refrigerator for several hours, or until thoroughly chilled, to improve flavor before serving. Add cucumbers and Mayonnaise or Cooked Salad Dressing, to taste. Serve on crisp salad greens, surrounded with hard-cooked eggs and tomatoes.

TOMATO SALAD

INGREDIENTS:

4 medium-sized tomatoes
6 to 12 lettuce leaves (or
   1½ cups shredded cabbage)

¼ cup French Dressing
   (page 214)
   or Mayonnaise (page 211)
2 tablespoons minced parsley

DIRECTIONS: Slice or cut peeled or unpeeled tomatoes into eighths. Serve on salad greens. Sprinkle with minced parsley. Serve dressing separately.

VEGETABLE GELATIN SALAD
(BASIC RECIPE)

INGREDIENTS:

1 envelope (1 tablespoon)
   granulated gelatin
½ cup cold water
1 cup boiling water
⅓ cup sugar
   (or less)
¼ teaspoon salt

¼ cup lemon juice
   (or cider vinegar)
¼ cup chopped or shredded carrots
1 cup chopped celery
2 tablespoons chopped
   green pepper
2 tablespoons chopped pimiento

DIRECTIONS: Soften gelatin in cold water and dissolve in boiling water. Add sugar and salt; stir until dissolved. Stir in lemon juice and place in refrigerator to chill. (Up to this point of preparation, recipe is foundation for all jellied vegetable or fruit salads. Any desired vegetables may be used, not merely the ones suggested in this list of ingredients.)

When mixture begins to set, add vegetables. Turn into 1-quart mold or individual molds and chill until set. Turn out on bed of lettuce, watercress or any other salad green; serve with Mayonnaise.

BALANCED MEAL SUGGESTIONS: *Lunch—Sliced Cucumber Salad, Combination Salad or Carrot and Raisin Salad;* Toasted Cheese Canapés; Fruit Cup; Molasses Cookies; Milk.

Dinner—Mixed Greens Salad, Coleslaw or Tomato Salad; Broiled Pork Chops; Sweet Potatoes and Apples; Broccoli; Canned Plums.

Supper—Vegetable Juices; *Potato Salad or Vegetable Gelatin Salad;* Hard-Cooked Eggs; Canned or Fresh Pears; Cookies; Milk.

FRUIT SALADS

This Chart Gives Approximate Food Values for MIXED FRUIT SALAD. For Vitamin Values of Specific Recipes, See Charts Accompanying Them.

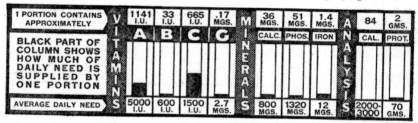

1 PORTION CONTAINS APPROXIMATELY	VITAMINS				MINERALS			ANALYSIS	
	1141 I.U.	33 I.U.	665 I.U.	.17 MGS.	36 MGS.	51 MGS.	1.4 MGS.	84	2 GMS.
BLACK PART OF COLUMN SHOWS HOW MUCH OF DAILY NEED IS SUPPLIED BY ONE PORTION	A	B	C	G	CALC.	PHOS.	IRON	CAL.	PROT.
AVERAGE DAILY NEED	5000 I.U.	600 I.U.	1500 I.U.	2.7 MGS.	800 MGS.	1320 MGS.	12 MGS.	2000-3000	70 GMS.

COMMENTS: Fruit salads offer a delightful medium for bringing vitamins and other essential food factors into any meal. They are of particular value in getting members of the family who do not care particularly for vegetables to eat enough protective foods.

Complicated or grotesque arrangements of fruit salads are a heritage of the days when fruits were served as a fancy. Today, when we appreciate the value of vitamins, the fruit salad has become as important as—if not more important than—the protein and starch dishes in a meal.

Certain fruits are admirably suited for use as salads. They can be arranged on shredded lettuce or tender cabbage or served in gelatin. Again, like raw vegetable salads, they should be used to introduce a meal.

In mixing fruits for salads, always combine some suitable and desirable raw fruit with the canned or dried variety. In that way, you can enhance the virtues of canned apricots, for example, with the taste appeal of bananas, the crispness of apples, the piquancy of persimmons, or the wonderful Vitamin C values of the citrus fruits.

MIXED FRUIT SALAD

INGREDIENTS:

1 banana
3 oranges (or 1 grapefruit)
½ cup seedless grapes
   (or halved, seeded grapes)

6 to 12 lettuce leaves (or
   1½ cups shredded cabbage)
¼ cup Cooked Fruit Juice
   Dressing (page 213)

DIRECTIONS: Dice banana into bowl. Prepare and dice oranges or grapefruit over bananas so juice will cover bananas and prevent discoloration. Add grapes. Combine with dressing and serve on salad greens.

VITAMINS	1 PORTION CONTAINS APPROXIMATELY	DAILY NEED
A	1142	5000 I.U.
B	39	600 I.U.
C	234	1500 I.U.
G	.17	2.7 MGS.

AVOCADO SALAD

INGREDIENTS:

2 avocados
6 to 12 lettuce leaves
   (or 1½ cups shredded cabbage)

¼ cup French Dressing
   (page 214) or lemon juice

DIRECTIONS: Chill avocados and do not cut until served. Divide each avocado into thirds (⅓ per portion). Remove pit but do not peel. Arrange on salad greens, and fill hollow places in each piece with 1 teaspoon (or more) dressing or lemon juice. Sprinkle greens with dressing. Avocados may also be peeled and diced to combine with any mixed vegetable salad. In that case, sprinkle with lemon juice as prepared, to prevent discoloration.

CANTALOUPE SALAD

Each Portion Contains Approximately:
Vit. A—1198 I.U.; Vit. B₁—28 I.U.; Vit. C—670 I.U.; Vit. G—.13 Mg.

INGREDIENTS:

1½ cups cantaloupe balls
1 cup sliced fresh strawberries
1 cup diced pineapple

¼ cup Cooked Fruit Juice
   Dressing (page 213)
salad greens

DIRECTIONS: Prepare thoroughly chilled fruit. Combine with dressing and serve on salad greens. Garnish with watercress, if desired.

GRAPEFRUIT SALAD

Each Portion Contains Approximately:
Vit. A—1000 I.U.; Vitamin B₁—17 I.U.; Vit. C—388 I.U.; Vit. G—.2 Mg.

INGREDIENTS:

2 grapefruits (or 1 can grapefruit wedges)

6 to 12 lettuce leaves (or 1½ cups shredded cabbage)

2 pimientos, cut into strips

¼ cup French Dressing (page 214) or Cooked Fruit Juice Dressing (page 213)

DIRECTIONS: Prepare grapefruit and segment sections. Arrange grapefruit on greens and garnish with pimiento. Serve dressing separately.

Grapefruit-Avocado Salad—Chill and peel 1 avocado and cut into slices. Serve on greens. Arrange slices alternately with canned or fresh grapefruit sections (1 grapefruit or 1 small can).

PEAR (PEACH OR PINEAPPLE) SALAD

Each Portion Contains Approximately:
Vit. A—1041 I.U.; Vit. B₁—43 I.U.; Vit. C—260 I.U.; Vit. G—.4 Mg.

INGREDIENTS:

6 fresh or canned pears (peaches or pineapple slices)

2 medium-sized apples

2 tablespoons lemon juice

¼ cup seedless raisins

¼ cup Mayonnaise (page 211) or Cooked Salad Dressing (page 213)

6 to 12 lettuce leaves (or 1½ cups shredded cabbage)

DIRECTIONS: Dice pears and apples. Add lemon juice. Chill. Soak raisins in just enough water to cover and place in refrigerator about 30 minutes to plump. Combine fruit with dressing and serve on salad greens. Pears also combine well with citrus fruits, grapes or cooked cranberries.

PEAR (PEACH OR PINEAPPLE) CHEESE BALL SALAD

INGREDIENTS:

1 4-ounce package cream cheese

3 tablespoons minced parsley

6 canned pear halves, peach halves or pineapple slices

6 to 12 lettuce leaves (or 1½ cups shredded cabbage)

¼ cup French Dressing (page 214)

DIRECTIONS: Divide cheese into 6 portions. Shape into balls and roll in minced parsley. Place in center (hollow) of fruit arranged on salad greens. Serve dressing separately.

204

	1 PORTION CONTAINS APPROXIMATELY	DAILY NEED
A	1488	5000 I.U.
B	38	600 I.U.
C	250	1500 I.U.
G	.27	2.7 MGS.

WALDORF SALAD

INGREDIENTS:

3 medium-sized apples, diced
2 tablespoons lemon juice
1½ cups diced celery
¼ cup nut meats (optional)

¾ cup Cooked Salad or Fruit
Juice Dressing or Mayonnaise
(page 213 or 211)
shredded salad greens

DIRECTIONS: Use firm "eating" apples. If skins are red and free from blemishes, they need not be pared. Sprinkle apples with lemon juice and combine with celery, nuts and dressing. Toss lightly and serve on shredded salad greens.

	1 PORTION CONTAINS APPROXIMATELY	DAILY NEED
A	1096	5000 I.U.
B	22	600 I.U.
C	318	1500 I.U.
G	.15	2.7 MGS.

FRUIT GELATIN SALAD

INGREDIENTS:

1 tablespoon (1 envelope)
granulated gelatin
½ cup cold water
1 cup boiling water (or fruit
juice drained from fruit)
¼ cup sugar
¼ teaspoon salt

¼ cup lemon juice
1½ cups diced fresh or canned
fruit (except fresh pineapple)
salad greens
¼ cup Mayonnaise (page 211) or
Cooked Fruit Juice Dressing
(page 213)

DIRECTIONS: Soften gelatin in cold water and dissolve in boiling water or fruit juice. Add sugar and salt; stir until dissolved. Cool. Stir in lemon juice and place in refrigerator to chill. When mixture begins to set, add fruit (if canned, drained of juice). Any of the following fruits may be used, alone or in combination: cherries, oranges, grapes, canned (not fresh) pineapple, apples or bananas. Turn into mold or individual molds and chill until set. Turn out on bed of lettuce, watercress or any suitable salad green. Serve dressing separately.

BALANCED MEAL SUGGESTIONS: *Lunch*—Spring Consommé; *Fruit Gelatin Salad* or *Pear Cheese Ball Salad;* Wheat-Raisin Bread; Stewed Rhubarb; Milk.

Dinner—*Waldorf Salad* or *Avocado Salad;* Cheese Omelet; Corn Bread; Stewed Tomatoes; Deep-Dish Cherry Pie.

Supper—Vegetable Juices; *Mixed Fruit Salad* or *Pineapple Salad;* Cheese-Egg Canapés; Nut Meringue; Milk.

MEAT, CHEESE, AND FISH SALADS

This Chart Gives Approximate Food Values for CHICKEN SALAD.
For Vitamin Values of Specific Recipes, See Charts Accompanying Them.

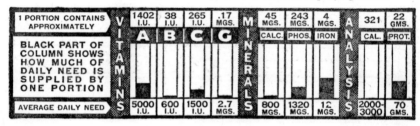

1 PORTION CONTAINS APPROXIMATELY	VITAMINS	A	B	C	G	MINERALS	CALC.	PHOS.	IRON	ANALYSIS	CAL.	PROT.
		1402 I.U.	38 I.U.	265 I.U.	.17 MGS.		45 MGS.	243 MGS.	4 MGS.		321	22 GMS.
BLACK PART OF COLUMN SHOWS HOW MUCH OF DAILY NEED IS SUPPLIED BY ONE PORTION												
AVERAGE DAILY NEED		5000 I.U.	600 I.U.	1500 I.U.	2.7 MGS.		800 MGS.	1320 MGS.	12 MGS.		2000-3000	70 GMS.

COMMENTS: Because of protein content, cheese, fish and meat (including poultry) salads are really main dishes, not salads in the usual sense of that word. Should be served at lunch or supper (or light dinner) with tomato or fruit juice, a starchy food such as bread, and a simple fruit dessert. If heavier dinner is desired, balance with a soup, and include a more filling dessert. These protein salads provide excellent dinner dishes during hot weather, when the body needs light foods only.

Chicken Salad recipe is basic for all leftover meats, such as chicken, ham or veal, and for seafood, such as lobster and shrimp. Both chicken and fish salad may be used to stuff large tomatoes (centers of tomatoes should be chopped with the salad). This is an attractive and popular main-dish salad for special summertime luncheons.

In general, protein salads supply less Vitamin C than fruit or vegetable salads; hence, should be supplemented with tomatoes, fruit cups, etc. All are good sources of Vitamin B complex, and cheese salads are rich in Vitamin A (if the cheese is of the whole-milk type).

206

CHICKEN SALAD (BASIC MEAT SALAD RECIPE)

INGREDIENTS:

2 cups cooked, diced chicken
salt and pepper
1 cup diced celery
1 tablespoon minced onion
1 tablespoon minced parsley

½ cup French Dressing
(page 214)
1 small head lettuce (or other
salad green)
½ pimiento
½ cup Mayonnaise (page 211)

DIRECTIONS: Chicken should be free from fat, skin and gristle. Sprinkle diced pieces with salt and pepper, and add celery, onion, parsley and French Dressing. Chill for ½ hour or longer. Arrange on lettuce leaves; garnish with pimiento. Serve Mayonnaise separately (or put some on each plate).

Jellied Chicken Salad—Soften 1 tablespoon granulated gelatin in cold water; dissolve in 1½ cups boiling chicken stock. Add ¼ teaspoon salt, stir until dissolved, stir in 2 tablespoons lemon juice and place in refrigerator to chill. When mixture begins to set, add 1 cup cooked, diced chicken, ¼ cup diced celery, 2 tablespoons each chopped green pepper and chopped pimiento. Turn into 1-quart mold or individual molds and chill until set. Turn out on bed of lettuce leaves or shredded lettuce; serve with Mayonnaise.

V I T A M I N S	1 PORTION CONTAINS APPROXIMATELY	DAILY NEED
Ⓐ	1903	5000 I.U.
Ⓑ 12		600 I.U.
Ⓒ 184		1500 I.U.
Ⓖ .4		2.7 MGS.

COTTAGE CHEESE SALAD

INGREDIENTS:

1 pound cottage cheese
1 teaspoon salt
2 tablespoons minced onion
(or chopped chives)
3 tablespoons minced parsley

paprika
6 to 12 lettuce leaves (or 1½
cups shredded cabbage)
¼ cup French Dressing
(page 214)

DIRECTIONS: Mix cottage cheese with salt, onion or chives, and parsley. If cheese is dry, moisten with sweet or sour cream. Pack in small bowl and chill half an hour or more. Unmold on large plate, sprinkle with paprika and surround with lettuce which has been sprinkled with French dressing. Mounds of sliced cucumbers and radishes may be arranged on the lettuce.

CREAM CHEESE SALAD

	1 PORTION CONTAINS APPROXIMATELY	DAILY NEED
A	2218	5000 I.U.
B₁	12	600 I.U.
C	637	1500 I.U.
G	.13	2.7 MGS.

INGREDIENTS:

½ pound cream cheese
2 tablespoons thin cream (or rich milk)
1 tablespoon minced parsley
2 tablespoons minced pimiento
paprika

½ teaspoon salt
6 to 12 lettuce leaves (or 1½ cups shredded cabbage)
¼ cup French Dressing (page 214)

DIRECTIONS: Blend cream and cheese until smooth. Add parsley, pimiento and seasonings. Form in mounds and chill. Serve on shredded lettuce or cabbage which has been tossed lightly with French Dressing. Sprinkle each portion with French Dressing.

COTTAGE CHEESE AND PEPPER SALAD

	1 PORTION CONTAINS APPROXIMATELY	DAILY NEED
A	1941	5000 I.U.
B₁	26	600 I.U.
C	1030	1500 I.U.
G	.3	2.7 MGS.

INGREDIENTS:

1 cup cottage cheese
2 green peppers
¼ cup thinly sliced scallions (or 1 teaspoon minced chives)
¼ cup thinly sliced radishes
½ teaspoon salt

2 tablespoons milk (or more)
1 small head lettuce (or other salad green)
2 tablespoons Mayonnaise (page 211)
paprika

DIRECTIONS: Cut tops from peppers, remove seeds, and wash. Cut into 6 ½-inch rings and mince remaining pepper. Add minced pepper to cheese with scallions, radishes and salt. Moisten with milk and use steel fork to mix ingredients well. Place pepper rings on shredded lettuce and fill with cheese mixture; garnish with Mayonnaise, a sprinkling of paprika and a few additional radish slices.

	1 PORTION CONTAINS APPROXIMATELY	DAILY NEED
A	1518	5000 I.U.
B	13	600 I.U.
C	1400	1500 I.U.
G	.24	2.7 MGS.

INGREDIENTS:

2 cups cooked or canned salmon (tuna or shrimp)
½ cup finely chopped celery
¼ cup minced pimiento
1 small onion, minced or grated
½ cup diced cucumber
¼ cup minced green pepper
3 tablespoons lemon juice
2 tablespoons minced parsley
salt and pepper to taste
½ pimiento, cut into strips

DIRECTIONS: Drain fish, reserving liquor, and separate into flakes with a fork. Combine with celery, minced pimiento, onion, cucumber and green pepper; use fork to toss together lightly. Add lemon juice, parsley and seasoning to 4 tablespoons reserved fish liquor and mix thoroughly. Combine with fish and vegetables and chill at least 30 minutes before serving. Place on large platter, garnish with pimiento strips and surround with salad greens, tomato slices, etc.

BALANCED MEAL SUGGESTIONS: *Lunch* or *Supper*—Grapefruit Juice; *Cottage Cheese Salad* or *Cream Cheese Salad;* Peanut Butter Canapés; Baked Apples; Milk.

Lunch or *Supper*—Hot Consommé; *Chicken Salad* or *Vitamin Fish Salad;* Whole Wheat Rolls; Cantaloupe or Berries; Milk.

209

SALAD DRESSINGS

This Chart Gives Approximate Food Values for MAYONNAISE.
For Vitamin Values of Specific Recipes, See Charts Accompanying Them.

1/4 CUP CONTAINS APPROXIMATELY	VITAMINS	A 83 I.U.	B 3 I.U.	C 13 I.U.	G .02 MGS.	MINERALS	CALC. 6 MGS.	PHOS. 15 MGS.	IRON .1 MGS.	ANALYSIS	CAL. 346	PROT. 1 GMS.
BLACK PART OF COLUMN SHOWS HOW MUCH OF DAILY NEED IS SUPPLIED BY ONE PORTION												
AVERAGE DAILY NEED		5000 I.U.	600 I.U.	1500 I.U.	2.7 MGS.		800 MGS.	1320 MGS.	12 MGS.		2000-3000	70 GMS.

COMMENTS: Flavorful, well-blended salad dressings can do much toward making salads popular in any household. Plain shredded greens and vegetables particularly need to be artfully blended with properly mixed salad dressings. Many people's dislike of salads comes from early experience with flat-tasting or wilted salads, or with salads too saturated with oily or strongly flavored ingredients, carelessly proportioned.

Dressings add nutritive value as well as taste appeal. Many ingredients rich in vitamin and mineral contents.

Salads themselves ideal dishes for reducers, but often made high in calorie content through excess use of rich dressing. Even small amount of any dressing with oil base extremely high in calorie content; reducers should stick to tasteful Reducing Dressing. See page 215 for list of calorie values of salad dressings.

Follow directions in salad section (page 195) carefully to be certain when to add dressing to salad. Some salad ingredients need marinating (blending with dressing) for half an hour or so to blend flavors, whereas the average salad is not combined with the dressing until just before serving. This is to prevent wilting of greens. Either salad is tossed at the table or dressing is passed with service of salad.

Wherever cider or tarragon vinegar is mentioned in list of ingredients for

French Dressing, lemon juice to taste may be substituted. In any salad dressing, lemon juice to taste may be added just before service for its refreshing quality. However, if lemon juice is used, salad dressing will not keep. Must be served as soon as possible after juice is added to other ingredients. If vinegar is used, always select mild cider vinegar or one seasoned with tarragon.

Store any dressing in tightly covered jar to be used as needed. Never store in an extremely cold or hot place. Always shake well or beat thoroughly any French Dressing just before serving.

Salad oil is specified throughout, rather than olive oil. The latter gives a finer, more delicate flavor to any dressing, but contributes nothing materially in nutritive value and is considerably more expensive than other oils.

MAYONNAISE

INGREDIENTS:

¾ teaspoon salt	2 cups salad oil
½ teaspoon dry mustard	2½ tablespoons mild cider or
⅛ teaspoon paprika	tarragon vinegar
1 egg	lemon juice to taste

DIRECTIONS: Place seasonings in small bowl and mix thoroughly. Add egg and beat well. Carefully and slowly add oil, drop by drop, at first, beating constantly. When about ¼ cup oil has been added, beat in larger amounts of oil, about 1 tablespoon at a time. If oil is added too rapidly, Mayonnaise will curdle. (Should Mayonnaise curdle, beat curdled mixture into second egg yolk and proceed.)

When ½ cup oil has been added, slowly add 1 tablespoon vinegar, beating constantly. Add remaining oil, continuing to beat constantly, and thin mixture with remaining vinegar, until all of each is used. Store Mayonnaise in a covered jar in moderately cold place in refrigerator. Add small amount lemon juice to Mayonnaise as used, to add piquancy and Vitamin C value. Yield: about 2¼ cups dressing.

Russian Dressing—To ½ cup Mayonnaise, add 1 tablespoon minced green pepper, 1 tablespoon minced pimiento, 1 tablespoon minced chives or onion, 1 tablespoon capers or minced sour pickles and 4 tablespoons chili sauce. Yield: about ¾ cup dressing. *Green pepper and pimiento add Vitamins A and C to Mayonnaise.*

211

Thousand Island Dressing—To ½ cup Mayonnaise, add 1 tablespoon tarragon vinegar, 1 tablespoon minced parsley, 1 tablespoon minced pimiento, 1 tablespoon minced green pepper, 1 tablespoon minced onion or chives, 1 minced hard-cooked egg, 2 tablespoons chili sauce and ¼ cup sour or sweet cream, whipped. Combine ingredients and mix well. Yield: about 1¼ cups dressing.

Vitamin C Mayonnaise—To 1 cup Mayonnaise, add 4 tablespoons minced green pepper, 2 tablespoons each minced pimiento and parsley, 1 tablespoon minced onion, 2 teaspoons lemon juice, ⅛ teaspoon pepper, ⅛ teaspoon paprika, ¼ teaspoon salt. Yield: about 1½ cups dressing. *Approximate vitamin values per portion: Vit. A—916 I.U.; Vit. B:—7 I.U.; Vit. C— 802 I.U.; Vit. G—.03 Mg.*

BEST USE SUGGESTIONS: *Mayonnaise*—Serve with combinations of vegetables and fruits (such as Apple Coleslaw); meat, cheese or fish salads in general; gelatin salads; plain fruit salads; pear (or peach) and cheese salads; plain vegetable salads (such as sliced tomatoes, cucumbers and shredded cabbage).

Mayonnaise Variations—Serve with plain lettuce; vegetable salads; meat, cheese and fish salads.

SOUR CREAM DRESSING

VITAMINS	1/4 CUP CONTAINS APPROXIMATELY	DAILY NEED
A	440	5000 I.U.
B	6	600 I.U.
C	105	1500 I.U.
G	.002	2.7 MGS.

INGREDIENTS:

½ teaspoon salt
⅛ teaspoon pepper
½ teaspoon paprika
1 tablespoon lemon juice (or mild cider or tarragon vinegar)

½ cup sour cream, whipped
1 tablespoon chopped chives or minced onion

DIRECTIONS: Mix seasonings thoroughly. Add lemon juice or vinegar and stir until well blended. Whip cream and add vinegar mixture slowly, beating constantly until mixture thickens slightly and is thoroughly blended. Add chives or onion. For a milder flavor, add ¼ teaspoon sugar, and for a smoother consistency, beat in 1 tablespoon salad oil. Yield: ½ cup dressing.

BEST USE SUGGESTIONS: Serve with Coleslaw and its variations.

1/4 CUP CONTAINS APPROXIMATELY		DAILY NEED
Ⓐ 393		5000 I.U.
Ⓑ 12		600 I.U.
Ⓒ 10		1500 I.U.
Ⓖ .17		2.7 MGS.

COOKED SALAD DRESSING

INGREDIENTS:

1½ teaspoons salt	1 cup scalded milk
1 teaspoon dry mustard	2 eggs, slightly beaten
⅛ teaspoon paprika	⅓ cup mild cider vinegar
4 teaspoons sugar	2 tablespoons melted butter
2 tablespoons flour	

DIRECTIONS: Mix dry ingredients thoroughly and add to slightly beaten eggs. Scald milk and add to egg mixture with the vinegar, stirring until well blended. Cook in top of double boiler, over hot (not boiling) water, stirring constantly until thick, about 8 to 10 minutes. Stir in butter and chill. Thin with fruit juices or milk before serving, if desired; or, when mixture is thoroughly chilled, add ½ to 1 cup sweet or sour cream, whipped. Yield (for recipe given): 1½ cups dressing.

BEST USE SUGGESTIONS: Serve with Coleslaw and its variations; citrus fruit salads; Waldorf Salad.

1/4 CUP CONTAINS APPROXIMATELY		DAILY NEED
Ⓐ 565		5000 I.U.
Ⓑ 16		600 I.U.
Ⓒ 189		1500 I.U.
Ⓖ .04		2.7 MGS.

COOKED FRUIT JUICE DRESSING

INGREDIENTS:

2 egg yolks	¼ cup orange juice
¼ cup sugar	2 tablespoons lemon juice
¼ cup pineapple juice	½ cup sour or sweet cream

DIRECTIONS: Beat egg yolks. Add sugar and stir until well blended. Combine with fruit juices in top of double boiler and cook, stirring constantly, over hot (not boiling) water just until slightly thick, about 8 to 10 minutes. (For a sharper salad dressing, use 3 tablespoons lemon juice.) Cool and fold in whipped sour or sweet cream. Yield: about 1 cup dressing.

FRENCH DRESSING

	1/4 CUP CONTAINS APPROXIMATELY	DAILY NEED
A		5000 I.U.
B[1]		600 I.U.
C	123	1500 I.U.
G	.001	2.7 MGS.

INGREDIENTS:

½ teaspoon salt
⅛ teaspoon pepper
½ teaspoon sugar
¼ teaspoon dry mustard
½ teaspoon paprika

½ cup salad oil
2 tablespoons lemon juice or mild cider vinegar (or 1 tablespoon each)
1 teaspoon onion juice

DIRECTIONS: Mix dry ingredients thoroughly. Add oil and stir until well blended. Add lemon juice or vinegar and onion juice and shake or beat well until mixture thickens slightly. For additional flavor, add ½ teaspoon celery salt and a peeled clove of garlic. Remove garlic before serving. For thinner consistency, add lemon juice to taste. Yield: about ¾ cup dressing.

Vitamin French Dressing—To recipe for French Dressing, add 2 table-spoons minced watercress (or parsley), 2 tablespoons diced celery, 2 tablespoons minced green pepper and 2 tablespoons minced pimiento. Increase lemon juice to ½ cup. Yield: about 1¼ cups dressing. *Added ingredients give dressing high value in Vitamins A and C.*

Herb French Dressing—To recipe for French Dressing, add about 2 tablespoons minced fresh herbs, either of one kind or mixed. Parsley, chives, tarragon, sweet basil, sweet marjoram or thyme are a few suggestions. Dried instead of fresh herbs may be used; in this case, use only 2 teaspoons of them.

Chiffonade Dressing—To recipe for French Dressing, add 1 minced hard-cooked egg, 1 tablespoon each minced green pepper, minced pimiento, minced celery and minced olives. *Pepper and pimiento add considerable amounts of Vitamins A and C to dressing.*

Roquefort (or Danish Bleu) Dressing—To recipe for French Dressing, add mashed Roquefort or Danish Bleu cheese to taste. For a mild dressing, use 2 tablespoons cheese; for a stronger one, use ¼ cup. Crumble cheese, and cream with a small amount of the dressing before gradually stirring in remaining dressing.

BEST USE SUGGESTIONS: Serve with plain lettuce (especially Chiffon-ade and Roquefort Dressings) ; all mixed vegetable or mixed greens salads.

214

VITAMINS	1/4 CUP CONTAINS APPROXIMATELY	DAILY NEED
A	527	5000 I.U.
B	4	600 I.U.
C	329	1500 I.U.
G	.03	2.7 MGS.

REDUCING DRESSING

INGREDIENTS:

½ cup skim milk
1 teaspoon onion juice
1 tablespoon lemon juice

1 tablespoon minced parsley
1 tablespoon minced pimiento

DIRECTIONS: Combine milk with lemon juice and flavoring agents, and shake thoroughly in small jar with tightly fitting lid. More or less fruit juice may be used according to taste. Use at once. Yield: ½ cup dressing.

BEST USE SUGGESTIONS: Serve with all salads if individual is following reducing diet.

COMPARATIVE CALORIE VALUES OF SALAD DRESSINGS

Mayonnaise	¼ cup	346
Russian Dressing	¼ cup	271
Thousand Island Dressing	¼ cup	215
Vitamin C Mayonnaise	¼ cup	239
Sour Cream Dressing	¼ cup	242
Cooked Salad Dressing	¼ cup	97
Cooked Fruit Juice Dressing	¼ cup	213
French Dressing	¼ cup	258
Vitamin French Dressing	¼ cup	169
Herb French Dressing	¼ cup	260
Chiffonade Dressing	¼ cup	174
Roquefort Dressing	¼ cup	221
Reducing Dressing	¼ cup	34

SAUCES, GRAVIES, STUFFINGS

This Chart Gives Approximate Food Values for CREAM SAUCE.
For Vitamin Values of Specific Recipes, See Charts Accompanying Them.

1/4 CUP CONTAINS APPROXIMATELY	VITAMINS	215 I.U.	8 I.U.	14 I.U.	.11 MGS.	MINERALS	81 MGS.	60 MGS.	.3 MGS.	ANALYSIS	94	2 GMS.
BLACK PART OF COLUMN SHOWS HOW MUCH OF DAILY NEED IS SUPPLIED BY ONE PORTION		A	B	C	G		CALC.	PHOS.	IRON		CAL.	PROT.
AVERAGE DAILY NEED		5000 I.U.	600 I.U.	1500 I.U.	2.7 MGS.		800 MGS.	1320 MGS.	12 MGS.		2000-3000	70 GMS.

COMMENTS: Sauces may contribute real nutritional value to diet, as well as flavor and color, if prepared with proper ingredients and cooked correctly. May be used to add vitamins to a meal. Minced parsley, watercress, green peppers, pimientos, tomato juice, lemon juice, eggs, milk and cheese all logical additions to sauces, and are concentrated sources of various vitamins and minerals.

Choose sauces first for nutritional value, then for flavor and color. If a given food lacks Vitamin A, for example, select a sauce high in that vitamin to serve with it, provided the flavor and color are compatible with the food. Minced vegetables, such as parsley, green peppers, etc., and lemon and tomato juice, used to give sauce high Vitamin C value, should be added at last minute, so vitamin is not destroyed by cooking.

The following sauces selected for digestibility; they contain comparatively little starch or fat. Apart from nutritional value, sauce should pass three tests to be good: flavor, texture and color. If food has characteristic flavor, sauce should be subtly flavored so as not to detract from food itself. If food is bland and lacking in flavor, sauce should be piquant and definitely flavored. Never serve rich, greasy concoction made with too much butter, fat, cream or cheese, and never serve a thick, colorless, pasty substance—similar to wallpaper paste—made with too much flour or cornstarch.

Basic recipe for Cream Sauce is foundation recipe for all simple sauces.

216

Other ingredients added to basic cream sauce contribute important vitamins and minerals which the cream sauce itself lacks. Pot liquors supply certain quantities of whatever vitamins and minerals were contained in the vegetable cooked, except for Vitamin A which is not water-soluble. Tomato juice added to cream sauce supplies Vitamins A and C. Vitamin Cream Sauce contains important amounts of all the vitamins, and the minerals, iron and copper. Chicken, veal or fish stock cream sauce (plus egg yolk) yields small amounts of all the vitamins, as well as some protein and fat.

Correct blending of ingredients is whole secret of good sauce making. Hollandaise Sauce, for example, often considered difficult to make. If directions are followed exactly, sauce will be of proper smoothness and consistency.

CREAM SAUCE

INGREDIENTS:
- 2 tablespoons butter
- 2 tablespoons flour
- 1/2 teaspoon salt
- 1/8 teaspoon pepper
- 1 cup milk

DIRECTIONS: Melt butter in small saucepan. Do not permit it to bubble. Reduce heat and gradually stir in flour and seasonings, stirring constantly until mixture is smooth and well blended. Add milk slowly, continuing to stir constantly over low heat until mixture thickens and boils. If cream sauce is not used at once, cover and keep warm over hot water; if egg yolk is used in any of the variations, this is not possible—sauce must be served immediately. Yield: about 1 cup.

Vegetable Pot Liquor Cream Sauce—Replace 1/2 cup milk with 1/2 cup vegetable pot liquor, or measure pot liquor available, and add enough milk to make 1 cup. After sauce has thickened, stir in 1/2 teaspoon onion juice (or minced onion) and 2 tablespoons minced parsley. *This variation adds 739 I.U. of Vitamin A and 153 I.U. of Vitamin C to Cream Sauce.*

Tomato Juice Cream Sauce—Replace milk with 1 cup tomato juice. Season with 1/2 teaspoon sugar, 1 teaspoon lemon juice and 1 teaspoon onion juice. *This variation adds 1322 I.U. of Vitamin A and 222 I.U. of Vitamin C to Cream Sauce.*

Vitamin Cream Sauce—After sauce has thickened, add 2 tablespoons of any of the following vegetables: minced parsley, pimiento or green pepper. *Using parsley, this variation adds 778 I.U. of Vitamin A, 9 I.U. of Vitamin B_1, 51 I.U. of Vitamin C and .11 Mg. of Vitamin G.*

217

Chicken, Veal or Fish Cream Sauce—Replace milk with 1 cup chicken, veal or fish stock. After sauce has thickened, remove from heat. Beat 1 egg yolk with $\frac{1}{4}$ cup rich milk, and gradually add to thickened sauce, stirring constantly. Return to low heat about 1 minute, just until reheated. Do not boil. Add 2 tablespoons minced parsley or pimiento. Season with $\frac{1}{8}$ teaspoon nutmeg or $\frac{1}{4}$ teaspoon celery salt for chicken or veal; 1 tablespoon lemon juice for fish.

BEST USE SUGGESTIONS: *Vegetable Pot Liquor Cream Sauce*—Combine with vegetables (spinach, cabbage, chard, asparagus, etc.) for creamed vegetables.

Tomato Juice Cream Sauce—Serve with meat loaves, tripe, fish or egg dishes.

Vitamin Cream Sauce—Combine with chicken, eggs or fish; serve with fish or egg casseroles.

Chicken or Veal Cream Sauce—Serve with chicken or veal loaves; combine with cooked chicken, veal, brains, sweetbreads, etc., for creamed dishes.

Fish Cream Sauce—Serve with poached (boiled) fish; combine with any cooked fish and vegetables for creamed or casserole dishes, etc.

CHEESE SAUCE

VITAMINS	1 PORTION CONTAINS APPROXIMATELY	DAILY NEED
A	510	5000 I.U.
B	8	600 I.U.
C	10	1500 I.U.
G	.20	2.7 MGS.

INGREDIENTS:

2 tablespoons butter
2 tablespoons flour
1 cup milk (or $\frac{1}{2}$ cup milk and $\frac{1}{2}$ cup pot liquor)
$\frac{1}{4}$ teaspoon salt

$\frac{1}{2}$ teaspoon prepared mustard
$\frac{1}{2}$ teaspoon Worcestershire sauce
$\frac{1}{4}$ pound grated or shredded American cheese

DIRECTIONS: Melt butter in heavy skillet. Reduce heat and gradually stir in flour until well blended and smooth. Add milk gradually, stirring constantly over low heat until mixture thickens and boils. (If served with vegetables, use $\frac{1}{2}$ cup vegetable pot liquor to replace $\frac{1}{2}$ cup milk.) Add cheese and seasonings and stir constantly until cheese is melted. Yield: $1\frac{1}{2}$ cups sauce.

Quick Cheese Sauce—Heat 1 cup milk in top part of double boiler. Add ¼ pound (1 cup) shredded or diced processed American cheese and stir constantly over hot water until cheese melts. This sauce is of thinner consistency than basic Cheese Sauce. Yield: 1¼ cups.

BEST USE SUGGESTIONS: *Cheese Sauce*—Serve with vegetables like asparagus, broccoli, cauliflower, etc.; with combination fish or egg dishes.

Quick Cheese Sauce—Serve with broiled tomatoes; cooked or canned asparagus on toast; any recipe specifying cheese sauce. Garnish dish with minced parsley or pimiento strips.

Cheese sauces are a quick and easy way to increase the milk intake, especially of underweight children who need extra nourishment.

VITAMINS	1 PORTION CONTAINS APPROXIMATELY	DAILY NEED
A	498	5000 I.U.
B	8	600 I.U.
C	40	1500 I.U
G	.09	2.7 MGS.

MUSHROOM SAUCE

INGREDIENTS:

1 cup (¼ pound) sliced mushrooms
1 tablespoon minced onion
¼ cup water
1 cup rich milk (or meat stock) combined with mushroom pot liquor

2 tablespoons butter
2 tablespoons flour
salt and pepper
2 tablespoons minced parsley (or pimiento)
1 teaspoon lemon juice (optional)

DIRECTIONS: Wash mushrooms and separate caps and stems. Slice caps and chop stems. Combine mushrooms, onion and water in small saucepan and simmer over medium heat 10 minutes. Drain, reserving pot liquor. Add enough milk (or meat stock) to pot liquor to make 1 cup liquid. Melt butter in skillet, reduce heat and add flour and seasoning, stirring constantly until mixture thickens and boils. Stir in mushrooms, parsley and lemon juice. Yield: about 1½ cups.

BEST USE SUGGESTIONS: Serve with boiled rice; egg, meat, fish or vegetable dishes; combine with fish, chicken, veal, brains, or sweetbreads in casserole or creamed dishes.

HOLLANDAISE
SAUCE

VITAMINS	1 PORTION CONTAINS APPROXIMATELY	DAILY NEED
A	2181	5000 I.U.
B₁	30	600 I.U.
C	63	1500 I.U.
G	.08	2.7 MGS.

INGREDIENTS:

2 egg yolks, slightly beaten
½ cup (¼ pound) butter

1 tablespoon lemon juice
¼ teaspoon salt

DIRECTIONS: Combine all ingredients in small saucepan. If butter is in ¼ pound print, break or cut into small pieces. Hold saucepan over larger one containing hot (not boiling) water and stir constantly, just until mixture is thick and smooth. Remove from heat at once. Do not overcook. Serve immediately. Yield: about ½ cup sauce.

Water over which sauce is cooked must never reach the boiling point. Should mixture begin to curdle, quickly remove saucepan from heat, and gradually, drop by drop, beat in 1 to 2 tablespoons cream.

BEST USE SUGGESTIONS: Serve with poached (boiled) fish; with vegetables such as asparagus, artichokes, broccoli and cauliflower.

MOCK HOLLANDAISE SAUCE

Each Portion Contains Approximately:
Vit. A—517 I.U.; Vit. B₁—14 I.U.; Vit. C—62 I.U.; Vit. G—.11 Mg.

INGREDIENTS:

4 tablespoons butter
1 tablespoon flour
½ teaspoon salt
⅛ teaspoon pepper

1 cup milk
2 egg yolks, slightly beaten
2 tablespoons lemon juice

DIRECTIONS: Melt 2 tablespoons of the butter in small saucepan. Reduce heat and gradually stir in flour and seasonings until smooth and well blended. Add milk slowly, stirring constantly over low heat until mixture thickens slightly and boils. Remove from heat and stir a small amount of the hot mixture into the slightly beaten egg yolks, stirring constantly. Pour egg mixture into remaining hot sauce and stir over low heat just until thick, about 1 minute. Do not boil. Remove from heat, add lemon juice and remaining 2 tablespoons butter and mix well. Serve at once. Yield: about 1¼ cups sauce.

TOMATO SAUCE

INGREDIENTS:

2 tablespoons salad oil
2 medium-sized onions, chopped
1 green pepper, chopped
1 peeled clove garlic (optional)
1 teaspoon salt

⅛ teaspoon pepper
1 6-ounce can tomato paste
2 cups boiling water
1 teaspoon sugar
1 bay leaf

DIRECTIONS: Heat oil in heavy skillet and sauté onions, green pepper and garlic until onions are yellow, about 3 minutes. Remove garlic and add remaining ingredients. Simmer uncovered over low heat about 15 minutes, or until onions are soft. Remove bay leaf. Yield: about 2 cups.

Italian Spaghetti Sauce—Add ½ pound chopped beef or veal and ½ pound sliced mushrooms (optional) to onions, green pepper and garlic. Sauté in oil until light brown. Add 2 cups canned tomatoes with remaining ingredients and simmer, uncovered, about 20 to 25 minutes, just until meat and vegetables are cooked. Serve with boiled spaghetti, and garnish with grated cheese. *Approximate vitamin values per portion: Vit. A—954 I.U.; Vit. B₁—28 I.U.; Vit. C—713 I.U.; Vit. G—.17 Mg.*

Creole Sauce—Replace tomato paste in basic recipe with 2 cups canned tomatoes, and omit water. Proceed as in basic recipe. *Approximate vitamin values per portion: Vit. A—746 I.U.; Vit. B₁—11 I.U.; Vit. C—601 I.U.; Vit. G—.03 Mg.*

BEST USE SUGGESTIONS: *Tomato Sauce*—Serve with fish, meat or egg dishes; boiled rice; boiled spaghetti. *Italian Spaghetti Sauce*—Serve with boiled spaghetti. *Creole Sauce*—Serve with fish, meat, tripe, or egg dishes.

COCKTAIL SAUCE

INGREDIENTS:

1 cup ketchup
2 tablespoons chili sauce

2 tablespoons lemon juice
1 tablespoon horseradish

DIRECTIONS: Mix ingredients well and chill thoroughly before serving. Yield: about 1½ cups sauce. Serve with seafood cocktail.

MOLDED CRANBERRY SAUCE

	1 PORTION CONTAINS APPROXIMATELY	DAILY NEED
V I T A M I N S	Ⓐ 3	5000 I.U.
	Ⓑ 4	600 I.U.
	Ⓒ 42	1500 I.U.
	Ⓖ .02	2.7 MGS.

INGREDIENTS:

4 cups firm cranberries
1 cup water

2 cups sugar

DIRECTIONS: Wash cranberries and remove bits of stems and wilted or bruised fruit. Add water and cook just until skins burst. Remove from heat, add sugar, and stir until sugar is thoroughly dissolved. Pour into 1-quart mold or individual molds and let cool. Place in refrigerator to chill thoroughly, or pour into hot sterilized glasses and seal. Yield: 4 8-ounce glasses or a 1-quart mold.

Cranberry Jelly—After removing sauce from heat, force pulp through coarse strainer or sieve. Add sugar to juice and stir until sugar is dissolved. Proceed as in basic recipe.

BEST USE SUGGESTIONS: *Cranberry Sauce*—Serve with pork, duck or goose, or any other meat or poultry. Also cut into cubes to combine with mixed fruit salads or fruit cups.

LEMON BUTTER

	1 PORTION CONTAINS APPROXIMATELY	DAILY NEED
V I T A M I N S	Ⓐ 2235	5000 I.U.
	Ⓑ 14	600 I.U.
	Ⓒ 285	1500 I.U.
	Ⓖ .02	2.7 MGS.

INGREDIENTS:

4 tablespoons butter
1 tablespoon lemon juice

1 tablespoon minced parsley
dash of paprika

DIRECTIONS: Place butter in small skillet and stir constantly over low heat just until butter melts. Remove from heat and stir in remaining ingredients. Serve at once.

Brown Butter—Follow basic recipe, but continue stirring butter after it melts until it is well browned, and decrease lemon juice to $\frac{1}{2}$ teaspoon.

222

Parsley Butter—Follow basic recipe but increase parsley to 3 tablespoons and omit lemon juice or decrease to ½ teaspoon. *This variation yields 4485 I.U. of Vitamin A, 15 I.U. of Vitamin B₁, 351 I.U. of Vitamin C and .04 Mg. of Vitamin G.*

Vitamin Butter—Add 1 tablespoon minced pimiento, 1 tablespoon minced green pepper and 1 teaspoon minced onion to basic recipe. *This variation yields 3403 I.U. of Vitamin A, 21 I.U. of Vitamin B₁, 2137 I.U. of Vitamin C and .05 Mg. of Vitamin G.*

BEST USE SUGGESTIONS: Serve these butters with broiled steak or fish; boiled vegetables.

GRAVIES

COMMENTS: Gravies one of foods most unnecessarily harmed in preparation and cooking. Usual gravy is pasty, fatty substance which detracts from instead of adding to value of meat it accompanies. Most of indigestion caused by gravies due to fat and/or flour added to meat juice.

Actually, gravies—like sauces—can be used as vehicles for carrying high-vitamin foods. Meat extractives, parsley, pot liquors and milk used as ingredients of pan gravy make it valuable source of Vitamins A, B₁, C and G, and minerals dissolved into pot liquors from vegetables. Absence of additional fat and flour makes such gravy readily digested.

Gravies used, of course, with those meats which yield drippings. Meat-vegetable combinations like loaves, stews, etc., will naturally have juices served along with them.

PAN MEAT GRAVY

INGREDIENTS:

juice from cooked meat	salt and pepper to taste
½ cup vegetable pot liquors	2 teaspoons minced parsley

DIRECTIONS: Remove meat from pan to hot serving platter and set in warm place. If the cut of meat is fatty, pour off fat and add ½ cup hot vegetable pot liquors, water, meat stock or consommé to the sediment which remains on the bottom or clings to sides of the pan. Add seasoning and let gravy boil 1 minute, stirring constantly to loosen brown particles which adhere to sides and bottom of pan. Strain, add minced parsley and serve. Bones from the meat may be boiled to furnish further flavor and nutriment.

223

STUFFINGS

This Chart Gives Approximate Food Values for BREAD STUFFING.
For Vitamin Values of Specific Recipes, See Charts Accompanying Them.

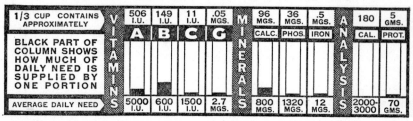

1/3 CUP CONTAINS APPROXIMATELY	VITAMINS	506 I.U.	149 I.U.	11 I.U.	.05 MGS.	MINERALS	96 MGS.	36 MGS.	.5 MGS.	ANALYSIS	180	5 GMS.
		A	B	C	G		CALC.	PHOS.	IRON		CAL.	PROT.
BLACK PART OF COLUMN SHOWS HOW MUCH OF DAILY NEED IS SUPPLIED BY ONE PORTION												
AVERAGE DAILY NEED		5000 I.U.	600 I.U.	1500 I.U.	2.7 MGS.		800 MGS.	1320 MGS.	12 MGS.		2000-3000	70 GMS.

COMMENTS: Stuffings made with added fruit or vegetable ingredients are not only flavorful—also good sources of vitamins and important minerals. Only Vitamin C may be missing, as this vitamin is easily destroyed by long cooking and high heat to which stuffings are subjected. All bread used is of whole grain variety (chiefly whole wheat).

Parsley should be used liberally in all stuffings; adds necessary flavor and insures Vitamin A and iron values. Giblet Stuffing a superior source of Vitamin A and iron; provides a good way to get giblets into diet of those who do not enjoy them alone. Vitamin Stuffing lives up to its name; has, in addition, important minerals. Fruit stuffings for goose, duck or pork help cut very fatty character of these meats.

BREAD STUFFING

INGREDIENTS:

6 tablespoons butter, melted
4 cups dry or soft bread crumbs
3 tablespoons minced parsley

1 teaspoon salt
1/4 teaspoon pepper

DIRECTIONS: Melt butter in large skillet. Add bread crumbs, parsley and seasoning, and use steel fork to mix lightly. If moist stuffing is desired, add small amount of water or slightly beaten egg. Yield: 4 cups stuffing, enough for a 4-pound bird.

Herb Stuffing—Add minced onion to taste, 1 teaspoon mixed poultry seasoning (or ½ teaspoon sage, ¼ teaspoon thyme, ⅛ teaspoon marjoram) and ½ cup chopped celery to basic recipe.

Watercress Stuffing—Add 1½ cups chopped watercress, ¼ cup chopped celery, and minced onion (optional) to basic recipe. *Watercress adds 60 I.U. of Vitamin A, 3 I.U. of Vitamin B₁, 34 I.U. of Vitamin C and .03 Mg. of Vitamin G.*

Corn Bread Stuffing—Replace 2 cups bread crumbs in basic recipe with 2 cups dry corn bread crumbs. *Approximate vitamin values per portion: Vit. A—1029 I.U.; Vit. B₁—8 I.U.; Vit. C—25 I.U.; Vit. G—.04 Mg.*

Raisin Stuffing—Add 1 cup chopped seedless raisins and 1 cup chopped celery to basic recipe. *Raisins add 80 I.U. of Vitamin A, 9 I.U. of Vitamin B₁, 4 I.U. of Vitamin C and .03 Mg. of Vitamin G.*

Giblet Stuffing—Follow basic recipe but add cooked gizzard, heart and liver, all chopped fine (page 192), and ½ cup giblet stock. If desired, use ¼ cup chopped onion, ¼ cup chopped celery and ½ teaspoon poultry seasoning

VITAMINS	1 PORTION CONTAINS APPROXIMATELY	DAILY NEED	
A	2256	5000 I.U.	
B	60	600 I.U.	**VITAMIN STUFFING**
C	180	1500 I.U.	
G	.19	2.7 MGS.	

INGREDIENTS:

1 cup finely chopped raw spinach
½ cup grated raw carrot
3 tablespoons minced onion
1 green pepper, minced
½ cup finely chopped celery
4 tablespoons minced parsley
1 cup dry bread crumbs, cooked rice, or ground meat
¼ pound grated cheese (optional)

1 teaspoon salt
¼ teaspoon paprika
¼ teaspoon sage
¼ teaspoon thyme
⅛ teaspoon marjoram
2 tablespoons melted butter, bacon fat or salad oil
1 egg, slightly beaten

DIRECTIONS: Combine all ingredients and mix thoroughly. Yield: about 3 cups.

BEST USE SUGGESTIONS: Use for stuffing eggplant; tomatoes; peppers (omit pepper in ingredients of stuffing); lamb breast; heart.

FISH STUFFING

	1 PORTION CONTAINS APPROXIMATELY	DAILY NEED
A	999	5000 I.U.
B	113	600 I.U.
C	40	1500 I.U.
G	.04	2.7 MGS.

INGREDIENTS:

1½ cups bread crumbs
1 teaspoon salt
⅛ teaspoon pepper
⅛ teaspoon celery salt
4 tablespoons finely minced parsley

1 teaspoon onion juice (or more)
4 tablespoons melted butter
1 tablespoon chopped pickles or capers

DIRECTIONS: Combine ingredients and mix thoroughly. If desired, replace chopped pickles with 1 to 2 tablespoons lemon juice. Yield: about 1½ cups stuffing, enough for a 4-pound fish.

BEST USE SUGGESTIONS: Use for stuffing fresh cod, bluefish, mackerel, bonito, etc.

ORANGE STUFFING

	1 PORTION CONTAINS APPROXIMATELY	DAILY NEED
A	874	5000 I.U.
B	158	600 I.U.
C	105	1500 I.U.
G	.13	2.7 MGS.

INGREDIENTS:

3 cups dry bread cubes, toasted
½ cup hot water
1 teaspoon grated orange rind
1 cup diced orange pulp
2 cups diced celery
3 tablespoons minced parsley

4 tablespoons melted butter
1 egg, slightly beaten
½ teaspoon salt
⅛ teaspoon pepper
½ teaspoon poultry seasoning

DIRECTIONS: Combine ingredients and mix lightly. If desired, sauté celery in butter about 3 minutes before combining with other ingredients. Yield: about 3 cups stuffing—enough for a 4- to 5-pound duck.

BEST USE SUGGESTIONS: Use for stuffing duck or goose.

226

PRUNE-APPLE STUFFING

INGREDIENTS:

½ cup chopped cooked prunes
1 medium-sized apple, diced
½ cup diced celery
1 cup bread crumbs
2 tablespoons minced parsley
2 tablespoons chopped walnuts

1 teaspoon salt
¼ teaspoon pepper
¼ teaspoon thyme
4 tablespoons melted butter
2 tablespoons prune juice
(approximate)

DIRECTIONS: Prepare fruit, vegetables, bread crumbs and nut meats. Combine and add seasonings. Melt butter and mix with other ingredients. Add prune juice and mix well. (If a less sweet stuffing is desired, replace butter and prune juice with 1 slightly beaten egg.) Yield: 2 cups stuffing.

BEST USE SUGGESTIONS: Use for stuffing veal or pork.

SOUPS

This Chart Gives Approximate Food Values for BROWN SOUP STOCK.
For Vitamin Values of Specific Recipes, See Charts Accompanying Them.

1 PORTION CONTAINS APPROXIMATELY	VITAMINS	1843 I.U.	77 I.U.	181 I.U.	.70 MGS.	MINERALS	54 MGS.	683 MGS.	.1 MGS.	ANALYSIS	551	62 GMS.
		A	B	C	G		CALC.	PHOS.	IRON		CAL.	PROT.
BLACK PART OF COLUMN SHOWS HOW MUCH OF DAILY NEED IS SUPPLIED BY ONE PORTION												
AVERAGE DAILY NEED		5000 I.U.	600 I.U.	1500 I.U.	2.7 MGS.		800 MGS.	1320 MGS.	12 MGS.		2000-3000	70 GMS.

COMMENTS: All these soups, with exception of clear consommé, are main dishes for substantial luncheons and suppers. Too filling to use as complement to main meal. Should always be balanced with a fresh fruit or vegetable salad, some starchy food such as whole wheat toast, cornbread, etc., and a fruit dessert. Meat consommé or broth permissible for use at dinner, especially for people who welcome a warm liquid before meal begins.

In food-wise households, bones are never thrown away, but are crushed and boiled in water. Stock produced is a veritable mine of available calcium and phosphorus, since all bones contain these minerals in soluble form. Add bone stock to regular soup stock.

Clarification of meat soup stocks removes particles of solidified albumin. Best not to clarify stock to be certain of getting full complement of nutrients in soup. Clarified stock (broth) called bouillon; with diced or shredded vegetables added, called consommé. Use stocks for dressings and sauces as well as soups. In preparing bland-tasting vegetables, like squash, add stock to cooking water to enhance flavor.

Use great care in removing all excess fat from stock. Cool stock uncovered before storing. Then keep in refrigerator in glass container, with tightly fitting cover. Remove fat before reheating. Canned consommés or bouillons often used as convenient soup stock do not, in our estimation, compare

228

favorably from nutritional viewpoint with homemade kind which can be continually fortified and improved.

All protein soups contain valuable protein derivatives dissipated into liquid as the meat or fish simmers. Addition of vegetables raises vitamin and mineral contents. Protein chowders or stews made with milk, such as New England Clam Chowder, especially important as a means of incorporating more milk into the diet. Protein soups using liver, giblets or other organ meats are recommended for children and all adults who need to increase hemoglobin content of blood. Liver a prime source of iron, the mineral which—together with copper—builds rich, red blood. Reducers in general should choose protein soups made with meat stock and non-starchy vegetables.

All meat and fish soups contained here especially beneficial for winter meals, rather than summer. Consommé, however, good to begin cold summer supper.

BROWN SOUP STOCK
(Consommé or Bouillon)

INGREDIENTS:

3 to 4 pounds shin or shoulder of beef
1 large marrow bone
1 knuckle of veal
water—1 pint to each pound meat and bone
¼ teaspoon pepper (or 4 peppercorns)

1 teaspoon salt
1 quartered carrot
4 stalks celery and leaves
4 sprigs parsley
1 sprig marjoram (or a pinch)
2 sprigs thyme (or a pinch)
1 bay leaf

DIRECTIONS: Have beef cut into 1-inch pieces. (Shoulder will be less expensive than shin.) Remove marrow from bone and melt in kettle in which soup is to be cooked. Add half of meat and sear (brown) on all sides. Add water, remaining meat and bones. Knuckle of veal gives stock a jelly-like consistency when cold. Cover and let come to a boil. Reduce heat and simmer over low heat about two to three hours. Half an hour before meat is tender, add seasoning, vegetables and spices. When done, strain through sieve lined with wet cheesecloth. Cool uncovered and then chill in refrigerator. When cold, use skimmer to remove fat which has solidified on top of soup. Heat and serve as bouillon or use as foundation for vegetable soup. Noodles, rice, barley, or marrow balls are good additions to bouillon.

White Soup Stock—Substitute veal for beef and do not sear (brown) it. Just cover meat and bones with water and follow directions in basic recipe for Brown Soup Stock.

Meat-Vegetable Soup—To 6 cups Brown or White Soup Stock, add 2 diced carrots, 1 cup diced turnip, 2 diced potatoes, and 2 diced leeks or minced onions. (Small amounts of any other fresh vegetables, like string beans or peas, may also be added if desired.) Simmer about 20 minutes, and add 4 peeled, quartered tomatoes or 2 cups canned tomatoes, or less, if desired. Cook 5 minutes longer, season and serve garnished with minced parsley. *Approximate vitamin values per portion: Vit. A—3019 I.U.; Vit. B₁—64 I.U.; Vit. C—752 I.U.; Vit. G—.7 Mg.*

CHICKEN SOUP

VITAMINS	1 PORTION CONTAINS APPROXIMATELY	DAILY NEED
A	1950	5000 I.U.
B	50	600 I.U.
C	147	1500 I.U.
G	.19	2.7 MGS.

INGREDIENTS:

1 5-pound fowl
3 pints water
bay leaf (optional)
4 cloves
6 peppercorns
2 tablespoons salt

¼ cup chopped carrot
3 sprigs parsley
1 onion, sliced
2 stalks celery, diced
celery leaves
3 tablespoons minced parsley

DIRECTIONS: Have chicken cleaned and cut in pieces for serving by dealer. Wash thoroughly and place in large saucepan with water, seasonings and vegetables. Let come to a boil, reduce heat, cover and simmer until tender, about 1½ hours or longer. Time for cooking may be longer, depending upon tenderness of fowl. Strain and serve garnished with minced parsley as a plain broth. Use chicken meat for fricassée, creamed dishes, loaves, salads, or any other desired dish.

If desired, add noodles or rice to the soup; if cooked separately, add them to soup just before serving. If cooked in the soup, add ¼ cup uncooked rice to strained stock and cook 30 minutes longer; or add 1 cup uncooked noodles to strained stock and cook 15 minutes longer. For a thickened chicken soup, prepare Chicken Stock Cream Sauce (page 218) and dilute with remaining broth.

LIVER-VEGETABLE SOUP

INGREDIENTS:

1 pound beef or calf liver, sliced ½ inch thick
4 tablespoons butter
1 medium-sized onion, minced
¼ cup finely diced celery
½ cup finely chopped mushrooms
2 tablespoons flour

1 teaspoon salt
¼ teaspoon pepper
4 cups meat stock (or 4 cups water and 2 bouillon cubes)
2 cups milk
3 tablespoons minced parsley

DIRECTIONS: Sauté liver in butter about 5 minutes. Remove from pan and chop fine. Sauté vegetables in pan drippings about 3 minutes. Add flour and seasoning and stir until well blended. Add stock and chopped liver, cover, reduce heat and simmer about 20 minutes. Add milk. Do not boil. Just heat milk, then add parsley and serve.

TURKEY SOUP

INGREDIENTS:

bones of leftover turkey
½ cup shredded celery leaves
4 sprigs parsley
1 leek, sliced
1 onion, sliced

2 carrots, quartered
3 celery stalks, sliced
¾ cup brown rice
salt and pepper

DIRECTIONS: Put bones in cold water to cover (about 2 quarts) with celery leaves, parsley, leek, onion, carrots and celery stalks, and simmer until a rich full flavor is reached, about 1 hour. Strain and add rice. Season to taste and simmer until rice is tender. Or replace rice with 2 cups canned corn, and simmer just until corn is heated.

CHICKEN GIBLET SOUP

INGREDIENTS:

chicken giblets
1 small onion, minced
½ cup finely diced celery
3 tablespoons flour
3 tablespoons butter

1 quart cold water (or part chicken broth)
2 sprigs parsley
2 hard-cooked eggs, sliced
2 tablespoons minced parsley

DIRECTIONS: Wash, clean and chop gizzard, heart and liver. Combine with minced onion and celery, sprinkle with flour and sauté in butter until light brown. Add water and parsley and simmer gently for about 30 minutes, or until giblets are tender. Add more water if necessary during cooking. Season to taste with salt and pepper. Serve garnished with sliced hard-cooked eggs and minced parsley.

MANHATTAN CLAM CHOWDER

VITAMINS	1 PORTION CONTAINS APPROXIMATELY	DAILY NEED
A	1933	5000 I.U.
B	41	600 I.U.
C	1310	1500 I.U.
G	.14	2.7 MGS.

INGREDIENTS:

1 pint shelled clams or 2 quarts (about 48) clams in shell
3 tablespoons butter (or 3 slices bacon, diced)
2 medium-sized onions, minced
¼ cup chopped celery
2 tablespoons minced green pepper

2 cups diced potatoes
2 teaspoons salt
3 cups boiling water
6 medium-sized tomatoes, peeled (or 3 cups canned tomatoes)
½ teaspoon thyme
3 tablespoons minced parsley

DIRECTIONS: Scrub clams and open, if not shelled. Drain, reserving liquor. Pick over clams, removing bits of shell. Place clams in colander or sieve, wash under running water, drain and chop fine. Strain clam liquor through fine sieve or cheesecloth. Melt butter or pan-broil bacon in large skillet. Remove bacon to paper towel and when cool break or cut in small pieces. In melted butter or bacon drippings, sauté onions, celery and green pepper about 2 minutes, until onions are yellow. Add potatoes, salt and boiling water. Cover and cook 10 minutes. Add tomatoes, clams, clam liquor, bacon and thyme; cook 10 minutes. Garnish with parsley.

NEW ENGLAND CLAM CHOWDER

Each Portion Contains Approximately:
Vit. A—381 I.U.; Vit. B₁—41 I.U.; Vit. C—591 I.U.; Vit. G—.38 Mg.

INGREDIENTS:

1 pint shelled clams or 2 quarts (about 48) clams in shell
3 tablespoons butter
2 medium-sized onions, minced
3 cups diced potatoes
2 teaspoons salt
⅛ teaspoon pepper
2 cups boiling water
4 cups scalded milk

DIRECTIONS: Scrub clam shells and open, if not shelled. Drain, reserving liquor. Pick over clams, removing bits of shell. Wash clams in colander under running water, drain and chop fine. Melt butter in large saucepan and sauté onions about 2 minutes, until yellow. Add potatoes, seasoning and boiling water. Cover and cook about 12 to 15 minutes, just until potatoes are soft. Strain clam liquor through fine sieve or cheesecloth. Heat clams and clam liquor just to boiling. Add scalded milk to potato mixture, and stir in heated clams and liquor. Bring just to a boil but do not boil—and serve at once, garnished with minced parsley.

BALANCED MEAL SUGGESTIONS: *Lunch*—Pimiento Coleslaw; *Meat-Vegetable Soup;* Johnnycake; Citrus Fruit Cup; Milk.

Supper—Mixed Vegetable Salad; *New England Clam Chowder;* Pumpernickel Toast; Deep-Dish Apple Pie; Milk.

VEGETABLE SOUPS

This Chart Gives Approximate Food Values for VEGETABLE SOUP STOCK. For Vitamin Values of Specific Recipes, See Charts Accompanying Them.

	VITAMINS				MINERALS			ANALYSIS	
	A	B	C	G	CALC.	PHOS.	IRON	CAL.	PROT.
1 PORTION CONTAINS APPROXIMATELY	2196 I.U.	40 I.U.	747 I.U.	.33 MGS.	32 MGS.	42 MGS.	1.6 MGS.	200	2 GMS.
BLACK PART OF COLUMN SHOWS HOW MUCH OF DAILY NEED IS SUPPLIED BY ONE PORTION									
AVERAGE DAILY NEED	5000 I.U.	600 I.U.	1500 I.U.	2.7 MGS.	800 MGS.	1320 MGS.	12 MGS.	2000-3000	70 GMS.

COMMENTS: With the exception of the vegetable consommé, all these soups are best suited for use at hearty luncheons or suppers, balanced with a raw salad, canapés or toast, and a fruit dessert. Too heavy for beginning a regular dinner. Vegetable consommé itself ideal for those individuals who need a warm and relaxing light soup to start main meal of the day; it is very low in calorie content and will not dull the appetite.

Vegetable soups made with meat stock contain some of nutritive qualities of meats from which they are made. In addition, have extra flavor of meat juices. Those made with milk highly nutritious, especially for children; good way to incorporate more milk into daily meals. Pot liquors added to soups provide extra vitamins and minerals. Cabbage pot liquor, however, should be used as soon as possible, as it spoils readily.

Vegetable soups using meat stock or vegetable pot liquors are best choice for reducers. Cream soups naturally highest in calorie content because of flour and butter used; excellent energy-producers for growing children. Vegetable pot liquors used in making soup cream sauce add valuable vitamins and minerals. Recipe as given is not thick or starchy; soup has characteristic flavor of vegetable.

VEGETABLE SOUP STOCK

VITAMINS	1 PORTION CONTAINS APPROXIMATELY	DAILY NEED
A	2196	5000 I.U.
B	40	600 I.U.
C	747	1500 I.U.
G	.33	2.7 MGS.

INGREDIENTS:

2 carrots
2 parsnips
2 small white turnips, or ½ large turnip
4 potatoes
2 leeks
3 stalks celery
1 large onion

1 bay leaf (optional)
3 quarts water (or part pot liquors)
6 peeled tomatoes (or 2 cups canned tomatoes)
2 teaspoons salt
⅛ teaspoon pepper
3 tablespoons minced parsley

DIRECTIONS: Shred or cut carrots, parsnips, turnips and potatoes in thin strips. Slice leeks and celery in ½-inch pieces, and mince onion. Heat water (mixed with pot liquors, if available), add prepared vegetables and bay leaf, and cook uncovered until a full, rolling boil is reached. Cover, reduce heat, and simmer gently about 20 minutes, just until root vegetables are almost tender. Add tomatoes and cook 5 minutes longer. Add seasoning and butter to taste, if desired. (Reducers should omit butter.) Serve at once, garnished with minced parsley, as a vegetable julienne soup, or strain and use as vegetable stock base for other soups. Do not keep, as stock will spoil.

SPRING CONSOMMÉ

Each Portion Contains Approximately:
Vit. A—2509 I.U.; Vit. B₁—20 I.U.; Vit. C—394 I.U.; Vit. G—.2 Mg.

INGREDIENTS:

1 bunch (4 ounces) watercress	1 bunch celery leaves
6 tablespoons chopped parsley	3 cups boiling water
3 large carrots	3 cups tomato juice
1 cup carrot tops	salt and pepper to taste
1 bunch scallion tops	3 tablespoons minced parsley

DIRECTIONS: Wash vegetables. Slice or shred carrots and chop greens. Add boiling water to vegetables and cook covered about 20 minutes, just until carrots are tender. Strain. Add tomato juice and seasoning to strained consommé. Reheat just to boiling point, about 1 minute, and serve hot, garnished with minced parsley, or cold with lemon wedges as a vegetable cocktail, or jellied as cold consommé. Yield: 12 cups.

Jellied Consommé—Soften 2 tablespoons granulated gelatin in ½ cup cold water. Add 3 cups hot strained consommé to softened gelatin and stir constantly until gelatin is dissolved. Turn into bouillon cups. Add 4 tablespoons lemon juice. Cool, and then chill in refrigerator until set. Just before serving, beat slightly with a fork. Serve with lemon wedges.

VITAMINS	1 PORTION CONTAINS APPROXIMATELY	DAILY NEED
A	1327	5000 I.U.
B	53	600 I.U.
C	617	1500 I.U.
G	.31	2.7 MGS.

BORSHT

INGREDIENTS:

1 small onion, minced	2 cups shredded cabbage
2 tablespoons butter	3 fresh tomatoes (or 1 cup canned tomatoes)
2 quarts meat stock	
2 cups shredded beets	1 tablespoon lemon juice (or vinegar)
1 cup shredded carrots	
½ cup diced celery	salt and pepper
2 potatoes, diced	½ cup sour cream

DIRECTIONS: Mince onion and sauté in butter until yellow, about 3 minutes. Add to meat stock with remaining vegetables. Simmer about 15 to 20 minutes, just until vegetables are tender. Season with lemon juice or vinegar, salt and pepper. Serve garnished with sour cream.

FRENCH ONION SOUP

INGREDIENTS:

3 tablespoons butter
6 medium-sized onions, sliced
6 cups stock (meat or vegetable)
salt and pepper
4 slices toast
½ cup grated cheese

DIRECTIONS: Sauté onions in butter until light brown, add soup stock and bring to boil. (If meat or vegetable stock or vegetable pot liquors are not available, use 6 cups boiling water and 4 bouillon cubes.) Reduce heat and simmer about 15 to 20 minutes, just until onions are tender. Cube toast or cut slices in halves, and place in serving dishes. Cover with soup, and garnish with grated cheese. Season to taste. Serve at once, to be certain soup is piping hot.

LEEK-POTATO SOUP

INGREDIENTS:

3 bunches leeks
6 medium-sized potatoes, diced
4 cups boiling water
1 egg yolk, slightly beaten
1 cup cream or rich milk
2 teaspoons salt
¼ teaspoon pepper
⅛ teaspoon nutmeg
2 tablespoons butter
3 tablespoons minced parsley

DIRECTIONS: Remove green tops of leeks to within 4 inches of bulb, reserving cut tops for use in other dishes. Cut leeks in ½-inch pieces. Place in large saucepan with potatoes, cover with boiling water and cook until tender, about 20 minutes. In a bowl, beat cream into egg yolk, and very slowly stir in about 1 cup of leek and potato pot liquor. Remove soup from heat and gradually stir in egg mixture. Add seasonings and butter. Reheat but do not boil. Serve at once, garnished with minced parsley.

CREAM SAUCE BASE FOR CREAM SOUPS

INGREDIENTS:

4 tablespoons butter
3 tablespoons flour
3 cups liquid (vegetable pot liquors and milk)
1 teaspoon salt

1/8 teaspoon pepper
2 tablespoons minced onion, parsley, pimiento, green pepper or diced celery

DIRECTIONS: Melt butter in large skillet, reduce heat and add flour, stirring constantly until mixture is smooth and well blended. Gradually add milk and vegetable pot liquors, stirring constantly until mixture boils and thickens. Add seasoning. For best flavor, do not use more than 1½ cups pot liquor. (In most instances, however, there will be only about 1 cup pot liquor.) Use this cream sauce base for variations which follow. Prepare vegetables as suggested and add to the cream sauce. Cook just until vegetables are reheated, add desired seasonings (onion, parsley, etc.), and serve at once. If not served at once, keep hot in double boiler.

VITAMINS	1 PORTION CONTAINS APPROXIMATELY	DAILY NEED
A	421	5000 I.U.
B	33	600 I.U.
C	577	1500 I.U.
G	.31	2.7 MGS.

CREAM OF ASPARAGUS SOUP

Cream of Asparagus Soup—Combine cream sauce with 2 cups cooked or canned asparagus, diced.

Cream of Celery Soup—Combine cream sauce with 2 cups cooked celery, diced. *Approximate vitamin values per portion: Vit. A—574 I.U.; Vit. B₁—27 I.U.; Vit. C—389 I.U.; Vit. G—.24 Mg.*

Cream of Mushroom Soup—Combine cream sauce with ½ pound (2 cups) sliced mushrooms, sautéed. *Approximate vitamin values per portion: Vit. A—297 I.U.; Vit. B₁—29 I.U.; Vit. C—362 I.U.; Vit. G—.27 Mg.*

Cream of Spinach Soup (or Chard)—Combine cream sauce with 2 cups cooked spinach, chard or other greens, chopped. *Approximate vitamin values per portion: Vit. A—5078 I.U.; Vit. B₁—30 I.U.; Vit. C—684 I.U.; Vit. G—.33 Mg.*

BALANCED MEAL SUGGESTIONS: *Lunch*—Lettuce with Russian Dressing; *Borsht;* Toasted Cheese Canapés; Milk.

237

LEGUME SOUPS

This Chart Gives Approximate Food Values for SPLIT PEA SOUP.
For Vitamin Values of Specific Recipes, See Charts Accompanying Them.

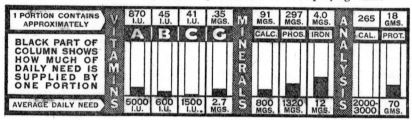

1 PORTION CONTAINS APPROXIMATELY	VITAMINS	A 870 I.U.	B 45 I.U.	C 41 I.U.	G .35 MGS.	MINERALS	CALC. 91 MGS.	PHOS. 297 MGS.	IRON 4.0 MGS.	ANALYSIS	CAL. 265	PROT. 18 GMS.
BLACK PART OF COLUMN SHOWS HOW MUCH OF DAILY NEED IS SUPPLIED BY ONE PORTION												
AVERAGE DAILY NEED		5000 I.U.	600 I.U.	1500 I.U.	2.7 MGS.		800 MGS.	1320 MGS.	12 MGS.		2000-3000	70 GMS.

COMMENTS: Legume soups are main-dish soups, high in vegetable protein and the Vitamin B complex. All very filling foods of the "stick-to-the-ribs" type, and should be considered as meat substitutes for a hearty supper or lunch. Dried Lima Bean Soup especially important in this respect, as the protein it contains is far superior in quality to that of other legume soups. All fairly high in calorie content; should not be eaten by reducers.

SPLIT PEA SOUP

INGREDIENTS:

2 cups split peas
½ cup diced carrots
2 celery stalks, diced
2 medium-sized onions, sliced
celery leaves
6 peppercorns

1 bay leaf
pinch of thyme
2 quarts boiling water
½ cup evaporated milk
¾ teaspoon sugar
salt and pepper

DIRECTIONS: Peas do not require soaking. Wash, drain and put peas, vegetables, spices and water in saucepan. Cover and simmer over low heat until peas are soft, about 40 minutes to 1 hour, stirring occasionally to prevent burning. Strain soup by rubbing peas through a coarse sieve. Return strained soup to heat. Add just enough milk or cream to give desired consistency, stirring constantly to prevent burning. Stir in sugar, and season to taste. Heat just to boiling but do not boil.

VITAMINS	1 PORTION CONTAINS APPROXIMATELY	DAILY NEED
A	581	5000 I.U.
B₁	42	600 I.U.
C	253	1500 I.U.
G	.31	2.7 MGS.

LENTIL SOUP

INGREDIENTS:

2 cups dried lentils
1 bay leaf
2 carrots
1 potato
2 medium-sized onions
6 peppercorns
celery leaves

2 quarts water
5 tablespoons cold water
2 tablespoons flour
1½ teaspoons salt
2 hard-cooked eggs, sliced
1 lemon, sliced

DIRECTIONS: Wash and soak lentils in cold water to cover about 5 hours. Wash and cut vegetables. Combine lentils, vegetables, bay leaf, peppercorns and water. Cover and simmer until lentils are tender, about 45 minutes. (If lentils are not soaked, they will take longer to cook, about 1½ hours.) Strain soup by rubbing lentils through a coarse sieve. Heat strained soup to boiling. Meanwhile add cold water gradually to flour, stirring constantly to make a smooth thin paste. Add this to boiling soup, stirring to prevent burning. Cook about 3 minutes, add salt and garnish with lemon.

BLACK BEAN SOUP

Each Portion Contains Approximately:
Vit. A—360 I.U.; Vit. B₁—294 I.U.; Vit. C—396 I.U.; Vit. G—1.5 Mg.

INGREDIENTS:

2 cups black beans
2 quarts boiling water
2 medium-sized onions, sliced
½ cup chopped celery
celery leaves

6 peppercorns
1 teaspoon salt
4 tablespoons lemon juice
2 hard-cooked eggs
1 lemon

DIRECTIONS: Soak beans about 10 hours in cold water to cover. Add boiling water, onions, celery, celery leaves and peppercorns. Cover and simmer until beans are soft, from 1¼ to 1½ hours, adding more water if needed. Stir occasionally to prevent burning. When tender, press through coarse sieve or ricer. Return strained soup to heat, and stir in salt and lemon juice. Bring to a boil. Garnish with sliced eggs and lemon.

PEA OR NAVY BEAN SOUP

VITAMINS	1 PORTION CONTAINS APPROXIMATELY	DAILY NEED
A	591	5000 I.U.
B	284	600 I.U.
C	149	1500 I.U.
G	1.43	2.7 MGS.

INGREDIENTS:

2 cups navy or pea beans
2 quarts boiling water
2 medium-sized onions, minced
½ cup diced celery
1 carrot, shredded
celery leaves

6 peppercorns
½ teaspoon thyme
5 tablespoons cold water
2 tablespoons flour
1 teaspoon salt
3 tablespoons minced parsley

DIRECTIONS: Soak beans about 10 hours in cold water to cover. Add remaining ingredients except cold water, flour, parsley. Cover and simmer until beans are tender, from 1 to 1¼ hours, adding more water if needed. When soft, rub beans through coarse sieve or put through a ricer. Heat strained soup to boiling. Meanwhile, add cold water gradually to flour, stirring constantly to make a smooth thin paste. Add this to boiling soup, stirring to prevent burning. Cook until thick and smooth, about 3 minutes. Add salt and serve garnished with minced parsley or chives.

Lima or Marrow Bean Soup—Replace navy beans with lima or marrow beans. Do not soak. Beans will become soft in 1½ to 2 hours. Soaking, of course, shortens cooking time, thereby reducing fuel consumption. Omit thyme. Add 3 tablespoons minced parsley just before serving. *Approximate vitamin values per portion: Vit. A—941 I.U.; Vit. B₁—46 I.U.; Vit. C—85 I.U.; Vit. G—.18 Mg.*

BALANCED MEAL SUGGESTIONS: *Lunch—Lentil Soup; Black Bean Soup* (or any other legume soup); Fruit Salad; Bran Muffins; Milk.

NOODLES

INGREDIENTS:

2 eggs, slightly beaten
½ teaspoon salt

1 cup flour (approximate)

DIRECTIONS: In medium-sized bowl, beat eggs slightly and add salt. Gradually add just enough flour to make a very stiff dough. Turn out on slightly floured board and knead dough until smooth, about 3 minutes. Roll out into paper-thin sheet, using just enough flour to prevent sticking. Cover with towel and let stand about 20 minutes, just until dry enough to handle. Roll up dough like jelly roll and with sharp knife cut in ⅛-inch strips for thin noodles or ¼-inch strips for broad noodles. Open (unroll) strips and spread out each strip to dry thoroughly. Drop slowly into boiling water or soup to cover, and when water again reaches boil, cover and cook about 10 to 15 minutes. Yield: 2 cups noodles. Store any uncooked noodles in tightly covered container.

VITAMINS	1 PORTION CONTAINS APPROXIMATELY	DAILY NEED
A	302	5000 I.U.
B	6	600 I.U.
C	1	1500 I.U.
G	.05	2.7 MGS.

EGG STRIPS

INGREDIENTS:

3 egg yolks
3 tablespoons milk

⅛ teaspoon salt

DIRECTIONS: Beat all ingredients just enough to blend milk and yolks of eggs. Pour mixture into small buttered pie plate or other small oven dish. Mixture should form ¼- to ½-inch layer. Set in pan of hot water and bake in moderate oven (350° F.) about 20 minutes, or until firm. Cool and cut in fine strips.

MARROW BALLS

Each Portion Contains Approximately:
Vit. A—323 I.U.; Vit. B₁—26 I.U.; Vit. C—12 I.U.; Vit. G—.04 Mg.

INGREDIENTS:

2 tablespoons marrow
4 tablespoons cracker crumbs
1 egg, well beaten
1 tablespoon chopped parsley

¾ teaspoon salt
⅛ teaspoon pepper
⅛ teaspoon nutmeg

DIRECTIONS: Place marrow in small bowl and stir until creamy. Add remaining ingredients and mix well. Place in refrigerator and let stand several hours until firm. Shape in small balls and drop in simmering water or soup. Do not let water boil furiously. Cook about 10 minutes.

241

VEGETABLES

Since vegetables are our most important all-'round source of all vitamins, proper care of them to preserve those vitamins is of particular significance in this food group. As you read in the introductory chapters, Vitamin A is harmed by drying and exposure to heat and air; Vitamin B_1, by high cooking temperatures and use of baking soda; Vitamin C, by exposure to air, use of baking soda and long cooking. These are the conditions that must be minimized as much as possible in the care and cooking of vegetables.

Selection—Choose vegetables which are bright in color and firm or crisp in texture. Be sure they are clean, free of bruises, discoloration and wilted leaves. Destruction of the vitamins, particularly Vitamin C, begins as soon as the vegetable leaves the ground or is removed from the plant. You cannot be absolutely certain it has been properly cared for in transit from farm to you, but you can tell much by its appearance. Good appearance, good flavor and high vitamin content almost always go together.

Choose tender, young products whenever possible. Hand-picked, home-grown vegetables are naturally fresher and of better flavor than those picked and shipped on a commercial scale.

Test green, leafy vegetables (spinach, lettuce, etc.) and seeds or pods (peas, strings beans, etc.) to be certain they are crisp. See that roots, tubers, bulbs and fruits (carrots, potatoes, onions, tomatoes, etc.) are firm, with unwrinkled skins. Onions and potatoes should be free of sprouts.

Choose canned vegetables by grade as often as possible; Grades A and B are usually more carefully selected vegetables than Grade C. Nationally advertised quick-frozen vegetables are uniformly reliable; do not buy cellophane bags of quick-frozen products without familiar labels. Canned and quick-frozen products are so processed today that they are often higher in vitamin content than ordinary market-fresh vegetables. Garden-fresh ones always best, of course.

Buy quality produce at all times even if cost is a little higher than that of slightly inferior vegetables. There will be less waste, less chance for hidden spoilage. If any vegetable is on the market in two varieties (green and white), always choose green type for highest vitamin content. This applies especially to green lettuce (in contrast to white iceberg lettuce), and green celery (in contrast to bleached "table" celery).

In general, use your eyes rather than your hands in judging quality, with the exception of weighing in your hand a head of lettuce or cabbage to make certain it is solid. Vegetables like tomatoes do not improve with pinching or other unnecessary handling.

Preparation—Wash all vegetables thoroughly; scrub roots and tubers. Remove blemishes, eyes, mold, etc., if present, from all vegetables.

After washing greens, flowers and heads, remove wilted leaves, stem ends, stalks or cores, and wash thoroughly in several waters to remove sand, soil, insects, sprays, etc. Shake and drain in colander or sieve.

Crisp in hydrator or ice water all vegetables to be eaten raw. Do not cut, dice, pare, shell, peel, scrape or in any manner break the outer covering of a vegetable until ready to use it. Destruction of Vitamin C begins and progresses rapidly once the food is cut and so exposed to air.

Storage—Wash, drain, and shake or pat until practically dry, all salad greens before storing. Refrigerate all appetizer or salad vegetables, greens, leafy or flower vegetables. Place all vegetables for chilling in hydrator or tightly covered container, oilskin or cellophane bags, damp cloth or waxed paper. Cold temperature of refrigerator inhibits destruction of Vitamin C.

Store mushrooms and pod vegetables without washing in tightly covered container in refrigerator.

Store potatoes, turnips, parsnips and dry onions in cool dry place, preferably a vegetable bin in which they can be spread out, rather than piled one on top of the other.

Use all vegetables as soon as possible rather than store for long periods. This rule excepts potatoes and dry onions, which keep for some time without serious deterioration or loss of vitamins.

General Cooking Directions—All vegetables should be quick-cooked; that is, for the shortest possible time to make them tender and palatable. Vitamins are destroyed by long cooking, as are color and flavor of vegetables. Drop prepared vegetables into required amount of rapidly boiling water. Vitamin C is preserved if this rule is carried out; it is destroyed if vegetables are started in cold water.

Use any utensils with tightly fitting covers, with the exception of copper or copper-lined pots. Copper completely destroys Vitamin C. Tightly fitting covers very important, so that small amount of water used will not boil away in steam.

Most vegetables require only very little water—a half inch or an inch in the bottom of the utensil. Follow specific water requirements for each vegetable. Any of the strongly flavored vegetables (onions, cabbage, etc.) are milder in taste when placed in water to cover and then cooked uncovered.

Water will stop boiling as vegetables are dropped into it. When it again reaches a full, rolling boil, cover utensil and cook just until vegetables are tender.

The cooking times suggested in each recipe are approximate only. Time depends upon age and tenderness of vegetable. Main rule of quick-cooking is: *Cook just until tender (but still a trifle crisp); do not overcook.*

Never use baking soda; it destroys Vitamins B_1, C and G.

Add salt just before removing vegetables from heat. Do not salt water before cooking.

Cook canned and quick-frozen vegetables according to directions on label. Be careful not to overcook.

Pot Liquors—Save and use all vegetable cooking waters. Vitamins B_1, C and G are dissolved in such waters during cooking, and if you throw them away, you will lose at least 30 per cent of the original water-soluble vitamin content of the vegetable, in addition to the percentage actually destroyed by cooking.

Serve most vegetables with a little of the pot liquor as sauce. Preserve other pot liquors by storing in tightly covered jars in refrigerator. Always use as soon as possible—preferably within next twenty-four hours—in soups, gravies, Vegetable Juice Cocktails (page 81), sauces, etc.

Use liquid on canned vegetables in same way, as it is equally rich in dissolved vitamins and minerals.

ARTICHOKES

COMMENTS: Artichokes not very high in any of the vitamins or minerals, but are enjoyed for distinctive flavor. Good for reducers, as low in calorie content when no butter or rich sauce is served with them. At one time were considered a delicacy too expensive for most budgets, but now are available in quantity to all but the lowest income groups. Do not confuse with Jerusalem artichokes, which are akin to the Irish potato.

Use as main vegetable for supper or dinner to balance concentrated foods in meal. Serve with yellow or white vegetable for color contrast. One whole artichoke per person served with Hollandaise Sauce a substantial dish.

QUICK-COOKED ARTICHOKES

This Chart Gives Approximate Food Values for ARTICHOKES.

1 PORTION CONTAINS APPROXIMATELY	VITAMINS	A 395 I.U.	B 22 I.U.	C 189 I.U.	G .24 MGS.	MINERALS	CALC. 61 MGS.	PHOS. 142 MGS.	IRON 2.9 MGS.	ANALYSIS	CAL. 148	PROT. 4 GMS.
BLACK PART OF COLUMN SHOWS HOW MUCH OF DAILY NEED IS SUPPLIED BY ONE PORTION												
AVERAGE DAILY NEED		5000 I.U.	600 I.U.	1500 I.U.	2.7 MGS.		800 MGS.	1320 MGS.	12 MGS.		2000-3000	70 GMS.

INGREDIENTS:
 6 small or medium-sized artichokes   4 tablespoons butter

DIRECTIONS: Wash thoroughly; remove any discolored outer leaves. Cut off sharp tips of leaves and stem about ½ inch below base of leaves. Drop artichokes into 2 inches boiling water. As soon as water boils again, cover utensil tightly; cook about 20 to 30 minutes, just until artichokes are tender (when outer leaf can easily be pulled from stem). Time of cooking depends upon size and freshness of artichokes. Serve whole with melted butter, Hollandaise Sauce (page 220) or Cheese Sauce (page 218). With fingers, dip large ends of leaves into sauce. Eat only white flesh part of leaves and heart. Discard spiny choke (the thistle-like portion) between leaves and above the heart.

BALANCED MEAL SUGGESTIONS: *Lunch* or *Supper*—Cold Borsht; Fish Salad; *Artichokes,* Hollandaise Sauce; Rye Toast; Pineapple; Milk.

ASPARAGUS

COMMENTS: Apart from excellent vitamin values in B_1, C and G, asparagus contains food factor called asparagin, which gently stimulates kidney function. In addition, high water content makes asparagus of particular value in cases of kidney disease, as it helps normalize water balance of body. High mineral content of asparagus helpful to sufferers from nutritional anemia. Best to buy green, unblanched stalks, as these contain Vitamin A. White stalks have practically none. Calorie content very low. Asparagus thus a good reducing dish if not served with butter or rich sauce.

Serve as main vegetable dish at dinner along with white or yellow vegetable for color contrast. Hot asparagus on toast, garnished with pimiento strips, makes excellent luncheon dish. Cold asparagus may be used for salads.

QUICK-COOKED ASPARAGUS

This Chart Gives Approximate Food Values for ASPARAGUS.

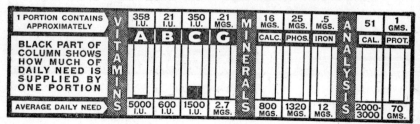

1 PORTION CONTAINS APPROXIMATELY	VITAMINS	A 358 I.U.	B 21 I.U.	C 350 I.U.	G .21 MGS.	MINERALS	CALC. 16 MGS.	PHOS. 25 MGS.	IRON .5 MGS.	ANALYSIS	CAL. 51	PROT. 1 GMS.
BLACK PART OF COLUMN SHOWS HOW MUCH OF DAILY NEED IS SUPPLIED BY ONE PORTION												
AVERAGE DAILY NEED		5000 I.U.	600 I.U.	1500 I.U.	2.7 MGS.		800 MGS.	1320 MGS.	12 MGS.		2000-3000	70 GMS.

INGREDIENTS:

30 stalks asparagus
1 teaspoon salt

3 tablespoons melted butter

DIRECTIONS: Wash stalks thoroughly under running water. Remove all of stem end which is hard and woody; scrape large scales from stalks when asparagus is very sandy. Do not bruise or knock off tender tips. Tie stalks in bunch with white cotton string; place stem-end down in bottom of double boiler containing 2 inches boiling water. Cover with upper part of double boiler (inverted), and cook 12 to 20 minutes, until tender. Add salt just before removing from heat. Drain asparagus, remove string, and dress with melted butter. Asparagus may also be dressed with Lemon Butter (page 222), Hollandaise Sauce (page 220) or Cheese Sauce (page 218).

	1 PORTION CONTAINS APPROXIMATELY	DAILY NEED	
A	662	5000 I.U.	
B	54	600 I.U.	
C	132	1500 I.U.	
G	.26	2.7 MGS.	

ASPARAGUS LOAF

INGREDIENTS:

2 cups cooked or canned asparagus
2 eggs
½ cup asparagus pot liquor
½ cup milk
1 tablespoon melted butter

½ cup soft bread crumbs
1 tablespoon minced onion
½ teaspoon salt
⅛ teaspoon paprika (optional)
3 teaspoons minced parsley

DIRECTIONS: Quick-cook asparagus according to basic recipe, or open canned asparagus and drain, reserving pot liquor. Cut asparagus into 1-inch pieces. Combine eggs, pot liquor, milk and melted butter; beat well. Add bread crumbs, onion, seasoning, parsley and asparagus, and turn into buttered casserole or loaf pan. Bake in a moderate oven (375° F.) about 25 to 30 minutes, just until center is firm and top is delicately browned. Garnish with pimiento strips, if desired.

ASPARAGUS AND MUSHROOMS ON TOAST

Each Portion Contains Approximately:
Vit. A—1140 I. U.; Vit. B₁—135 I. U.; Vit. C—620 I. U.; Vit. G—.45 Mg.

INGREDIENTS:

1 can condensed mushroom soup
¼ cup rich milk
1 egg yolk, well beaten
1 teaspoon lemon juice

salt and pepper
1 No. 2 can asparagus
6 slices buttered toast
2 tablespoons minced parsley

DIRECTIONS: Combine mushroom soup, milk, egg yolk, lemon juice and seasoning in top part of double boiler. Stir over boiling water until ingredients are well blended, and cook until thoroughly heated. Meanwhile, heat asparagus and prepare toast. Drain asparagus, reserving liquid, and arrange asparagus on toast. Pour mushroom sauce over asparagus and garnish with minced parsley (or pimiento strips). Reserved asparagus liquid may be added to mushroom sauce or used in Vegetable Juice Cocktail (page 81).

BALANCED MEAL SUGGESTIONS: *Dinner*—Green Pepper Cole-slaw; Baked Ham; *Asparagus,* Lemon Butter; Mashed Potatoes; Pears.

LIMA BEANS

COMMENTS: Lima beans, even those in green shell rather than dried, an excellent source of vegetable protein of high quality. Used with eggs or cheese in menu, can form a good meat substitute. Like meats, very rich in Vitamin B complex. Highly alkalinizing. Not very low in calorie content; reducers should choose snap rather than lima beans.

Traditional combination of lima beans with corn an excellent one from the flavor viewpoint; corn also adds considerable Vitamin A to lima beans. Carrot-lima bean dish even more fortified with this vitamin.

Serve as main dinner vegetable, preferably with meat or fish low in protein quality. Balance meal with light vegetable, high in water content.

QUICK-COOKED LIMA BEANS

This Chart Gives Approximate Food Values for GREEN LIMA BEANS.

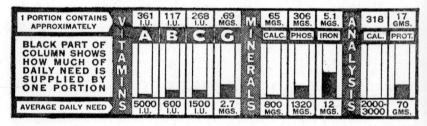

1 PORTION CONTAINS APPROXIMATELY	V I T A M I N S	361 I.U. A	117 I.U. B	268 I.U. C	.69 MGS. G	M I N E R A L S	65 MGS. CALC.	306 MGS. PHOS.	5.1 MGS. IRON	A N A L Y S I S	318 CAL.	17 GMS. PROT.
BLACK PART OF COLUMN SHOWS HOW MUCH OF DAILY NEED IS SUPPLIED BY ONE PORTION												
AVERAGE DAILY NEED		5000 I.U.	600 I.U.	1500 I.U.	2.7 MGS.		800 MGS.	1320 MGS.	12 MGS.		2000-3000	70 GMS.

INGREDIENTS:

3 pounds (unshelled)
   green lima beans

2 teaspoons salt
2 tablespoons butter

DIRECTIONS: Shell beans just before cooking. Wash shelled beans and drop into 1 inch boiling water. When water has again reached full boil, cover utensil and cook about 20 to 35 minutes, depending upon freshness and quality of beans. Add salt just before removing from heat. Serve with pot liquor and butter.

Lima Beans and Carrots—Combine 2 cups shelled green lima beans and 1½ cups diced carrots, and quick-cook as directed in basic recipe. If canned green limas are used, add to carrots when carrots have cooked about 15 minutes and are almost tender. Cook 5 minutes longer, just until beans are heated and carrots are tender. *Approximate vitamin values per portion: Vit. A—1037 I.U.; Vit. B₁—35 I.U.; Vit. C—76 I.U.; Vit. G—.21 Mg.*

BALANCED MEAL SUGGESTIONS: *Lunch* or *Supper* — Waldorf Salad; *Lima Beans and Carrots;* Whole Wheat Rolls; Custard; Milk.

STRING BEANS

COMMENTS: Green string (snap) beans a good source of all the vitamins; yellow wax beans contain smaller amounts. Unlike other members of the bean family, string beans eaten chiefly for their pods, rather than seeds. Hence they are classed as protective vegetable, rather than as legume. Low in calorie content and high in water content. Good food for reducers.

Many persons feel that string beans are difficult to digest. Answer usually is that beans are improperly prepared with lots of grease or meat. Quick-cooked beans rarely cause distress, except in persons allergic to them.

QUICK-COOKED STRING BEANS

This Chart Gives Approximate Food Values for STRING BEANS.

	VITAMINS				MINERALS			ANALYSIS	
	A	B	C	G	CALC.	PHOS.	IRON	CAL.	PROT.
1 PORTION CONTAINS APPROXIMATELY	1234 I.U.	26 I.U.	253 I.U.	.02 MGS.	78 MGS.	80 MGS.	1.7 MGS.	57	4 GMS.
BLACK PART OF COLUMN SHOWS HOW MUCH OF DAILY NEED IS SUPPLIED BY ONE PORTION									
AVERAGE DAILY NEED	5000 I.U.	600 I.U.	1500 I.U.	2.7 MGS.	800 MGS.	1320 MGS.	12 MGS.	2000-3000	70 GMS.

INGREDIENTS:

2 pounds green or yellow (wax) string beans
2 teaspoons grated onion
2 teaspoons salt
2 tablespoons butter
2 tablespoons minced parsley

DIRECTIONS: Wash thoroughly; break or cut off ends of beans; string if necessary. Shred by cutting each bean into fine strips or slivers (slice lengthwise or sidewise diagonally). Drop slivers into 1 inch of boiling water. When water again reaches full boil, cover utensil and cook beans until just tender. Add onion (or chives) during last 5 minutes of cooking. Strictly fresh, young and very finely cut beans will cook in 12 to 15 minutes. Ordinary market beans, sometimes neither too young nor too fresh, usually require 20 to 25 minutes. Add salt just before removing from heat (never salt during cooking). Serve in individual dishes with pot liquor and butter, and garnish with minced parsley.

String Beans and Corn—Quick-cook 1 pound shredded green or yellow string beans as directed in basic recipe. Separately, quick-cook 1½ cups fresh-cut corn in 1 inch boiling water about 6 minutes. Combine vegetables with pot liquors, add 2 tablespoons butter and 2 teaspoons salt. Serve in individual dishes. If canned or leftover cooked corn (cut from cob) is used, add to beans 5 minutes before they have finished cooking. *Approximate vitamin values per portion: Vit. A—798 I.U.; Vit. B₁—29 I.U.; Vit. C— 188 I.U.; Vit. G—.13 Mg.*

String Beans and Chard Stalks—Combine 1½ pounds shredded green or yellow string beans and 2½ cups diced chard stalks (from 3 pounds chard). Quick-cook as directed in basic recipe. If canned string beans are used, add to saucepan after chard stalks have cooked 10 minutes. This dish good way to serve chard to those who may not like it plain. *Approximate vitamin values per portion: Vit. A—3534 I.U.; Vit. B₁—28 I.U.; Vit. C—219 I.U.; Vit. G—.29 Mg.*

STRING BEANS PIQUANT

VITAMINS	1 PORTION CONTAINS APPROXIMATELY	DAILY NEED
A	962	5000 I.U.
B	28	600 I.U.
C	229	1500 I.U.
G	.13	2.7 MGS.

INGREDIENTS:

2 pounds (or 1 No. 2 can) string beans
¼ teaspoon salt
⅛ teaspoon white pepper
½ teaspoon dry mustard
¼ cup cream or rich milk
1 egg yolk
1 cup hot bean pot liquor
2 teaspoons lemon juice
1 tablespoon butter

DIRECTIONS: Quick-cook string beans as directed in basic recipe; drain when tender, reserving pot liquor. While beans are cooking, combine seasonings, cream and egg yolk in a bowl, and stir until well blended. Then add hot pot liquor slowly, stirring constantly. Pour over beans and reheat by bringing just to the boiling point. Do *not* boil. Stir in lemon juice and butter and serve. If there is less than 1 cup pot liquor, add milk to it to make 1 cup. If canned beans are used, heat, drain, and use liquid.

BALANCED MEAL SUGGESTIONS: *Dinner*—Mixed Greens Salad; Beef Patties; *String Beans;* Mashed Pimiento Potatoes; Orange Ice.

BEETS

COMMENTS: Beets usually cooked incorrectly by those who believe they should not be scraped or cut before cooking. Beets cooked whole take 40 to 80 minutes to become tender, depending upon size and freshness. Such long cooking tends to destroy valuable vitamins (especially Vitamin B_1). Best to quick-cook by slicing or dicing as directed in recipes given.

Serve beets as vegetable to balance dinner protein dish, along with another vegetable, white, yellow or green for color contrast. Should not accompany another sweet vegetable, like carrots, or the meal as a whole will be too sweet. For the same reason, do not serve with a very sweet dessert. Leftover beets, thoroughly chilled and pickled if desired, are appetizing in salads.

Beet greens should not be thrown away if they are young and crisp, as they are even higher in vitamin content (particularly Vitamin A) than the root of the vegetable, and very rich in the blood-building minerals, iron and manganese. Serve cooked with beets or with Mixed Greens (page 266) or alone.

QUICK-COOKED BEETS

This Chart Gives Approximate Food Values for BEETS.

	VITAMINS				MINERALS			ANALYSIS	
	A	B	C	G	CALC.	PHOS.	IRON	CAL.	PROT.
1 PORTION CONTAINS APPROXIMATELY	1243 I.U.	69 I.U.	221 I.U.	.35 MGS.	57 MGS.	86 MGS.	5.4 MGS.	109	5 GMS.
BLACK PART OF COLUMN SHOWS HOW MUCH OF DAILY NEED IS SUPPLIED BY ONE PORTION									
AVERAGE DAILY NEED	5000 I.U.	600 I.U.	1500 I.U.	2.7 MGS.	800 MGS.	1320 MGS.	12 MGS.	2000-3000	70 GMS.

INGREDIENTS:

18 small beets
2 tablespoons butter
1 teaspoon salt

2 tablespoons lemon juice
(or 6 orange segments, diced)

DIRECTIONS: Remove leaves and stems. Scrub beets. Scrape or pare thin skin from beets (if you do not have a scraper, pare skin as thin as possible); dice, slice, or cut into quarters. Drop prepared beets into boiling water to cover. When water has again reached full boil, cover utensil and cook 20 to 25 minutes, just until beets are tender. All cooking times depend upon age of beets and size of pieces. Add butter, salt to taste, and fruit or fruit juice just before serving. Serve in individual dishes with pot liquor.

251

Young Fresh Beets—Rub thoroughly washed beets across fine shredder or grater, and place slivers in saucepan with only enough water to prevent burning. Cover and cook over low heat about 8 or 10 minutes, stirring occasionally. Season with salt and a few drops of lemon juice. Serve dotted with butter in individual dishes.

HARVARD BEETS

VITAMINS	1 PORTION CONTAINS APPROXIMATELY	DAILY NEED
A	360	5000 I.U.
B	21	600 I.U.
C	61	1500 I.U.
G	.10	2.7 MGS.

INGREDIENTS:

2 cups cooked or canned beets
4 tablespoons sugar
½ teaspoon salt
1 tablespoon cornstarch

1 cup beet liquor
3 tablespoons lemon juice
1 tablespoon butter

DIRECTIONS: Prepare and cook beets as directed in basic recipe, just until tender, or remove from can and slice or dice. Drain, reserving liquid. Mix sugar, salt and cornstarch in a saucepan. Stir in beet liquor gradually to prevent cornstarch from lumping. Cook, stirring constantly, until mixture is smooth and thick, about 8 minutes. Stir in lemon juice and butter. Add beets, reheat and serve.

BEETS PIQUANT

VITAMINS	1 PORTION CONTAINS APPROXIMATELY	DAILY NEED
A	575	5000 I.U.
B	35	600 I.U.
C	168	1500 I.U.
G	.17	2.7 MGS.

INGREDIENTS:

8 medium-sized cooked
    (or 1 No. 2 can) beets
1 cup beet liquor
¼ cup lemon juice

½ teaspoon salt
⅛ teaspoon pepper
1 teaspoon sugar
1 tablespoon minced onion

DIRECTIONS: Prepare, cook and drain beets (reserving liquid) as directed in basic recipe. Add beet liquor to remaining ingredients and stir until sugar dissolves. Pour over beets. Reheat to serve hot, or chill thoroughly to serve as cold pickled beets.

VITAMINS	1 PORTION CONTAINS APPROXIMATELY	DAILY NEED
A	15,809	5000 I.U.
B	44	600 I.U.
C	1128	1500 I.U.
G	.59	2.7 MGS.

INGREDIENTS:

1½ pounds beet greens	2 tablespoons butter
1 teaspoon salt	6 lemon wedges (1 lemon)

DIRECTIONS: Remove any coarse, wilted or discolored leaves and stems. Wash well in several waters to remove all traces of sand. Usually necessary to rinse 3 or 4 times in large pan of cold water (fresh each rinsing) to get thoroughly clean (see Spinach, page 291). Place greens in utensil containing ½ inch boiling water. Cover pan when water has again begun to boil and cook about 7 minutes—just until tender. Season with salt just before removing from heat. Drain, chop and add butter. Serve with lemon.

BALANCED MEAL SUGGESTIONS: *Dinner*—Parsley Coleslaw; Veal Loaf; *Beets and Greens;* Cauliflower; Deep-Dish Berry Pie.

Supper—Poached Eggs on Whole Wheat Toast; *Young Fresh Beets;* Citrus Fruit Cup; Milk.

BROCCOLI

COMMENTS: Broccoli practically a perfect protective food. Extremely rich in all vitamins, as well as calcium, sulphur, potassium and iron. When in season, a serving of broccoli at least once or twice a week will go far toward fulfilling that day's vitamin requirements. Low in calorie content; hence especially good for reducers, and for all others to balance a heavy or concentrated meal. Since it is of the cabbage group, overcooked or badly cooked broccoli often produces digestive distress. If correctly prepared, however, is well tolerated by those with normal digestive powers.

Tender stalks of broccoli may be used raw as appetizer, and tender leaves may be added to soup stock or cooked in Mixed Greens (page 266). Like asparagus, broccoli is especially good when served with Flavored Butter or Hollandaise Sauce. As such, it is more filling, and may be used for lunch or supper, or as main part of vegetable plate.

253

QUICK-COOKED BROCCOLI

This Chart Gives Approximate Food Values for BROCCOLI.

	VITAMINS	A	B	C	G	MINERALS	CALC.	PHOS.	IRON	ANALYSIS	CAL.	PROT.
1 PORTION CONTAINS APPROXIMATELY		14051 I.U.	62 I.U.	1610 I.U.	.97 MGS.		281 MGS.	136 MGS.	3.2 MGS.		96	7 GMS.
BLACK PART OF COLUMN SHOWS HOW MUCH OF DAILY NEED IS SUPPLIED BY ONE PORTION												
AVERAGE DAILY NEED		5000 I.U.	600 I.U.	1500 I.U.	2.7 MGS.		800 MGS.	1320 MGS.	12 MGS.		2000-3000	70 GMS.

INGREDIENTS:

3 pounds broccoli (approximate)   2 tablespoons butter
1 teaspoon salt

DIRECTIONS: Discard only the largest and heaviest leaves, and any woody part of stems if present. Separate flowers into suitable portions for serving. Wash well. Tie sections into bunch with white cotton string. Place stems downward in utensil containing 3 inches boiling water. When water has again reached a full boil, cover utensil and cook 15 to 30 minutes, depending upon tenderness of stems of broccoli. Salt just before removing from heat. Take broccoli from water, remove string and place vegetable in serving dish. Dress with butter and pot liquor, or with Hollandaise Sauce (page 220), Lemon Butter (page 222) or Cheese Sauce (page 218).

BALANCED MEAL SUGGESTIONS: *Lunch* or *Supper* — Grapefruit Juice; Vegetable Plate (*Broccoli* with Hollandaise Sauce, Beets, String Beans, Whole-Kernel Corn); Iron-Rich Tarts; Milk.

Dinner—Tomato Salad; Broiled Steak or Broiled Beef Patties; *Broccoli;* Parsley Potatoes; Baked Rhubarb.

BRUSSELS SPROUTS

COMMENTS: Brussels sprouts look like miniature cabbages, and actually are, nutritionally speaking. Valuable chiefly for their Vitamin C content (like cabbage), and when in season are a relatively inexpensive way to supply that factor to the diet. Very low in calorie content, so an excellent dish for reducers. Many persons who suffer digestive distress after eating Brussels sprouts may be sensitive merely to improperly cooked sprouts. Over-cooking generates sulphur compounds and often makes sprouts difficult to digest. Finely shredded raw sprouts, or quick-cooked ones, rarely cause distress, except in those actually allergic to this vegetable.

Serve as dinner vegetable to balance protein part of meal, along with a white or yellow vegetable for color contrast. Best combined with one like carrots, to supply Vitamin A in which sprouts are not especially rich.

QUICK-COOKED BRUSSELS SPROUTS

This Chart Gives Approximate Food Values for BRUSSELS SPROUTS.

		A	B	C	G		CALC.	PHOS.	IRON		CAL.	PROT.
1 PORTION CONTAINS APPROXIMATELY	VITAMINS	698 I.U.	54 I.U.	1099 I.U.	.47 MGS.	MINERALS	42 MGS.	186 MGS.	3.6 MGS.	ANALYSIS	111	7 GMS.
BLACK PART OF COLUMN SHOWS HOW MUCH OF DAILY NEED IS SUPPLIED BY ONE PORTION												
AVERAGE DAILY NEED		5000 I.U.	600 I.U.	1500 I.U.	2.7 MGS.		800 MGS.	1320 MGS.	12 MGS.		2000-3000	70 GMS.

INGREDIENTS:

1 quart Brussels sprouts
1 teaspoon minced onion
1 teaspoon salt
¼ teaspoon pepper
2 tablespoons minced parsley
2 tablespoons butter

DIRECTIONS: Remove any wilted leaves and stems; cut into quarters and wash well. Soaking is unnecessary and should be avoided because it destroys valuable vitamins. Core-like part extending from stem into sprouts may be cut out, as it requires considerably longer cooking to become tender than do the leaves. Drop quartered sprouts and onion into enough boiling water to cover. Do not cover utensil. Cook 8 to 10 minutes, just until tender. Add salt, pepper and parsley just before removing from heat. Never salt during cooking. Dress with butter, Lemon Butter (page 222) or rich milk; serve with pot liquor in individual dishes.

Brussels Sprouts and Celery—Quick-cook 1½ cups diced celery as directed on page 261. After it has boiled about 5 minutes, add 1 pint quartered Brussels sprouts and 1 teaspoon minced onion with just enough boiling water to cover. Continue cooking as in basic recipe for Brussels sprouts. Season, add butter and minced parsley, and serve in individual dishes with pot liquor. *Approximate vitamin values per portion: Vit. A—751 I.U.; Vit. B₁—31 I.U.; Vit. C—578 I.U.; Vit. G—.27 Mg.*

BALANCED MEAL SUGGESTIONS: *Dinner*—Lettuce and Tomato Salad; Broiled Kidneys; *Brussels Sprouts;* Carrots; Peaches.

CABBAGE

COMMENTS: Raw, shredded cabbage one of cheapest and best sources of Vitamin C. If budget does not permit use of citrus fruits to supply this factor, one generous six-ounce serving daily of coleslaw will fulfill the day's Vitamin C requirement. Green cabbage, of course, better in all vitamin respects than bleached cabbage. Very low in calorie content; good for reducers. Properly quick-cooked cabbage and *finely* shredded raw cabbage have been shown in clinical experiments to be well tolerated by persons who previously had suffered digestive distress upon eating cabbage. Should be shredded as fine as possible, chewed sufficiently and never overcooked.

Serve as raw salad to introduce any meal, or use in combination with other vegetables to make a large luncheon salad (for uses of cabbage served raw, see page 198). Serve cooked as main dinner vegetable along with meat dish and another vegetable of different color (white or yellow). Red cabbage prepared with apples a rather sweet dish; do not serve at same meal with other sweet vegetables, like carrots, beets or sweet potatoes.

QUICK-COOKED CABBAGE

This Chart Gives Approximate Food Values for CABBAGE.

1 PORTION CONTAINS APPROXIMATELY	VITAMINS	A	B	C	G	MINERALS	CALC.	PHOS.	IRON	ANALYSIS	CAL.	PROT.
		179 I.U.	52 I.U.	1293 I.U.	.45 MGS.		268 MGS.	247 MGS.	.1 MGS.		76	3 GMS.
BLACK PART OF COLUMN SHOWS HOW MUCH OF DAILY NEED IS SUPPLIED BY ONE PORTION												
AVERAGE DAILY NEED		5000 I.U.	600 I.U.	1500 I.U.	2.7 MGS.		800 MGS.	1320 MGS.	12 MGS.		2000-3000	70 GMS.

INGREDIENTS:

1 large head cabbage	2 tablespoons butter
½ teaspoon salt	½ cup rich milk (optional)
¼ teaspoon pepper	

DIRECTIONS: Remove any damaged leaves. Quarter, slice or shred (depending upon use) and wash under running water. Place in boiling water to cover and cook uncovered just until tender, 7 to 12 minutes, depending upon size of pieces. Quartered sections require longest cooking time. Add salt and pepper just before removing from heat. Drain, reserving pot liquor for future use. Add butter, and milk if desired.

CREAMED CABBAGE

INGREDIENTS:

3 cups shredded cabbage	3 tablespoons flour
1 cup cabbage pot liquor	½ teaspoon salt
½ cup evaporated or rich milk	⅛ teaspoon pepper
3 tablespoons butter	2 tablespoons minced parsley

DIRECTIONS: Quick-cook cabbage as directed in basic recipe; drain, reserving pot liquor. Combine pot liquor and milk. Melt butter in saucepan, reduce heat to medium, and stir in flour and seasonings until smooth and well blended. Add pot liquor and milk gradually, stirring constantly until mixture thickens and boils. Stir in parsley and cabbage and cook about 2 minutes, just until cabbage is reheated.

VITAMINS	1 PORTION CONTAINS APPROXIMATELY	DAILY NEED
A	76	5000 I.U.
B	43	600 I.U.
C	964	1500 I.U.
G	.33	2.7 MGS.

RED CABBAGE AND APPLES

INGREDIENTS:

3 cups finely shredded red cabbage	⅛ teaspoon ground cloves
2 cups sliced tart apples	3 tablespoons sugar
3 cups boiling water	1 teaspoon salt
¼ teaspoon nutmeg	3 tablespoons lemon juice (or ¼ cup vinegar)

DIRECTIONS: Combine cabbage, apples, water, nutmeg and cloves. Simmer uncovered over medium heat about 20 to 25 minutes, just until tender. Add sugar, salt and lemon juice just before removing from heat. Serve in individual dishes with a dab of butter, if desired.

Leftover red cabbage delicious served cold as a relish. Store in tightly covered jar in refrigerator. Add more lemon juice just before serving to give fresh flavor as well as additional Vitamin C.

BALANCED MEAL SUGGESTIONS: *Lunch* or *Supper*—Cheese Soufflé; *Red Cabbage and Apples;* Citrus Cup; Oatmeal Cookies; Milk.

Dinner—Carrot and Celery Salad; Lamb-Liver Patties; *Green Cabbage;* Mashed Potatoes; Baked Apples.

257

CARROTS

COMMENTS: Cheapness, availability and popularity make carrots one of most important protective vegetables. Higher in vitamin value when eaten raw in salads or as an appetizer, but still an excellent source of protective factors when cooked.

Recommended for reducers and the elderly because of very low calorie content and high water content. Latter virtue makes carrots good choice for serving at a meal with concentrated foods. One of best "combiners" among vegetables. Flavor blends well with almost any green vegetable, and is traditional for addition to vegetable soups and all sorts of stews.

Carrot tops are too often thrown away by housewives. Are a fine source of vitamins and minerals, and should always be saved for use in Cooked Mixed Greens (page 266), soups (especially Spring Consommé and Cream of Spinach Greens Soup, pages 235 and 237), or stews. Use tender leaves and stems. Flavor is characteristically strong and somewhat bitter; hence, combination dishes are recommended.

QUICK-COOKED CARROTS

This Chart Gives Approximate Food Values for CARROTS.

1 PORTION CONTAINS APPROXIMATELY	VITAMINS	3353 I.U. A	34 I.U. B	64 I.U. C	.23 MGS. G	MINERALS	71 MGS. CALC.	59 MGS. PHOS.	.9 MGS. IRON	ANALYSIS	78 CAL.	2 GMS. PROT.
BLACK PART OF COLUMN SHOWS HOW MUCH OF DAILY NEED IS SUPPLIED BY ONE PORTION												
AVERAGE DAILY NEED		5000 I.U.	600 I.U.	1500 I.U.	2.7 MGS.		800 MGS.	1320 MGS.	12 MGS.		2000-3000	70 GMS.

INGREDIENTS:

2 pounds (about 12 medium-sized) carrots

½ teaspoon salt

2 tablespoons butter

DIRECTIONS: Small-sized carrots intended for serving whole need not be scraped; larger, more mature ones can be skinned after cooking. Carrots to be sliced or diced should be scraped before cooking. Slice or quarter lengthwise. Drop into 1 inch boiling water. When water has again reached full boil, cover utensil; cook about 15 to 25 minutes, just until tender, depending upon size and maturity of carrots. Add salt and butter just before removing from heat. Serve with pot liquor in individual dishes.

Parsley Carrots—Quick-cook carrots as directed in basic recipe. When tender, drain, reserving pot liquor for future use. Add butter to drained carrots in pan. Gently turn carrots in melted butter until well coated. Sprinkle with 4 tablespoons minced parsley. *Approximate vitamin values per portion: Vit. A—4103 I.U.; Vit. B₁—34 I.U.; Vit. C—134 I.U.; Vit. G—.24 Mg.*

Carrots and Onions—Shred very fine 10 medium-sized carrots and mince 2 medium-sized onions. Place in pan with 1 cup boiling water, cover tightly and quick-cook about 8 to 10 minutes, just until tender. Add ½ teaspoon salt, 2 tablespoons butter, 2 tablespoons minced parsley and 1 cup rich milk just long enough before serving to heat milk. Serve in individual dishes with pot liquor. *Approximate vitamin values per portion: Vit. A—3779 I.U.; Vit. B₁—39 I.U.; Vit. C—132 I.U.; Vit. G—.31 Mg.*

Carrots and Peas—Dice 6 medium-sized carrots. Combine with 1½ cups shelled peas and quick-cook, according to directions in basic recipe, about 15 minutes. Sprinkle with 2 tablespoons minced parsley, season, dress with butter and serve in individual dishes with pot liquor. *Approximate vitamin values per portion: Vit. A—2481 I.U.; Vit. B₁—34 I.U.; Vit. C—228 I.U.; Vit. G—.23 Mg.*

VITAMINS	1 PORTION CONTAINS APPROXIMATELY	DAILY NEED	
A	3728	5000 I.U.	**CARROT RING**
B₁	28	600 I.U.	
C	72	1500 I.U.	
G	.23	2.7 MGS.	

INGREDIENTS:

3 cups diced carrots
2 tablespoons butter
¼ teaspoon salt

⅛ teaspoon pepper
2 tablespoons minced parsley

DIRECTIONS: Quick-cook carrots as directed in basic recipe. Drain, reserving pot liquor for future use, and rice or mash. Stir in remaining ingredients. Place in buttered ring mold and reheat in moderate oven (375° F.) about 10 minutes. Unmold and serve garnished with parsley.

BALANCED MEAL SUGGESTIONS: *Lunch* — Pineapple Coleslaw; *Carrot Ring* (with Creamed Peas); Whole Grain Toast; Stewed Rhubarb; Milk.

CAULIFLOWER

COMMENTS: Cauliflower rich source of all vitamins except Vitamin A; hence combinations with cheese, tomatoes or other foods high in Vitamin A, good nutritionally. High water content of cauliflower makes it suitable for balancing concentrated foods at meal. Excellent for reducers, as extremely low in calorie content.

Belongs to cabbage group of vegetables, and, like other members, is frequently a cause of allergic reactions. However, the digestive distress many people suffer after eating cauliflower is often due to improper cooking of vegetable. Correctly cooked, it rarely disturbs those not allergic to it.

Serve cauliflower at any balanced dinner along with a green vegetable for color contrast. Do not serve with pale squash, potatoes or turnips, unless bright-colored vegetable also accompanies them.

Make Vitamin C pot liquor (to add to soups, sauces, etc.) by dropping outside leaves of cauliflower into boiling water and boiling for 2 minutes.

QUICK-COOKED CAULIFLOWER

This Chart Gives Approximate Food Values for CAULIFLOWER.

	VITAMINS				MINERALS			ANALYSIS	
	A	B	C	G	CALC.	PHOS.	IRON	CAL.	PROT.
1 PORTION CONTAINS APPROXIMATELY	462 I.U.	58 I.U.	679 I.U.	.28 MGS.	187 MGS.	92 MGS.	2.4 MGS.	36	2 GMS.
BLACK PART OF COLUMN SHOWS HOW MUCH OF DAILY NEED IS SUPPLIED BY ONE PORTION									
AVERAGE DAILY NEED	5000 I.U.	600 I.U.	1500 I.U.	2.7 MGS.	800 MGS.	1320 MGS.	12 MGS.	2000-3000	70 GMS.

INGREDIENTS:

2-pound head of cauliflower
1 teaspoon salt
1 tablespoon butter
2 tablespoons minced parsley

DIRECTIONS: Remove leaves, stalks, stem and any discoloration on flowerets. Save leaves for making soups or pot liquors, and stems for eating raw. Break head into flowerets and wash well under running water; do not soak. Drop flowerets into 2 inches boiling water, and cook uncovered 15 to 20 minutes. Salt just before removing from heat. Serve in individual dishes with pot liquor to which has been added butter and parsley. For variety, dress cauliflower with Tomato Juice Cream Sauce (page 217).

Cauliflower au Gratin—Prepare and cook cauliflower as directed in basic recipe. Drain, place in casserole dish and cover with Cheese Sauce (page 218) or with ¼ cup grated cheese. Bake in moderate oven (375° F.) just until cheese is browned. *Approximate vitamin values per portion: Vit. A —558 I.U.; Vit. B₁—48 I.U.; Vit. C—403 I.U.; Vit. G—.31 Mg.*

BALANCED MEAL SUGGESTIONS: *Lunch*—Tomato Juice; Vegetable Plate (with *Cauliflower au Gratin*); Honey-nut Cookies; Milk.

CELERY

COMMENTS: Green celery 100 times richer in Vitamin A than white or blanched celery, which has practically none of this factor.

Apart from vitamin value, celery has a tonic effect on digestive system. Low in calorie content and high in water content, which makes it a good food for balancing concentrated foods at a meal. Adds to alkaline reserves. Fairly high in roughage; not recommended for soft diets.

QUICK-COOKED CELERY

This Chart Gives Approximate Food Values for CELERY.

	VITAMINS				MINERALS			ANALYSIS	
1 PORTION CONTAINS APPROXIMATELY	1571 I.U.	25 I.U.	142 I.U.	22 MGS.	105 MGS.	74 MGS.	1.1 MGS.	21 CAL.	.5 GMS.
	A	B	C	G	CALC.	PHOS.	IRON		
BLACK PART OF COLUMN SHOWS HOW MUCH OF DAILY NEED IS SUPPLIED BY ONE PORTION									
									PROT.
AVERAGE DAILY NEED	5000 I.U.	600 I.U.	1500 I.U.	2.7 MGS.	800 MGS.	1320 MGS.	12 MGS.	2000-3000	70 GMS.

INGREDIENTS:

3 cups diced celery

1 teaspoon salt

1 tablespoon butter

2 tablespoons minced parsley

DIRECTIONS: Scrub celery and remove any damaged stalks or leaves. Trim root. Quarter bunch and, holding quarters together, cut through all four sections at once to dice. Place diced celery in cold water to cover and move pieces about to remove any remaining sand. Drain. Drop diced celery into ½ inch boiling water. When water has again reached full boil, cover pan and cook 10 to 12 minutes, just until celery is tender. Salt before removing from heat. Serve in individual dishes with pot liquor to which has been added butter and minced parsley.

Celery, String Beans and Onion—Combine 1 cup diced celery, 1 pound string beans (shredded) and 1 small onion (minced); quick-cook as directed above in basic recipe, about 15 minutes, just until vegetables are tender. Season, add butter, and serve in individual dishes with pot liquor. *Approximate vitamin values per portion: Vit. A—948 I.U.; Vit. B₁—16 I.U.; Vit. C—167 I.U.; Vit. G—.09 Mg.*

BALANCED MEAL SUGGESTIONS: *Dinner*—Tomato Salad; Veal Loaf; Baked Potatoes; *Celery, String Beans and Onion;* Baked Apples.

CHARD

COMMENTS: Chard should be eaten chiefly for its superior richness in Vitamins A and G. Very low in calorie content, so recommended for reducers. Because of sulphur compounds, may cause stomach upsets in some individuals. Seems to be readily digested, however, if cooked with potatoes.

Chard really two vegetables; the leafy greens, and the firm, crisp stalks and midribs. Use together or separately, as desired.

QUICK-COOKED CHARD LEAVES

This Chart Gives Approximate Food Values for CHARD.

1 PORTION CONTAINS APPROXIMATELY	VITAMINS				MINERALS			ANALYSIS	
	A	B	C	G	CALC.	PHOS.	IRON	CAL.	PROT.
	19,826 I.U.	66 I.U.	603 I.U.	1.3 MGS.	206 MGS.	95 MGS.	9.4 MGS.	78	6 GMS.
BLACK PART OF COLUMN SHOWS HOW MUCH OF DAILY NEED IS SUPPLIED BY ONE PORTION									
AVERAGE DAILY NEED	5000 I.U.	600 I.U.	1500 I.U.	2.7 MGS.	800 MGS.	1320 MGS.	12 MGS.	2000-3000 CAL.	70 GMS.

INGREDIENTS:

3 pounds chard
1 teaspoon salt

1 tablespoon butter
6 lemon wedges

DIRECTIONS: Remove wilted or damaged leaves from chard plant. Wash well in several waters, and separate leaves from coarse midribs and stalks or stems. Drop chard leaves into ½ inch boiling water. When water has again reached full boil, cover utensil and cook about 7 minutes. Salt just before removing from heat. Drain, reserving pot liquor. Chop and serve in individual dishes with seasoned pot liquor to which butter has been added. Accompany with lemon wedges.

Chard Leaves and Potatoes—Combine 3 pounds chard leaves with 1 cup grated or minced raw potatoes and 1 small onion (grated). Quick-cook as directed in basic recipe. Season and serves. *Approximate vitamin values per portion: Vit. A—19,787 I.U.; Vit. B₁—67 I.U.; Vit. C—465 I.U.; Vit. G—1.29 Mg.*

Chard Stalks—Tie whole chard stalks together and cook as in basic recipe for Asparagus (page 246) ; or dice and place in ½ inch boiling water, cover and cook about 15 minutes, just until tender. Salt just before removing from heat. Dress with butter and serve with pot liquor. May be served alone, with Vegetable Pot Liquor Cream Sauce (page 217) or with leaves.

CORN

COMMENTS: Yellow corn an excellent source of Vitamin A; white corn probably contains none of this protective element. Corn itself not especially high in calorie content, as is usually supposed, and not very much of it is digested. Actually, the butter used with corn is what makes a dish taboo for reducers, who could eat corn safely with a bare minimum of butter. Not recommended for soft diets, as high in roughage.

QUICK-COOKED CORN

This Chart Gives Approximate Food Values for CORN.

	VITAMINS				MINERALS			ANALYSIS	
	A	B	C	G	CALC.	PHOS.	IRON	CAL.	PROT.
1 PORTION CONTAINS APPROXIMATELY	838 I.U.	29 I.U.	140 I.U.	.12 MGS.	8 MGS.	105 MGS.	.5 MGS.	180 CAL.	3 GMS.
BLACK PART OF COLUMN SHOWS HOW MUCH OF DAILY NEED IS SUPPLIED BY ONE PORTION									
AVERAGE DAILY NEED	5000 I.U.	600 I.U.	1500 I.U.	2.7 MGS.	800 MGS.	1320 MGS.	12 MGS.	2000-3000 CAL.	70 GMS.

INGREDIENTS: 6 to 12 ears corn

DIRECTIONS: In large kettle, boil enough water to cover ears of corn. Remove husks and silk of ears, trimming ends if necessary. Drop corn into boiling water and cook covered 5 to 10 minutes, depending upon age and freshness of corn. Remove from water as soon as milk in kernels is set; overcooking will make corn tough. Serve ears piping hot, to be buttered and seasoned individually at table.

Stewed Fresh-Cut Corn—Use 6 to 12 ears of corn as desired. Cut from cob and place kernels in upper part of double boiler with 3 to 6 tablespoons cream or rich milk, depending upon amount of corn, and 2 to 3 tablespoons butter. Cook about 10 to 15 minutes. Season with 1 teaspoon salt and ⅛ teaspoon pepper, and serve in individual dishes.

Succotash—Quick-cook separately 1 cup green lima beans (as directed in basic recipe on page 248) and 2 cups fresh-cut or canned corn (see recipe above). Combine vegetables, 2 tablespoons butter, bean pot liquor and ½ cup rich milk or cream. Reheat and season with 2 teaspoons salt. *Approximate vitamin values per portion: Vit. A—655 I.U.; Vit. B₁—36 I.U.; Vit. C—137 I.U.; Vit. G—.17 I.U.*

Scalloped Corn and Tomatoes—Combine 2 cups canned (whole-kernel style) or fresh-cut cooked corn, 1 cup canned or fresh tomatoes and ½ cup grated sharp cheese in a greased casserole dish. Bake in medium oven (375° F.) about 10 minutes, until cheese is melted. For additional flavor, add 3 tablespoons of minced and sautéed onion before baking.

CORN WITH GREEN PEPPERS

VITAMINS	1 PORTION CONTAINS APPROXIMATELY	DAILY NEED
A	1069	5000 I.U.
B₁	28	600 I.U.
C	809	1500 I.U.
G	.12	2.7 MGS.

INGREDIENTS:

3 slices bacon
(or 3 tablespoons butter)
4 tablespoons chopped green pepper

3 tablespoons minced onion
2 cups cooked or canned corn
3 tablespoons minced pimiento

DIRECTIONS: Pan-broil bacon until golden brown. Remove from pan and crisp on soft paper. When cool, break into small pieces. Add onion and pepper to melted fat in pan and sauté until onion is yellow, about 3 minutes. Add corn, minced bacon and pimiento. Cook just until corn is thoroughly heated, about 5 minutes. Stir occasionally to prevent burning.

BALANCED MEAL SUGGESTIONS: *Lunch* or *Supper*—Raw Carrot and Celery Strips; Broiled Bacon (optional); *Succotash;* Rye Bread; Stewed Prunes and Apricots; Milk.

Dinner—Combination Salad; Baked Fillets of Halibut; *Corn-on-the-Cob;* String Beans with Onion; Lemon Meringue Pie.

EGGPLANT

COMMENTS: Eggplant not high in any of the usual protective nutrients found in other vegetables, but estimated to be an outstanding source of Vitamin G, which is not found in great abundance in any other vegetable except turnip greens. Very low in calorie content and high in water content. Excellent for reducers and to balance concentrated foods at meal.

Reputation eggplant has for being difficult to digest is result of improper cooking methods. Old-fashioned cooks always fried or sautéed eggplant, thus making it a greasy dish. Much better nutritionally to add needed flavor with tomatoes, onion, mushrooms, etc.

Flavor of eggplant alone not especially enjoyable; hence it is usually combined with vegetables of compatible flavors, as in Eggplant Creole.

EGGPLANT CREOLE

This Chart Gives Approximate Food Values for EGGPLANT CREOLE.

1 PORTION CONTAINS APPROXIMATELY	VITAMINS	A 1086 I.U.	B 50 I.U.	C 707 I.U.	G 1.5 MGS.	MINERALS	CALC. 31 MGS.	PHOS. 94 MGS.	IRON 2.5 MGS.	ANALYSIS	CAL. 111	PROT. 3 GMS.
BLACK PART OF COLUMN SHOWS HOW MUCH OF DAILY NEED IS SUPPLIED BY ONE PORTION												
AVERAGE DAILY NEED		5000 I.U.	600 I.U.	1500 I.U.	2.7 MGS.		800 MGS.	1320 MGS.	12 MGS.		2000-3000	70 GMS.

INGREDIENTS:

- 1 medium-sized eggplant
- ½ pound (2 cups) mushrooms
- 4 tablespoons butter
- 1 medium-sized onion, minced
- 1 green pepper, chopped
- 1½ cups fresh or canned tomatoes
- ½ teaspoon salt
- ½ teaspoon sugar
- ⅛ teaspoon pepper

DIRECTIONS: Pare eggplant and chop or dice into small pieces. Wash and slice mushrooms. Melt butter in large skillet, add onions, peppers and mushrooms, and sauté until onions are yellow, about 3 minutes. Add eggplant and tomatoes, cover and simmer about 20 to 25 minutes, just until eggplant is tender. Add seasoning and serve.

BALANCED MEAL SUGGESTIONS: *Dinner*—Waldorf Salad; Broiled Liver; Parsley Potatoes; *Eggplant Creole;* Citrus Sherbet.

MIXED GREENS

COMMENTS: Many greens usually served raw (dandelion, escarole, lettuce, etc.) excellent when mixed with others in cooked mixed greens dish.

Because of bland flavor of some greens (lettuce, spinach, chard, kale, kohlrabi and broccoli) and strong flavor of others (chicory, endive, escarole, turnip tops, beet greens, carrot greens, dandelion greens and mustard greens), combination of greens often desirable. However, usually only two greens are combined—never more than three—as individual allergies must be guarded against.

From nutritional point of view, greens a superior dish to supply Vitamins A and C, and the minerals iron and copper. Low in calorie content, so excellent for reducers.

Many vegetable tops normally thrown away as just so much waste may go into mixed greens dish. Since tops are often even better protective foods than roots, mixed dish practical.

Serve at dinner meal to balance concentrated foods, along with white or yellow vegetable for color contrast.

QUICK-COOKED GREENS

This Chart Gives Approximate Food Values for MIXED GREENS.

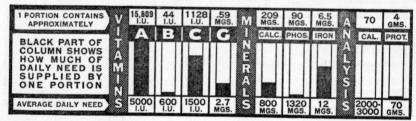

1 PORTION CONTAINS APPROXIMATELY	VITAMINS				MINERALS			ANALYSIS	
	A	B	C	G	CALC.	PHOS.	IRON	CAL.	PROT.
	15,809 I.U.	44 I.U.	1128 I.U.	.59 MGS.	209 MGS.	90 MGS.	6.5 MGS.	70	4 GMS.
AVERAGE DAILY NEED	5000 I.U.	600 I.U.	1500 I.U.	2.7 MGS.	800 MGS.	1320 MGS.	12 MGS.	2000-3000	70 GMS.

BLACK PART OF COLUMN SHOWS HOW MUCH OF DAILY NEED IS SUPPLIED BY ONE PORTION

INGREDIENTS:

3 pounds greens
1 teaspoon salt

2 tablespoons butter
1 teaspoon onion juice

DIRECTIONS: Prepare desired greens as directed under individual listing of vegetables, and wash thoroughly in several waters, removing any wilted or damaged leaves. Boil just enough water to cover greens in saucepan, then add selected greens according to following cooking times: escarole, chicory, endive, kale, kohlrabi and carrot tops about 15 to 20 minutes; beet greens, spinach, chard and dandelion greens about 7 to 10 minutes; lettuce about 5 minutes. Should take no longer than about 20 minutes for the coarsest leaves to become tender. Drain, reserving pot liquor for future use. Chop together and place in individual dishes with seasoned pot liquor to which butter and onion juice have also been added.

BALANCED MEAL SUGGESTIONS: *Dinner*—Lettuce Salad, Russian Dressing; Chicken Fricassée; *Mixed Greens;* Carrots; Berry Pie.

KALE

COMMENTS: Kale one of most outstanding sources of Vitamin A; in fact, superior food in all vitamins except D. Should be eaten often when in season, as one serving will supply more than the daily Vitamin A requirement, and go far toward satisfying all the other vitamin needs. Kale rich in minerals as well. Low in calorie content and alkaline in reaction.

Kale mixed with potatoes enjoyable way to use this vegetable. Onions cooked with kale add pleasant flavor for those who may not like kale alone. Use either plain and quick-cooked, or mixed with other vegetables.

QUICK-COOKED KALE

This Chart Gives Approximate Food Values for KALE.

1 PORTION CONTAINS APPROXIMATELY	VITAMINS				MINERALS			ANALYSIS		
	A	B	C	G	CALC.	PHOS.	IRON		CAL.	PROT.
	23,093 I.U.	34 I.U.	1087 I.U.	.92 MGS.	303 MGS.	111 MGS.	4 MGS.		65	3 GMS.
BLACK PART OF COLUMN SHOWS HOW MUCH OF DAILY NEED IS SUPPLIED BY ONE PORTION										
AVERAGE DAILY NEED	5000 I.U.	600 I.U.	1500 I.U.	2.7 MGS.	800 MGS.	1320 MGS.	12 MGS.		2000-3000	70 GMS.

INGREDIENTS:

2 pounds kale
1 teaspoon salt

¼ teaspoon pepper
2 tablespoons butter

DIRECTIONS: Remove root ends, coarse stems and any wilted or discolored leaves. Wash thoroughly in several waters. If leaves are large, cut into smaller pieces. Drop leaves into enough boiling water to cover and cook covered about 15 to 20 minutes, just until tender. Drain, reserving pot liquor, and chop. Add seasonings and butter to a little of the pot liquor (save most of it for other uses). Pour over chopped kale.

Kale and Onions—Prepare and cook kale as directed in basic recipe. Pan-broil 3 slices bacon in hot skillet. Drain on absorbent paper and dice. Mince 2 medium-sized onions and sauté in bacon drippings until golden brown. Drain and chop kale. Add onions and diced bacon. Season and serve. *Approximate vitamin values per portion: Vit. A—23,002 I.U.; Vit. B$_1$—36 I.U.; Vit. C—1097 I.U.; Vit. G—.93 Mg.*

BALANCED MEAL SUGGESTIONS: *Dinner* — Coleslaw; Baked Oysters; *Kale and Onions;* Carrots; Cheese Cake.

KOHLRABI

COMMENTS: Kohlrabi unusually high in Vitamin C; hence extra care should be taken in refrigerating and cooking vegetable to avoid destruction of this perishable vitamin. Nutritionally best eaten raw, cut into strips.

Combination of high Vitamin C content, high water content and low calorie content makes kohlrabies particularly good food for reducers and the elderly. As member of cabbage group, may produce flatulence when badly cooked.

Use as main dinner vegetable to offset concentrated foods at meal. Serve along with yellow or white vegetable for color contrast.

QUICK-COOKED KOHLRABI

This Chart Gives Approximate Food Values for KOHLRABI.

1 PORTION CONTAINS APPROXIMATELY	VITAMINS				MINERALS			ANALYSIS	
	507 I.U.	14 I.U.	1130 I.U.	.11 MGS.	110 MGS.	65 MGS.	.8 MGS.	39	2 GMS.
	A	B	C	G	CALC.	PHOS.	IRON	CAL.	PROT.
BLACK PART OF COLUMN SHOWS HOW MUCH OF DAILY NEED IS SUPPLIED BY ONE PORTION									
AVERAGE DAILY NEED	5000 I.U.	600 I.U.	1500 I.U.	2.7 MGS.	800 MGS.	1320 MGS.	12 MGS.	2000-3000	70 GMS.

INGREDIENTS:

1½ pounds kohlrabi (about 12 medium-sized kohlrabies)
1 teaspoon salt

1 tablespoon butter
3 tablespoons evaporated or rich milk (optional)

DIRECTIONS: Remove root ends, stems and leaves of kohlrabi, reserving tender stems and leaves for future use (see Quick-Cooked Greens, page 266).

Wash, pare and dice or slice thin. Drop into enough boiling water to cover, and cook uncovered about 20 to 30 minutes, just until tender. Drain and place in individual dishes. To a little of the pot liquor (save most of it for other uses), add seasoning, butter and, if desired, evaporated or rich milk. Pour over kohlrabi and serve in individual dishes.

BALANCED MEAL SUGGESTIONS: *Dinner*—Mixed Greens Salad; Baked Fish; *Kohlrabi;* Baked Potatoes; Citrus Sherbet.

LEEKS

COMMENTS: Germicidal quality of whole onion family (garlic, scallions, etc.) shared by leeks. Good protective vitamin values also. Very low in calorie content; hence of great value to reducers. Excellent in soups.

QUICK-COOKED LEEKS

This Chart Gives Approximate Food Values for LEEKS.

	VITAMINS				MINERALS			ANALYSIS	
1 PORTION CONTAINS APPROXIMATELY	748 I.U.	29 I.U.	245 I.U.	.25 MGS.	86 MGS.	79 MGS.	.6 MGS.	52	3 GMS.
	A	B	C	G	CALC.	PHOS.	IRON	CAL.	PROT.
BLACK PART OF COLUMN SHOWS HOW MUCH OF DAILY NEED IS SUPPLIED BY ONE PORTION									
AVERAGE DAILY NEED	5000 I.U.	600 I.U.	1500 I.U.	2.7 MGS.	800 MGS.	1320 MGS.	12 MGS.	2000-3000	70 GMS.

INGREDIENTS:

12 leeks
½ teaspoon salt
1 tablespoon butter

3 tablespoons evaporated or rich milk (optional)

DIRECTIONS: Remove green tops from leeks to within 2 inches of white stalks (save tops for use in soups, stews and gravies). Remove root end and thin, paper-like covering of stalks and any wilted or discolored portions. Wash thoroughly. Cut into 1-inch slices. Drop sliced leeks into enough boiling water to cover vegetable, and cook uncovered about 10 to 15 minutes. Salt just before removing from heat. Drain, reserving liquid, and place leek slices in individual dishes. To part of pot liquor (save most of it for other uses), add butter, and milk if desired. Pour over leeks and serve.

Leeks and Potatoes—Dice 3 medium-sized potatoes, and quick-cook together with 1½ cups sliced leeks, as directed in basic recipe, about 15 to 18 minutes. Season, add butter and 2 tablespoons minced parsley. Serve in individual dishes. *Approximate vitamin values per portion: Vit. A—606 I.U.; Vit. B₁—16 I.U.; Vit. C—174 I.U.; Vit. G—.1 Mg.*

BALANCED MEAL SUGGESTIONS: *Lunch*—Vegetable Juice Cocktail; Scrambled Eggs; *Leeks and Potatoes;* Fresh Berries; Milk.

Dinner—Lettuce and Tomato Salad; Roast Leg of Lamb; *Leeks,* Hollandaise Sauce; Baked Sweet Potatoes; Fruit Cup.

LEGUMES

COMMENTS: Beans, peas and lentils are known as legumes, and are the only vegetable group high in protein content. When dried, they are sufficiently rich in this food factor to serve occasionally as meat substitutes, although no legume but soybeans is considered Class A protein. Like other protein dishes (meats, fish, etc.) legumes rich in the Vitamin B complex and high in calcium and phosphorus; should not be used in menus as a potato substitute.

Because of type of protein they contain, dried legumes may sometimes be used during week's menus to provide variety, and allow one meatless, fishless day. Soybeans, above all other legumes, outstanding for protein content, as well as richness in Vitamin B complex. However, there are so many varieties of soybeans, each with its own texture and varying cooking time, that no recipes have been given. Until certain standards for this product have been set up, and wider distribution achieved, soybeans will not have the place they should in the American diet. Navy beans have inferior quality of protein; combine with other legumes to use as meat substitute.

Legume dishes are heavy and filling. Use them as main course of dinner meal, balanced with light, leafy or root vegetables low in calorie content. Legumes are concentrated foods, especially good for cold-weather meals. High in calorie value, though not much higher than meats for which they substitute. May be used occasionally by reducers to replace meat course.

Most legumes lend themselves to making of main-dish soups (page 238), loaves, casserole dishes, etc., although favorite way of preparing them is baked, often combined with tomatoes for flavor. Any legume dish may be substituted for one mentioned in Balanced Meal Suggestions.

BAKED NAVY BEANS

This Chart Gives Approximate Food Values for BAKED NAVY BEANS.

1 PORTION CONTAINS APPROXIMATELY	VITAMINS	A 30 I.U.	B 169 I.U.	C 33 I.U.	G 1.0 MGS.	MINERALS	CALC. 84 MGS.	PHOS. 287 MGS.	IRON 5 MGS.	ANALYSIS	CAL. 314	PROT. 18 GMS.
BLACK PART OF COLUMN SHOWS HOW MUCH OF DAILY NEED IS SUPPLIED BY ONE PORTION												
AVERAGE DAILY NEED		5000 I.U.	600 I.U.	1500 I.U.	2.7 MGS.		800 MGS.	1320 MGS.	12 MGS.		2000-3000	70 GMS.

INGREDIENTS:

2 cups dried navy (white pea) or marrow beans

6 cups boiling water (approximate)

¼ pound bacon (or 4 tablespoons butter or rendered, seasoned poultry fat)

¼ cup brown sugar (or ¼ to ½ cup molasses)

2 teaspoons salt

½ teaspoon dry mustard

1 cup bean pot liquor

DIRECTIONS: Long soaking is not necessary but soaking overnight does shorten cooking time; hence is more economical of fuel. Navy or marrow beans soaked overnight cook in 1½ to 2 hours; unsoaked beans require 2 to 3 hours to become mealy.

Wash and pick over beans carefully, especially those purchased in bulk, to remove any small stones or gravel. If beans are soaked, use soaking water for cooking as it contains water-soluble Vitamin B_1. Those to be baked need less actual cooking than those used for soups.

Simmer beans in a covered utensil about 1 hour, if soaked overnight; and 1½ to 2 hours, if not soaked. Test for tenderness by blowing on a spoonful of beans; if skins burst, beans are sufficiently tender for baking. Drain beans, reserving pot liquor, and place in casserole or bean pot. Bury bacon in beans, leaving rind exposed. Mix sugar (or molasses), salt and mustard with 1 cup bean liquor. Pour over beans, and bake covered in slow oven (250° F.) 6 to 8 hours. Add enough extra water or bean liquor to keep beans covered. During last hour of baking, remove cover so that beans will have brown crust on top, and bacon will become brown and crisp.

Canned Baked Bean Stew—Pan-broil 2 strips bacon. Drain on paper towel. Sauté 1 green pepper, minced, and 1 medium-sized onion, minced, in bacon drippings in skillet about 5 minutes, stirring occasionally. Add tomatoes, beans and diced bacon, and cook until heated, about 10 minutes.

271

BAKED DRIED LIMA BEANS

INGREDIENTS:

1½ cups dried lima beans
4 cups boiling water
 (approximate)
¼ pound sliced bacon
 (or 2 tablespoons butter)
¼ cup diced onion

¼ cup diced green pepper
½ cup bean pot liquor
1 teaspoon salt
½ cup evaporated or rich milk
3 tablespoons chopped parsley

DIRECTIONS: Long soaking is not necessary. Simply wash beans thoroughly and place in saucepan with water. Simmer, do not boil. Add more water if needed, but remember to use just enough water so that there will not be more than about 1 cup to drain off when beans are tender.

When tender (in about 1½ to 2½ hours, depending upon type and age of beans), drain beans, reserving pot liquor. In skillet, pan-broil bacon about 3 minutes. Remove to paper towel, drain and dice. Sauté onion and green pepper in 2 tablespoons bacon drippings (or butter) over medium heat about 5 minutes, stirring occasionally. Add beans, pot liquor, salt and milk, mix well and turn into casserole. Bake about 1 hour in moderate oven (350° F.) until liquid has thickened slightly. Garnish with parsley.

Baked Lima Beans with Tomato Sauce—Follow directions in basic recipe. Omit milk and use 1 cup (1 can) condensed tomato soup.

BAKED KIDNEY BEANS WITH CHEESE

VITAMINS	1 PORTION CONTAINS APPROXIMATELY	DAILY NEED
A	681	5000 I.U.
B	45	600 I.U.
C	37	1500 I.U.
G	.41	2.7 MGS.

INGREDIENTS:

2 cups dried kidney beans
6 cups boiling water
 (approximate)
1 medium-sized onion, minced

2 teaspoons salt
2 tablespoons butter
1 cup condensed tomato soup
¼ cup grated cheese (optional)

DIRECTIONS: Wash and pick over beans. Soaking is not necessary. Add water and onion to beans, cover and simmer just until beans are mealy yet still keep their shape—about 1½ to 2 hours. Add more water after 1 hour, only if necessary. Simmer in just enough water as needed, so there will be not more than 1 cup to drain off when beans are cooked. Add salt, butter and condensed tomato soup to cover. Sprinkle with cheese if desired. Place in baking dish and bake in moderate oven (350° F.) about 1 hour.

V I T A M I N S	1 PORTION CONTAINS APPROXIMATELY	DAILY NEED
A	1975	5000 I.U.
B	411	600 I.U.
C	671	1500 I.U.
G	1.1	2.7 MGS.

PIMIENTO-BEAN LOAF

INGREDIENTS:

2 cups dried beans (lima, navy or lentils)
2 quarts boiling water
1 cup soft bread crumbs
2 eggs, slightly beaten
1 tablespoon minced onion

6 tablespoons chopped pimiento
4 tablespoons minced parsley
1 teaspoon salt
1/4 teaspoon pepper
1/4 teaspoon thyme (optional)

DIRECTIONS: Simmer beans (or lentils) in boiling water until tender. Drain, mash and add remaining ingredients. Mix well and turn into buttered loaf pan. Bake in moderate oven (350° F.) about 30 to 40 minutes.

KIDNEY BEAN LOAF

INGREDIENTS:

2 cups dried kidney beans
2 quarts boiling water
2 tablespoons butter
1 green pepper, minced
1 medium-sized onion, minced
1 teaspoon salt

1/8 teaspoon pepper
1 cup (1 8-ounce can) tomato sauce
4 tablespoons peanut butter (optional)

DIRECTIONS: Simmer kidney beans in boiling water until tender. Drain and mash. Melt butter in skillet and sauté green pepper and onion about 5 minutes. Add tomato sauce, seasoning and peanut butter. Stir constantly until smooth and well blended. Add to beans and mix well. Turn into buttered loaf pan and bake in moderate oven (350° F.) about 40 minutes.

BALANCED MEAL SUGGESTIONS: *Lunch* or *Supper*—Green Pepper Coleslaw; *Kidney Beans with Cheese;* Brown Bread; Cherries; Milk.

MUSHROOMS

COMMENTS: Mushrooms used most frequently to give additional flavor to meat, vegetable or soup combinations, or to serve with steak, but delicious as a separate vegetable.

One of vegetables lowest in calorie content; almost no calories in cooked mushrooms (excluding butter or cream sauce, of course); hence, excellent for reducers. High water content makes mushrooms good to balance concentrated foods. This factor, plus easy digestibility of mushrooms, makes them recommended choice for elderly.

Fortification of mushrooms with foods rich in Vitamin A (peppers, pimiento, etc.) rounds out protective value of vegetable. Serving with cream sauce gives mushrooms staying qualities—hence suitable for luncheon dishes.

Mushrooms should not be picked in wild state except by experts. Danger of mistaking poisonous toadstools for edible fungus is too great.

BROILED MUSHROOMS

This Chart Gives Approximate Food Values for MUSHROOMS.

1 PORTION CONTAINS APPROXIMATELY	VITAMINS	159 I.U. A	18 I.U. B	I.U. C	.18 MGS. G	MINERALS	11 MGS. CALC.	75 MGS. PHOS.	2 MGS. IRON	ANALYSIS	43 CAL.	.1 GMS. PROT.
BLACK PART OF COLUMN SHOWS HOW MUCH OF DAILY NEED IS SUPPLIED BY ONE PORTION												
AVERAGE DAILY NEED		5000 I.U.	600 I.U.	1500 I.U.	2.7 MGS.		800 MGS.	1320 MGS.	12 MGS.		2000-3000	70 GMS.

INGREDIENTS:

1 pound mushrooms
3 tablespoons butter, melted

(or salad oil)
salt and pepper to taste

DIRECTIONS: Cut off woody ends of stems if present. Wash thoroughly, under running water, using a soft brush to remove dirt from top and bottom of rounded tops it necessary. Move back and forth in cold water several times. Drain and dry. Remove stems, reserving for other dishes. Dip caps in melted butter or olive oil and place round-side up on broiling pan. Broil for 2 minutes. Turn, drop small piece of butter into hollows, and season; broil about 7 or 8 minutes longer, just until tender.

274

VITAMINS	1 PORTION CONTAINS APPROXIMATELY	DAILY NEED
A	1126	5000 I.U.
B	114	600 I.U.
C	671	1500 I.U.
G	.3	2.7 MGS.

CREAMED MUSHROOMS WITH GREEN PEPPER

INGREDIENTS:

½ pound fresh mushrooms
  (2 cups, sliced)
4 tablespoons butter
½ green pepper, minced
1 tablespoon minced onion
3 tablespoons flour
½ teaspoon salt

⅛ teaspoon nutmeg
2 cups milk
¼ cup cream
1 egg yolk
6 slices toast
3 pimientos, cut into strips

DIRECTIONS: Wash and slice mushrooms. Melt butter in large skillet, add mushrooms, green pepper and onion, and cook over medium heat 5 minutes. Stir in flour, salt and nutmeg until well blended. Add milk gradually, stirring constantly over low heat until mixture thickens and boils. Add cream to slightly beaten egg yolk, beat well and stir into the sauce until blended. Cover toast with sauce, and garnish with pimiento strips.

VITAMINS	1 PORTION CONTAINS APPROXIMATELY	DAILY NEED
A	916	5000 I.U.
B	109	600 I.U.
C	35	1500 I.U.
G	.2	2.7 MGS.

MUSHROOMS IN SOUR CREAM

INGREDIENTS:

1 pound fresh mushrooms
  (4 cups, sliced)
4 tablespoons butter
1 cup sour cream

½ teaspoon salt
2 tablespoons minced parsley
6 slices toast or 1½ cups
  Boiled Rice (page 289)

DIRECTIONS: Wash and slice mushrooms. Sauté in butter about 5 minutes. Add sour cream and salt, and stir just until cream is heated. Do not boil. Stir in parsley. Serve on toast or boiled rice.

BALANCED MEAL SUGGESTIONS: *Lunch* — Asparagus Salad; *Creamed Mushrooms with Green Pepper* on Toast; Fruit Cup; Milk.

OKRA

COMMENTS: Because of bland flavor, okra generally eaten in combination dishes, such as Okra Creole, other mixtures of tomatoes, corn, green peppers and onions, or in soups (particularly chicken-rice). Nutritive value—as well as taste appeal—enhanced by such methods of cooking, as okra not very rich in any one vitamin.

Important chiefly for its vegetable mucin content. This substance of therapeutic value in cases of digestive disturbances, like stomach ulcers, because it is soothing and helps to neutralize hydrochloric acid. Okra very low in calorie content. Excellent for reducers.

OKRA CREOLE

This Chart Gives Approximate Food Values for OKRA.

1 PORTION CONTAINS APPROXIMATELY	VITAMINS	1101 I.U. A	44 I.U. B	501 I.U. C	.19 MGS. G	MINERALS	47 MGS. CALC.	120 MGS. PHOS.	1 MGS. IRON	ANALYSIS	122 CAL.	4 GMS. PROT.
BLACK PART OF COLUMN SHOWS HOW MUCH OF DAILY NEED IS SUPPLIED BY ONE PORTION												
AVERAGE DAILY NEED		5000 I.U.	600 I.U.	1500 I.U.	2.7 MGS.		800 MGS.	1320 MGS.	12 MGS.		2000-3000	70 GMS.

INGREDIENTS:

- ½ pound okra (or 2 cups canned okra)
- 1 cup green lima beans
- 6 large tomatoes (or 2 cups canned tomatoes)
- 1 cup cut or canned whole kernel corn
- ½ teaspoon salt
- ¼ teaspoon pepper
- 2 tablespoons butter

DIRECTIONS: Cut okra into ¼-inch slices and shell beans. Place in saucepan with just enough boiling water to cover. Cook in tightly covered pan 20 minutes. Add tomatoes and corn and simmer just until all fresh vegetables are tender or canned vegetables are thoroughly heated, about 10 minutes longer. If all vegetables used are canned, combine vegetables and simmer about 15 minutes. Add seasoning and butter and serve.

BALANCED MEAL SUGGESTIONS: *Dinner*—Cucumber Salad; Roast Veal or Broiled Veal Cutlet; *Okra Creole;* Parsley Potatoes; Blueberries.

ONIONS

COMMENTS: Mild onions and scallions used primarily as additions (raw or cooked) to other vegetables, soups, salads, stews, meat dishes, etc., but both stronger-flavored onions and scallions may be served plain boiled or creamed. All onions contain protective vitamin values as well as a special chemical called allyl aldehyde which makes onions a natural bactericide. Quick-cooked onion soup valuable therapeutically for both these reasons.

Sulphur compounds in onions not tolerated well by some people. Best for such individuals to eat mature onions cooked or young onions (scallions) raw. Plain onions low in calorie content; excellent for reducers.

Onions intended for flavoring agents in soups, vegetable combination dishes, etc., should be sautéed in a slight amount of butter for two or three minutes before adding to dish. This makes onions tender without long cooking.

Garlic, shallots and chives also members of the onion group; used chiefly as flavoring agents. Always use them sparingly, as taste is pungent.

BOILED ONIONS

This Chart Gives Approximate Food Values for ONIONS.

1 PORTION CONTAINS APPROXIMATELY	VITAMINS	655 I.U.	6 I.U.	214 I.U.	.04 MGS.	MINERALS	39 MGS.	54 MGS.	.8 MGS.	ANALYSIS	73	2 GMS.
		A	B	C	G		CALC.	PHOS.	IRON		CAL.	PROT.
BLACK PART OF COLUMN SHOWS HOW MUCH OF DAILY NEED IS SUPPLIED BY ONE PORTION												
AVERAGE DAILY NEED		5000 I.U.	600 I.U.	1500 I.U.	2.7 MGS.		800 MGS.	1320 MGS.	12 MGS.		2000-3000	70 GMS.

INGREDIENTS:

1½ pounds white onions	Vegetable Pot Liquor
salt and pepper	Cream Sauce, page 217)
2 tablespoons butter (or 1 cup	3 tablespoons minced parsley

DIRECTIONS: Wash and peel onions. Cook uncovered in plenty of water 20 to 30 minutes, until tender. Drain, reserve pot liquor, season and dress with butter. Serve with pot liquor and minced parsley in individual dishes. Or prepare Pot Liquor Cream Sauce, combine sauce and onions, and garnish with minced parsley.

CREAMED SCALLIONS OR LEEKS ON TOAST

INGREDIENTS:

3 bunches scallions or leeks
   (approximately 2 cups cut)
1 cup Pot Liquor Cream Sauce

6 thick slices fresh tomatoes
6 slices toast
2 tablespoons minced parsley

DIRECTIONS: Remove root ends, peel paper-like skin covering bulbs, and remove green tops to within 3 inches of white bulbs. Cut into 1-inch pieces and measure 2 cups. Quick-cook, uncovered, in just enough boiling water to cover, until tender, about 10 minutes. Drain, reserving pot liquor. Prepare Pot Liquor Cream Sauce, using reserved pot liquor; mix with scallions. Place tomatoes on toast; pour mixture over each portion. Sprinkle with parsley.

PARSNIPS

COMMENTS: Parsnips valuable for balancing concentrated starch or protein foods; have very high water content, and are low in calorie content. When combined with potatoes, have lower calorie content than potatoes alone.

Fortification of parsnips with parsley, eggs, etc. not only increases vitamin and mineral richness but also makes vegetable more popular. Parsnips cheap and easily available; most flavorfully used in combination dishes.

QUICK-COOKED PARSNIPS

This Chart Gives Approximate Food Values for PARSNIPS.

		VITAMINS				MINERALS			ANALYSIS	
1 PORTION CONTAINS APPROXIMATELY		489 I.U.	27 I.U.	259 I.U.	.15 MGS.	49 MGS.	62 MGS.	1 MGS.	67	1 GMS.
		A	B	C	G	CALC.	PHOS.	IRON	CAL.	PROT.
BLACK PART OF COLUMN SHOWS HOW MUCH OF DAILY NEED IS SUPPLIED BY ONE PORTION										
AVERAGE DAILY NEED		5000 I.U.	600 I.U.	1500 I.U.	2.7 MGS.	800 MGS.	1320 MGS.	12 MGS.	2000-3000	70 GMS.

INGREDIENTS:

6 medium-sized parsnips
1 teaspoon salt

2 tablespoons melted butter
2 tablespoons minced parsley

DIRECTIONS: Wash well. If old, pare very thin. If young, scraping unnecessary as thin skin may be easily removed by peeling under cold water after boiling. Cut in halves, or pare and dice or cut into strips. Cook uncovered, in boiling water to cover, about 30 to 50 minutes, until tender. Salt before removing from heat. Drain, reserving pot liquor; remove woody core. Peel, if this has not previously been done. Serve with melted butter and minced parsley.

Creamed Parsnips—Prepare, cook, drain and peel as directed in basic recipe. Combine with Pot Liquor Cream Sauce (page 217). Garnish with parsley.

Parsnips and Potatoes—Dice 3 medium-sized parsnips and 3 medium-sized potatoes. Quick-cook together as directed in basic recipe. Drain, and mash or rice. Season with 1 teaspoon salt and dash of pepper. Add ½ cup heated milk, 1 tablespoon butter and beat. *Approximate vitamin values per portion: Vit. A—92 I.U.; Vit. B₁—24 I.U.; Vit. C—193 I.U.; Vit. G—.15 Mg.*

VITAMINS	1 PORTION CONTAINS APPROXIMATELY	DAILY NEED	
A	1159	5000 I.U.	
B	72	600 I.U.	PARSNIP LOAF
C	306	1500 I.U.	
G	.29	2.7 MGS.	

INGREDIENTS:

4 cups cooked mashed parsnips
2 tablespoons butter
1 teaspoon salt
¼ teaspoon pepper
2 eggs

½ cup parsnip pot liquor
3 tablespoons minced parsley
½ cup buttered bread crumbs
2 tablespoons finely minced green pepper (or pimiento)

DIRECTIONS: Quick-cook parsnips as directed in basic recipe and drain, reserving pot liquor. Scrape skins and mash parsnips with butter and seasonings. Combine pot liquor and eggs and beat well, then add to mashed parsnips with minced parsley. Stir until thoroughly mixed. Place in buttered casserole or loaf pan and top with buttered crumbs. Bake in a hot oven (400° F.) about 20 to 25 minutes, until center is firm and top is delicately browned. Unmold on hot platter and garnish with finely minced green peppers or pimiento.

BALANCED MEAL SUGGESTIONS: *Lunch* or *Supper*—Lettuce and Tomato Salad; *Parsnip Loaf;* Fresh or Canned Peaches; Milk.

Dinner—Green Pepper Coleslaw; Broiled Kidneys; *Parsnips and Potatoes;* String Beans; Deep-Dish Berry Pie.

PEAS

COMMENTS: One of the most popular of all vegetables. A member of the legume group; hence, comparatively high in vegetable protein. Also medium in calorie content (not low, like leafy, watery greens, tomatoes, etc.). Reducers should choose very young peas—the younger they are, the lower their calorie content.

Should be used with less concentrated vegetables in a meal; may be served occasionally as meat substitute. Lend themselves admirably to combining with other vegetables, meats, etc.

QUICK-COOKED GREEN PEAS

This Chart Gives Approximate Food Values for PEAS.

1 PORTION CONTAINS APPROXIMATELY	V I T A M I N S	1243 I.U.	50 I.U.	483 I.U.	.35 MGS.	M I N E R A L S	62 MGS.	292 MGS.	4 MGS.	A N A L Y S I S	226	15 GMS.
		A	B	C	G		CALC.	PHOS.	IRON		CAL.	PROT.
BLACK PART OF COLUMN SHOWS HOW MUCH OF DAILY NEED IS SUPPLIED BY ONE PORTION												
AVERAGE DAILY NEED		5000 I.U.	600 I.U.	1500 I.U.	2.7 MGS.		800 MGS.	1320 MGS.	12 MGS.		2000-3000	70 GMS.

INGREDIENTS:

3 pounds (3 cups shelled) peas
2 tablespoons butter
½ teaspoon salt
¼ teaspoon pepper
4 tablespoons rich milk
(optional)

DIRECTIONS: Shell peas. Discard all but a few pods. Place in 1 inch boiling water; let water return to full boil and cover; cook 10 to 15 minutes, just until tender. Add butter, salt and pepper and, if desired, rich milk to pot liquor; bring to boil and serve pot liquor with peas in individual dishes.

Peas and Lettuce—Reduce peas in basic recipe to 2 cups shelled peas. Melt butter in heavy utensil. Add 1 tablespoon water, 1 medium-sized minced onion, 1 tablespoon minced parsley and ¼ teaspoon nutmeg, and cook over low heat 2 minutes. Add peas and ½ cup boiling water and cook covered about 8 to 12 minutes, until peas are almost tender. Add 8 shredded lettuce leaves and cook about 5 minutes longer, until peas are tender. Add seasoning and butter to taste. *Approximate vitamin values per portion: Vit. A—1760 I.U.; Vit. B₁—40 I.U.; Vit. C—393 I.U.; Vit. G—.29 Mg.*

Peas and Onions—Follow directions in basic recipe for quick-cooked peas. Add 1 minced onion with the peas at start of cooking. Increase amount of rich milk to ½ cup. Serve in individual dishes with pot liquor.

BALANCED MEAL SUGGESTIONS: *Dinner*—Mixed Greens Salad; Broiled Veal Cutlets; Turnips; *Peas and Onions;* Apple Pie.

PEPPERS

COMMENTS: Peppers extremely valuable for richness in Vitamins A and C. Red and green peppers have highest Vitamin C contents of all foods. Recommended for use raw (minced and added to salads, sauces, other vegetables, dressings, etc.), so that all Vitamin C content will be preserved.

Plain cooked peppers not particularly palatable. Best when stuffed whole, or minced and used as ingredient of loaves, stews and vegetable combination dishes. Low in calorie content and high in water content; excellent for reducers, and good to balance starchy or concentrated foods.

STUFFED GREEN PEPPERS

This Chart Gives Approximate Food Values for STUFFED PEPPERS.

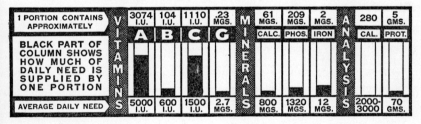

1 PORTION CONTAINS APPROXIMATELY	VITAMINS	3074 I.U. A	104 I.U. B	1110 I.U. C	.23 MGS. G	MINERALS	61 MGS. CALC.	209 MGS. PHOS.	2 MGS. IRON	ANALYSIS	280 CAL.	5 GMS. PROT.
BLACK PART OF COLUMN SHOWS HOW MUCH OF DAILY NEED IS SUPPLIED BY ONE PORTION												
AVERAGE DAILY NEED		5000 I.U.	600 I.U.	1500 I.U.	2.7 MGS.		800 MGS.	1320 MGS.	12 MGS.		2000-3000 CAL.	70 GMS.

INGREDIENTS:

6 green peppers
4 tablespoons butter
1 cup (¼ pound) chopped mushrooms
¼ cup minced onion
¼ cup diced celery

1½ cups Boiled Rice (page 289)
3 tablespoons minced parsley
1 teaspoon salt
¼ teaspoon pepper
¼ cup buttered bread crumbs (or 3 strips bacon, diced)

DIRECTIONS: Remove stem end of each pepper by slicing crosswise, or cut peppers (if large) lengthwise. Remove seeds and white fibrous portions.

Melt butter in large skillet. Add mushrooms, onion and celery, and sauté over medium heat about 3 minutes, stirring occasionally to prevent burning. Stir in rice, parsley and seasoning, and mix well. (If desired, add a bit of ketchup or tomato soup to moisten stuffing.) Stuff peppers, cover with buttered bread crumbs or bits of diced bacon and place in buttered baking dish. Bake uncovered in hot oven (400° F.) about 25 minutes.

Additional Stuffings—Other suggested stuffings for green pepper are cooked rice, tomatoes and mushrooms; cooked or canned corn and tomatoes; okra, rice and tomatoes; peas and mushrooms.

BALANCED MEAL SUGGESTIONS: *Lunch or Supper*—Raw Carrot Strips; *Green Peppers Stuffed with Corn and Tomatoes;* Cherries; Milk.

Dinner—Lettuce with Russian Dressing; *Stuffed Green Peppers* (basic recipe); Parsley Potatoes; Asparagus; Citrus Sherbet.

POTATOES

COMMENTS: Potatoes a real staple food—the vegetable eaten more often than any other in this country. Contain only relatively small amounts of necessary vitamins and minerals but large quantities of potatoes consumed make total supply of Vitamins B_1, C and G, and the mineral iron, considerable.

Proper cooking important for preserving these nutrients. Follow directions closely; cook in jackets as often as possible.

Low in roughage, so important source of Vitamin C for people on soft diets. Medium in calorie content when prepared as directed (fried or chips high because of addition of fat). Reducers should eat sparingly, but should choose potatoes in preference to bread because the vegetable is more "filling" per amount eaten, and, weight for weight, much lower in calorie content.

Fortification of potatoes with vitamin-rich vegetables, cheese, milk, etc. highly recommended. In the case of parsley, pimiento, etc., mince the vegetable and combine it with the potato so it will actually be eaten—separate sprigs of parsley, strips of pimiento, etc., may be pushed aside.

Usually recommended for main meal of day three or more days a week, but if food budget is limited, potatoes may be eaten much oftener, as they are cheap, nutritious and filling. Always balance with leafy green vegetable, salad, fruit or fruit juice to offset starch in potatoes, and to add vitamins.

1 PORTION CONTAINS APPROXIMATELY	DAILY NEED	
A 594	5000 I.U.	
B₁ 17	600 I.U.	
C 110	1500 I.U.	
G .08	2.7 MGS.	

BAKED POTATOES

INGREDIENTS:

6 medium-sized baking potatoes
7 tablespoons butter

4 teaspoons minced parsley
paprika

DIRECTIONS: Scrub potatoes thoroughly, dry, and rub with butter. Place in moderately hot oven (425° F.) and bake 50 to 60 minutes, depending upon size of potatoes, until soft when pressed with fingers. Remove from oven; break open at once to avoid sogginess. Spread liberally with butter, sprinkle with paprika and minced parsley, and serve to be seasoned at table.

Baked Stuffed Potatoes—Bake potatoes as directed in basic recipe. Remove from oven and cut large potatoes into halves lengthwise, or cut slices from sides. Remove potato with a teaspoon, being careful not to break skins, and put through ricer. Add 4 tablespoons butter and about 1/3 to ½ cup hot milk—just enough to give a creamy consistency. Beat until light and fluffy and season to taste. Return potato mixture to shells, piling lightly so that top is heaped high and uneven. Do not pack down the mixture. Garnish with paprika. Sprinkle each half with 1 to 2 teaspoons grated cheese. Arrange in baking pan and bake in hot oven (450° F.) about 10 minutes.

1 PORTION CONTAINS APPROXIMATELY	DAILY NEED	
A 909	5000 I.U.	
B₁ 18	600 I.U.	
C 222	1500 I.U.	
G .1	2.7 MGS.	

BOILED PARSLEY POTATOES

INGREDIENTS:

6 potatoes

salt and pepper

DIRECTIONS: Scrub potatoes well; place in covered utensil containing 1 inch boiling water. When water again boils, cover pan tightly and boil 25 to 30 minutes, until potatoes are soft. Take from water and remove skins. Always save pot liquor for soups, etc. Season to taste, and prepare in following ways:

Parsley or Paprika Potatoes—Cook, drain, peel and season as directed in basic recipe, and place in hot buttered serving dish. Add 3 tablespoons melted butter and turn potatoes until well coated with butter. Sprinkle with ¼ cup minced parsley (or paprika to taste) and turn potatoes until well covered. Serve immediately.

Mashed Potatoes—Cook as directed in basic recipe. Drain, reserving pot liquor, and shake over low heat to dry. Peel and rice or mash. Add 4 tablespoons butter, 1 teaspoon salt, ¼ teaspoon pepper and ¼ to ½ cup hot rich milk. Beat until creamy for fluffy potatoes and serve at once, garnished with 2 tablespoons minced parsley or chopped chives. For additional flavor, add 1 teaspoon onion juice, 3 tablespoons minced pimiento or grated cheese to taste, and use steel fork to distribute evenly. *Approximate vitamin values per portion: Vit. A—605 I.U.; Vit. B₁—20 I.U.; Vit. C—191 I.U.; Vit. G—.12 Mg.*

SCALLOPED POTATOES

VITAMINS	1 PORTION CONTAINS APPROXIMATELY	DAILY NEED
A	846	5000 I.U.
B₁	25	600 I.U.
C	139	1500 I.U.
G	.32	2.7 MGS.

INGREDIENTS:

6 medium-sized potatoes
2 tablespoons minced onion
3 tablespoons flour
3 tablespoons butter
1 teaspoon salt

¼ teaspoon pepper
2½ cups milk (approximate)
¼ cup grated cheese (optional)
2 tablespoons minced parsley

DIRECTIONS: Scrub, pare and slice potatoes thin. Arrange in buttered baking dish in layers, sprinkling each layer with onion, flour, butter, salt and pepper. Add milk, cover dish and bake in moderate oven (375° F.) 30 minutes. Then remove cover, sprinkle with cheese, if desired, and continue baking until potatoes are tender, about 15 minutes longer. Serve garnished with minced parsley.

BALANCED MEAL SUGGESTIONS: *Lunch*—Vegetable Juice Cocktail; *Baked Stuffed Potatoes with Cheese;* Grapefruit or Berries; Milk.

Dinner—Carrot and Raisin Salad; Baked Oysters; Stewed Tomatoes and Onions; *Parsley Potatoes;* Fruit Cup.

SWEET POTATOES

COMMENTS: In many ways, superior in nutritive value to white potatoes. Higher in protein content, 100 times richer in Vitamin A, and slightly better in Vitamin B complex. Less Vitamin C. Richness in available sugar and ease of digestion makes sweet potatoes excellent for children and elderly. Much higher than white potatoes in roughage—must be mashed and puréed for soft diet. Higher in calorie content; not advisable for reducers.

Combination of sweet potatoes with watery fruits, low in calorie content, recommended for weight-watchers (see Scalloped Sweet Potatoes and Apples). Vegetable best used as starch dish of main meal of day, with green leafy vegetable and fruit dessert, or as main luncheon dish.

Sweet potatoes of two varieties; dry and firm-textured (flesh yellow in color); moist and soft-textured (flesh yellow to orange in color). Many people prefer moist for all uses; definitely better for baking. Very yellow, soft type often called yams, although this name actually not correct. True yams are a tropical vegetable, rarely available in American markets. The so-called "yams" are generally, however, the most brilliantly colored and sweetest of all sweet potatoes.

BAKED SWEET POTATOES

This Chart Gives Approximate Food Values for SWEET POTATOES.

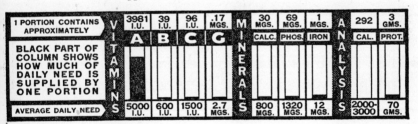

1 PORTION CONTAINS APPROXIMATELY	VITAMINS	A	B	C	G	MINERALS	CALC.	PHOS.	IRON	ANALYSIS	CAL.	PROT.
		3981 I.U.	39 I.U.	96 I.U.	.17 MGS.		30 MGS.	69 MGS.	1 MGS.		292	3 GMS.
BLACK PART OF COLUMN SHOWS HOW MUCH OF DAILY NEED IS SUPPLIED BY ONE PORTION												
AVERAGE DAILY NEED		5000 I.U.	600 I.U.	1500 I.U.	2.7 MGS.		800 MGS.	1320 MGS.	12 MGS.		2000-3000	70 GMS.

INGREDIENTS:

6 medium-sized, moist-type sweet potatoes

5 tablespoons butter

DIRECTIONS: Scrub potatoes thoroughly, dry and rub with butter. Place in moderately hot oven (425° F.) and bake about 30 to 45 minutes, just until soft when pressed with fingers. Remove from oven, break open at once to prevent sogginess, and butter liberally.

BOILED
SWEET POTATOES

INGREDIENTS:

6 sweet potatoes

1 teaspoon salt

3 tablespoons butter

2 tablespoons minced parsley

DIRECTIONS: Scrub potatoes thoroughly. Place potatoes in utensil containing enough boiling water to cover potatoes. When water again boils, cover pan tightly and cook 30 to 40 minutes, until tender. Drain (reserving water for soups, stews, etc.) and remove skins. Season to taste and spread with butter. Serve plain; or sauté, glaze or mash. Sprinkle with parsley.

Candied Sweet Potatoes—Quick-cook potatoes as in basic recipe (or use 1 1-pound can of sweet potatoes). Cut potatoes in halves or quarters. Melt 4 tablespoons butter in heavy skillet. Reduce heat to medium. Add 3 tablespoons honey or ½ cup brown sugar and stir constantly until smooth. Add ¼ cup potato pot liquor or hot water and stir until sugar dissolves and forms a syrup. Add potatoes, and cover closely. Cook about 5 minutes on each side, just until well glazed. Uncover potatoes during last few minutes of cooking; be careful that syrup does not burn. Reduce heat if necessary.

SCALLOPED
SWEET POTATOES
AND APPLES

INGREDIENTS:

6 medium-sized sweet potatoes
(or 1 1-pound can)

4 pared, cored apples, sliced

4 tablespoons butter

¼ cup potato pot liquor

½ cup brown sugar

DIRECTIONS: Scrub potatoes and parboil in water to cover 15 minutes. Drain, reserving pot liquor, and peel (or open canned potatoes). Cut into ¼-inch slices. Arrange alternate layers of sweet potatoes and apples in buttered baking dish, dotting each layer with butter. Add brown sugar to

potato pot liquor (or hot water) and stir until dissolved. Pour over
potatoes. Cover and bake in moderate oven (375° F.) about 20 m
then remove cover and bake 10 minutes longer.

BALANCED MEAL SUGGESTIONS: *Lunch*—Green Pepper Coleslaw;
Scalloped Sweet Potatoes and Apples; Berries or Melon; Milk.

PUMPKIN

COMMENTS: Used much less frequently as a vegetable than formerly, but,
if liked, an excellent and usually cheap source of valuable vitamins. High
in water content and very low in calorie content. In addition, easy to digest.

Since pumpkin is not popular with most people as a vegetable, its chief
purpose seems to be to serve as pie filling. The recipe given for boiled
pumpkin may be used as a basis for such a filling. Always select small
pumpkins, either for cooking as a vegetable or pie filling.

QUICK-COOKED PUMPKIN

This Chart Gives Approximate Food Values for PUMPKINS.

1 PORTION CONTAINS APPROXIMATELY	VITAMINS				MINERALS			ANALYSIS	
	A	B	C	G	CALC.	PHOS.	IRON	CAL.	PROT.
	4931 I.U.	57 I.U.	161 I.U.	.35 MGS.	54 MGS.	107 MGS.	3 MGS.	88	2 GMS.
BLACK PART OF COLUMN SHOWS HOW MUCH OF DAILY NEED IS SUPPLIED BY ONE PORTION									
AVERAGE DAILY NEED	5000 I.U.	600 I.U.	1500 I.U.	2.7 MGS.	800 MGS.	1320 MGS.	12 MGS.	2000-3000	70 GMS.

INGREDIENTS:
    3 pounds pumpkin (approximate)   salt and pepper
    3 tablespoons butter

DIRECTIONS: Cut or break pumpkin into small pieces. Remove seeds and
stringy portions and pare. Cover with boiling water. Cook covered about
20 to 30 minutes, until tender. Drain. Mash or put through ricer. Season
with salt and pepper, and dot with butter. If mashed pumpkin is to be
used for pumpkin pie, do not add seasoning or butter.

BALANCED MEAL SUGGESTIONS: *Dinner* — Apple Coleslaw;
Broiled Fish; *Quick-Cooked Pumpkin;* Broccoli; Lemon Meringue Pie.

RADISHES

COMMENTS: Radishes best eaten raw, sliced, minced or grated, in salads. However, greens—much richer in vitamin and mineral content than roots—too sharp in flavor for eating raw in any appreciable amount. Tender fresh greens should always be saved and used in some form, either chopped and added to creamed roots or combined with other greens in mixed greens salad. Both roots and greens very low in calorie content; excellent for reducers. Tendency of this vegetable to cause flatulence can partially be averted by cutting radishes into fine pieces, and eating them in salad which precedes main course at dinner.

CREAMED RADISHES

This Chart Gives Approximate Food Values for RADISHES.

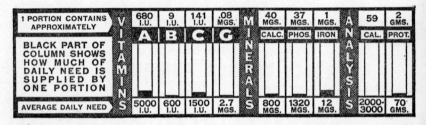

	VITAMINS				MINERALS			ANALYSIS	
1 PORTION CONTAINS APPROXIMATELY	680 I.U.	9 I.U.	141 I.U.	.08 MGS.	40 MGS.	37 MGS.	1 MGS.	59	2 GMS.
	A	B	C	G	CALC.	PHOS.	IRON	CAL.	PROT.
BLACK PART OF COLUMN SHOWS HOW MUCH OF DAILY NEED IS SUPPLIED BY ONE PORTION									
AVERAGE DAILY NEED	5000 I.U.	600 I.U.	1500 I.U.	2.7 MGS.	800 MGS.	1320 MGS.	12 MGS.	2000-3000	70 GMS.

INGREDIENTS:

3 cups red radishes (about 3 bunches)
2 tablespoons butter
2 tablespoons flour
1 cup radish pot liquor and milk
salt and pepper to taste
3 tablespoons minced parsley

DIRECTIONS: Wash radishes and slice (not too thin). Reserve greens. Place sliced radishes in saucepan, add boiling water to cover and let come to a boil again. Reduce heat, cover pan and cook about 5 minutes, just until radishes are tender. Drain, reserving pot liquor (there should be about 1/2 cup of liquid). Melt butter in large skillet, reduce heat and add flour, stirring constantly until well blended. Add reserved pot liquor and milk (to make 1 cup of liquid) gradually, stirring constantly until mixture boils and thickens. Add seasoning and radishes, and cook just until radishes are reheated, about 2 minutes. Serve garnished with minced parsley.

BALANCED MEAL SUGGESTIONS: *Dinner*—Grapefruit Salad; Liver-Beef Loaf; Broccoli; *Creamed Radishes;* Sour Cherry Pie.

288

RICE

COMMENTS: Although a cereal (not a vegetable), rice used in menus as a starchy component of creole dishes, curries, Beef-Rice, Casserole, etc., or plain, to take the place of potatoes. A concentrated food, relatively high in calorie content. Should be used sparingly by reducers.

Rice rich only in Vitamin B complex. This value destroyed by refining; hence, white rice absolutely valueless in vitamin content. Rice water need not be saved; starchy and unpleasant to taste, and some experiments have shown that Vitamin B complex is not dissolved in rice cooking water.

BOILED BROWN RICE

This Chart Gives Approximate Food Values for BROWN RICE.

	VITAMINS				MINERALS			ANALYSIS	
1 PORTION CONTAINS APPROXIMATELY	23 I.U.	34 I.U.	I.U.	.04 MGS.	34 MGS.	116 MGS.	.8 MGS.	140	3 GMS.
	A	B	C	G	CALC.	PHOS.	IRON	CAL.	PROT.
BLACK PART OF COLUMN SHOWS HOW MUCH OF DAILY NEED IS SUPPLIED BY ONE PORTION									
AVERAGE DAILY NEED	5000 I.U.	600 I.U.	1500 I.U.	2.7 MGS.	800 MGS.	1320 MGS.	12 MGS.	2000-3000	70 GMS.

INGREDIENTS:
- 1 cup brown rice
- 3 teaspoons salt

2 quarts boiling water

DIRECTIONS: Wash rice thoroughly in several waters until all loose starch is removed. Drain. Have boiling water ready in deep saucepan, add salt, slowly drop in rice, and boil for about 40 to 50 minutes. Rice is done when a grain, pressed between the thumb and finger, is entirely soft. In order to prevent rice from sticking to pan, stir occasionally with a steel fork, loosening from bottom of pan if necessary, but do not stir with a spoon. When tender, turn rice into colander or sieve. Run a little hot water through rice to wash off extra starch. Shake back and forth to drain off excess water and cover with a cloth. Set colander over pan of hot water or turn rice into a shallow pan and place in a warm oven for a short time. Cared for this way, grains swell and keep separate. Yield: 3 cups.

BALANCED MEAL SUGGESTIONS: *Lunch*—Cucumber Salad; *Green Peppers Stuffed with Rice and Mushrooms;* Fruit Cup; Milk.

SAUERKRAUT

COMMENTS: Sauerkraut is shredded cabbage fermented in salt brine. May be eaten raw, or cooked as directed. In either case, very low in calorie content. Recommended occasionally for reducers. Sauerkraut especially good to serve with spareribs or brisket of beef. Usually accompanied by mashed potatoes when cooked plain.

SAUERKRAUT AND APPLES

This Chart Gives Approximate Food Values for SAUERKRAUT.

1 PORTION CONTAINS APPROXIMATELY	VITAMINS	166 I.U. A	10 I.U. B	37 I.U. C	.01 MGS. G	MINERALS	33 MGS. CALC.	11 MGS. PHOS.	3 MGS. IRON	ANALYSIS	80 CAL.	1 GMS. PROT.
BLACK PART OF COLUMN SHOWS HOW MUCH OF DAILY NEED IS SUPPLIED BY ONE PORTION												
AVERAGE DAILY NEED		5000 I.U.	600 I.U.	1500 I.U.	2.7 MGS.		800 MGS.	1320 MGS.	12 MGS.		2000-3000	70 GMS.

INGREDIENTS:

3 cups sauerkraut
3 cups boiling water
1 peeled apple, quartered
1 teaspoon minced onion

salt and pepper
1 tablespoon sugar
3 tablespoons butter

DIRECTIONS: Combine ingredients and cook uncovered 30 to 40 minutes, until tender. Add 1 teaspoon caraway seeds for additional flavor, if desired.

BALANCED MEAL SUGGESTIONS: *Dinner*—Mixed Vegetable Salad; Brisket of Beef; *Sauerkraut and Apples;* Asparagus; Sponge Cake.

SPINACH

COMMENTS: Besides having superior vitamin content, spinach is also low in calorie content and high in water content; hence, a good choice for reducers and the elderly. Iron content of spinach, while quite high, is not readily available to the body. However, it is not necessary to rely on spinach for this mineral; many other foods supply it in assimilable form.

Spinach's lack of popularity usually the result of poor cooking; vegetable should never be overcooked. Variations suggested may help to win over spinach-haters in family. Always serve spinach with a more concentrated vegetable, as it does not have much "staying" quality. Spinach combined with eggs naturally is high in protein, and should be served as main luncheon or supper dish.

QUICK-COOKED SPINACH

This Chart Gives Approximate Food Values for SPINACH.

1 PORTION CONTAINS APPROXIMATELY	VITAMINS				MINERALS			ANALYSIS	
	A	B	C	G	CALC.	PHOS.	IRON	CAL.	PROT.
	19,213 I.U.	37 I.U.	1288 I.U.	.58 MGS.	113 MGS.	62 MGS.	6 MGS.	33	3 GMS.
AVERAGE DAILY NEED	5000 I.U.	600 I.U.	1500 I.U.	2.7 MGS.	800 MGS.	1320 MGS.	12 MGS.	2000-3000	70 GMS.

BLACK PART OF COLUMN SHOWS HOW MUCH OF DAILY NEED IS SUPPLIED BY ONE PORTION

INGREDIENTS:

2 pounds spinach
1 tablespoon butter

salt and pepper

DIRECTIONS: Wash spinach thoroughly under running water. Cut off roots and coarse stems, and remove any discolored or wilted leaves. Shake spinach leaves in large pan of cold water. Lift leaves to another pan of cold water, and continue this procedure, changing water each time, until spinach is free of sand. When leaves are clean, no sand will appear in bottom of pan. Usually 4 rinse waters will suffice. Place spinach in $\frac{1}{2}$ inch boiling water and cook covered about 7 minutes, stirring occasionally. Chop, butter and season. Add 1 tablespoon lemon juice for further flavor, if desired.

Creamed Spinach—Quick-cook spinach as in basic recipe (or use 2 cups canned spinach) and drain, reserving pot liquor. Chop spinach but do not season. Prepare Pot Liquor Cream Sauce (page 217), using $\frac{1}{4}$ cup spinach pot liquor as part liquid in making sauce. Combine sauce and chopped spinach, adding 2 teaspoons lemon juice just before serving.

Spinach and Egg—Quick-cook $1\frac{1}{2}$ pounds spinach as in basic recipe, or chop $1\frac{1}{2}$ cups canned spinach. Put 4 tablespoons spinach in bottoms of 6 buttered individual baking dishes and break a raw egg into each. Season eggs to taste and cover each with $1\frac{1}{2}$ tablespoons Cheese Sauce (page 218). Bake in moderate oven (375° F.) about 15 minutes, until eggs are set. Garnish with paprika. *Approximate vitamin values per portion: Vit. A— 15,256 I.U.; Vit. B₁—39 I.U.; Vit. C—554 I.U.; Vit. G—.7 Mg.*

291

Spinach and Mushrooms—Quick-cook spinach as in basic recipe. While spinach is cooking, prepare and sauté, over low heat, 1 cup (¼ pound) sliced mushrooms in 2 tablespoons butter about 5 minutes, stirring occasionally. Drain spinach, add sautéed mushrooms and chop together very fine. Add seasoning and butter to taste. *Approximate vitamin values per portion: Vit. A—19,310 I.U.; Vit. B₁—42 I.U.; Vit. C—1288 I.U.; Vit. G—.63 Mg.*

BALANCED MEAL SUGGESTIONS: *Lunch*—Carrot and Raisin Salad; *Spinach with Egg;* Rye or Pumpernickel Toast; Berries or Grapefruit.

SQUASH

COMMENTS: Squash an excellent vegetable for reducers and the elderly because of its very low calorie content and its high percentage of water. For these reasons, too, squash should be used to balance meals in which other foods are concentrated or rich. Summer squash best when it is well fortified with other vegetables higher in vitamin and mineral content, as it is not particularly rich in these vital factors. Also, because of its delicate, often bland taste and pale color, summer squash more appetizing when served combined with or in contrast to a bright-colored, more flavorful vegetable. Winter squash rich in Vitamin A only; serve with green vegetables.

BAKED HUBBARD SQUASH

This Chart Gives Approximate Food Values for HUBBARD SQUASH.

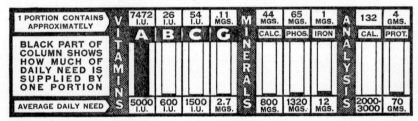

1 PORTION CONTAINS APPROXIMATELY	VITAMINS	A	B	C	G	MINERALS	CALC.	PHOS.	IRON	ANALYSIS	CAL.	PROT.
		7472 I.U.	26 I.U.	54 I.U.	.11 MGS.		44 MGS.	65 MGS.	1 MGS.		132	4 GMS.
BLACK PART OF COLUMN SHOWS HOW MUCH OF DAILY NEED IS SUPPLIED BY ONE PORTION												
AVERAGE DAILY NEED		5000 I.U.	600 I.U.	1500 I.U.	2.7 MGS.		800 MGS.	1320 MGS.	12 MGS.		2000-3000	70 GMS.

INGREDIENTS:

3 pounds Hubbard squash   salt and pepper
2 tablespoons butter

DIRECTIONS: Wash squash and break into pieces for serving, removing seeds and stringy portion. Arrange in greased baking dish, dot with butter, season and cover. Bake in moderate oven (375° F.) about 40 to 50 minutes.

Baked Acorn Squash—Scrub 6 small acorn squash. Leave whole for better flavor and texture. Place in baking dish and add water to depth of ½ inch. Bake in hot oven (400° F.) about 30 minutes, until skin is soft when touched. Serve like baked potatoes—to be dressed at table with seasonings.

V	1 PORTION CONTAINS APPROXIMATELY	DAILY NEED	
A	1406	5000 I.U.	
B	34	600 I.U.	**BOILED**
C	31	1500 I.U.	**SUMMER SQUASH**
G	.12	2.7 MGS.	

INGREDIENTS:

3 pounds squash
2 tablespoons butter

salt and pepper

DIRECTIONS: Wash squash. Do not pare or remove seeds. Slice thin and drop into ½ inch boiling water. Cook covered about 8 to 10 minutes, just until tender. Mash if desired. Add seasoning and butter, and serve with pot liquor in individual dishes.

CREOLE SQUASH

Each Portion Contains Approximately:
Vit. A—2901 I. U.; Vit. B₁—61 I. U.; Vit. C—755 I. U.; Vit. G—.24 Mg.

INGREDIENTS:

2 tablespoons butter
1 onion, minced
1 green pepper, minced
salt and pepper

6 tomatoes, peeled and sliced (or 2 cups canned tomatoes)
1 yellow or zucchini squash (approximately 2 cups sliced)

DIRECTIONS: Melt butter in large skillet. Add onion and pepper, and sauté about 3 minutes, just until onion is yellow. Add tomatoes. While tomatoes are heating, slice or dice squash without peeling. When tomatoes come to a boil, add squash, cover, and simmer about 8 minutes, just until squash is tender. Season and serve in individual dishes.

Baked Zucchini—Cut 6 zucchinis in halves lengthwise. Place in greased baking dish. Bake in moderately hot oven (400° F.) 15 to 25 minutes, until tender. Season and butter.

BALANCED MEAL SUGGESTIONS: *Dinner*—Lettuce Salad; Broiled Beef Patties; *Creole Squash;* Carrots and Peas; Baked Apples or Melon.

TOMATOES

COMMENTS: Tomatoes one of the best and cheapest sources of vitamins and minerals. Retain almost all of their valuable nutrients when canned, and so are well within even a limited budget the year 'round. Besides, tomatoes well liked by nearly everyone, and can be combined tastily with numerous other vegetables. Best nutritionally when eaten raw, but are still valuable when quick-cooked. Low in calorie content and high in water content; hence excellent for reducers. Should be used, either raw or cooked, to offset heavy, concentrated foods. Easily digested, and recommended for children, convalescents, etc., unless allergy to tomatoes is present.

STEWED TOMATOES

This Chart Gives Approximate Food Values for TOMATOES.

1 PORTION CONTAINS APPROXIMATELY	VITAMINS	1114 I.U.	23 I.U.	558 I.U.	.05 MGS.	MINERALS	18 MGS.	39 MGS.	.6 MGS.	ANALYSIS	69	1 GMS.
		A	B	C	G		CALC.	PHOS.	IRON		CAL.	PROT.
BLACK PART OF COLUMN SHOWS HOW MUCH OF DAILY NEED IS SUPPLIED BY ONE PORTION												
AVERAGE DAILY NEED		5000 I.U.	600 I.U.	1500 I.U.	2.7 MGS.		800 MGS.	1320 MGS.	12 MGS.		2000-3000	70 GMS.

INGREDIENTS:

8 large tomatoes (or 3 cups canned tomatoes)
1 small onion, minced

salt and pepper
3 tablespoons butter

DIRECTIONS: Peel and quarter tomatoes; place in saucepan with minced onion. Cover and cook 10 minutes over medium heat. Add remaining ingredients; stir until butter is melted. If desired, serve with whole wheat toast, cut into cubes, and a sprinkling of sharp cheese. Tomatoes may be combined and cooked with any or all of the following vegetables: diced celery, whole-kernel canned, fresh or quick-frozen corn, minced green peppers, minced onions or summer squash.

Tomato-Egg à la Mode—Prepare stewed tomatoes as in basic recipe, reducing tomatoes to 4 (or 1½ cups canned tomatoes). Then prepare a flour-water paste by gradually adding 3 tablespoons water to 1 tablespoon flour, stirring until smooth and well blended. Stir into stewed tomatoes and cook 2 minutes, pour over slices of toast and top each slice with a Poached Egg (page 123).

294

BAKED TOMATOES

Each Portion Contains Approximately:
Vit. A—1364 I. U.; Vit. B₁—19 I. U.; it. C—311 I. U.; Vit. G—.0518 Mg.

INGREDIENTS:

6 tomatoes
salt and pepper
¼ cup finely minced **onion**

3 tablespoons butter
2 tablespoons minced parsley

DIRECTIONS: Cut tomatoes into halves and place in shallow baking pan. Season, sprinkle with minced onion (or onion juice), and dot with butter. Bake in hot oven (450° F.) about 15 to 20 minutes, just until tender but still firm. Sprinkle with minced parsley. If desired, omit onion and sprinkle each tomato with 1 teaspoon grated cheese after 10 minutes' baking.

	1 PORTION CONTAINS APPROXIMATELY	DAILY NEED	
A	1604	5000 I.U.	
B	20	600 I.U.	**BROILED TOMATOES**
C	532	1500 I.U.	
G	.12	2.7 MGS.	

INGREDIENTS:

6 tomatoes
salt and pepper
2 tablespoons onion juice

¼ cup grated sharp cheese
3 tablespoons minced parsley

DIRECTIONS: Peel and cut tomatoes into ¼-inch slices. Place in greased broiler pan. Season and sprinkle with onion juice and sharp grated cheese. Broil 3 inches from medium heat, about 3 minutes. Sprinkle with parsley.

BALANCED MEAL SUGGESTIONS: *Dinner*—Celery and Apple Salad; Baked Ham Slices or Broiled Fish; Mashed Potatoes with Pimiento; *Stewed Tomatoes;* Fruit Sherbet.

TURNIPS

COMMENTS: Turnip roots excellent source of Vitamin C, but long cooking time needed to make turnips palatable causes large percentage to be dissolved into cooking water. Pot liquor thus very valuable. Turnip greens higher in vitamin and mineral contents than roots. Very inexpensive, too; in fact, can sometimes be obtained free, because many people thoughtlessly ask grocer to remove tops, if present, when they buy roots. However, in many large cities, turnips unfortunately arrive in market with greens already removed. Very low in calorie content (both roots and greens); excellent for reducers. Because of sharp, somewhat bitter flavor of greens, should be combined with mild greens, like spinach, in Mixed Greens (page 266).

QUICK-COOKED TURNIPS

This Chart Gives Approximate Food Values for TURNIPS.

1 PORTION CONTAINS APPROXIMATELY	VITAMINS	170 I.U.	20 I.U.	644 I.U.	.06' MGS.	MINERALS	99 MGS.	71 MGS.	1 MGS.	ANALYSIS	91	2 GMS.
		A	B	C	G		CALC.	PHOS.	IRON		CAL.	PROT.
BLACK PART OF COLUMN SHOWS HOW MUCH OF DAILY NEED IS SUPPLIED BY ONE PORTION												
AVERAGE DAILY NEED		5000 I.U.	600 I.U.	1500 I.U.	2.7 MGS.		800 MGS.	1320 MGS.	12 MGS.		2000-3000	70 GMS.

INGREDIENTS:

2 pounds white or yellow turnips (approximate)

salt and pepper
3 tablespoons butter

DIRECTIONS: Scrub thoroughly; pare; slice or dice. Place in boiling water to cover; cook uncovered about 20 to 30 minutes (until soft) if young—about 50 minutes or longer if old. Drain, rice or mash and season with salt, pepper and butter.

Turnips with Green Peppers—Cook as directed in basic recipe, drain and mash with 4 tablespoons minced green pepper which has been sautéed in 2 tablespoons butter over low heat for 5 minutes. *Approximate vitamin values per portion: Vit. A—446 I.U.; Vit. B₁—23 I.U.; Vit. C—804 I.U.; Vit. G—.07 Mg.*

Turnips with Peas—Dice 1 pound turnips and cook as directed in basic recipe. Quick-cook 1 cup shelled green peas separately, then drain (reserving liquid). To ½ cup milk, add cooking water drained from peas and turnips to make 1½ cups liquid. Use to make Pot Liquor Cream Sauce (page 217). Combine turnips, peas, and cream sauce. Reheat and add 2 tablespoons minced parsley before serving. *Approximate vitamin values per portion: Vit. A—1374 I.U.; Vit. B₁—32 I.U.; Vit. C—663 I.U.; Vit. G—.2 Mg.*

BALANCED MEAL SUGGESTIONS: *Dinner*—Mixed Greens Salad; Broiled Kidneys; String Beans; *Turnips with Green Peppers;* Apple Pie.

296

VITAMIN - RICH RECIPES

RECIPES HIGH IN VITAMIN A

Approximate Vitamin A content per portion, measured in International units.

Kale and Onions......23,002 I .U.
Liver-Vegetable
   Soup ....19,956 I. U.
Liver-Beef Loaf ....19,949 I. U.
Chard Leaves and
   Potatoes ....19,787 I. U.
Liver-Beef
   Spaghetti ....19,435 I. U.
Spinach and
   Mushrooms ....19,310 I. U.
Quick-Cooked
   Greens ....15,809 I. U.
Spinach and Egg.....15,256 I. U.
Chicken Livers with
   Mushrooms ....14,442 I. U.
Beef-Liver Loaf.......10,635 I. U.
Liver Canapés .... 9,910 I. U.
Fish Roe .... 7,018 I. U.
Cream of Spinach
   Soup .... 5,078 I. U.
Parsley Butter .... 4,485 I. U.
Boiled Sweet
   Potatoes .... 4,264 I. U.
Parsley Carrots........... 4,103 I. U.
Carrots and Onions 3,779 I. U.
Carrot Ring .... 3,728 I. U.
String Beans and
   Chard Stalks........... 3,534 I. U.
Vitamin Butter .... 3,403 I. U.
Hollandaise Sauce... 2,181 I. U.

Creamed Eggs with
   Cheese .... 2,175 I. U.
Deviled Crabs ....2,109 I. U.
Tomato Salad .... 2,000 I. U.
Mixed Greens Salad 3,342 I. U.
Meat-Vegetable
   Soup .... 3,019 I. U.
Creole Squash .... 2,901 I. U.
Scalloped Sweet Po-
   tatoes and Apples 2,717 I. U.
Broiled Lamb Liver
   Patties .... 2,534 I. U.
Spring Consommé ... 2,509 I. U.
Broiled Fish .... 2,427 I. U.
Carrots and Peas...... 2,481 I. U.
Creamed Eggs with
   Pimiento .... 2,412 I. U.
Beef and Kidney
   Stew .... 2,340 I. U.
Vitamin Stuffing........ 2,256 I. U.
Lemon Butter............ 2,235 I. U.
Tuna-Tomato
   Casserole .... 2,231 I. U.
Cream Cheese Salad 2,218 I. U.
Vegetable Soup
   Stock .... 2,196 I. U.
Carrot-Raisin Salad 1,977 I. U.
Pimiento Bean Loaf 1,975 I. U.

Chicken Soup	1,950 I. U.	Beef Meat Loaf	1,580 I. U.
Cottage Cheese and Pepper Salad	1,941 I. U.	Beef-Rice Casserole	1,574 I. U.
Manhattan Clam Chowder	1,933 I. U.	Tomato Rarebit	1,562 I. U.
Baked Stuffed Heart	1,921 I. U.	Boiled Hard-Shelled Crabs	1,558 I. U.
Turkey Soup	1,917 I. U.	Roast Stuffed Shoulder of Lamb	1,521 I. U.
Cottage Cheese Salad	1,903 I. U.	Waldorf Salad	1,488 I. U.
Creamed Eggs	1,807 I. U.	Chinese Chop Suey	1,475 I. U.
Lettuce Tomato Sandwich	1,762 I. U.	Veal Stew	1,457 I. U.
Peas and Lettuce	1,760 I. U.	Brunswick Stew	1,450 I. U.
Corn and Tomato Soufflé	1,626 I. U.	Asparagus Salad	1,434 I. U.
Baked Eggs, Mushroom Sauce	1,592 I. U.	Steamed Chicken	1,417 I. U.
		Boiled Summer Squash	1,406 I. U.
		Borsht	1,327 I. U.
		Shrimp Creole	1,323 I. U.

RECIPES HIGH IN VITAMIN B₁

Approximate Vitamin B₁ content per portion, measured in International units.

Broiled Pork Chops	769 I. U.	Veal Loaf	197 I. U.
Baked Ham with Fruit	504 I. U.	Chicken Canapés	196 I. U.
Roast Spareribs	481 I. U.	Roast Chicken with Stuffing	192 I. U.
Pimiento-Bean Loaf	411 I. U.	Ham and Cheese Casserole	190 I. U.
Lettuce-Tomato Sandwich	391 I. U.	Beef and Kidney Stew	176 I. U.
Baked Stuffed Heart	380 I. U.	Orange Stuffing	158 I. U.
Chinese Chop Suey	302 I. U.	Lamb-Fruit Grill	153 I. U.
Black Bean Soup	294 I. U.	Toasted Cheese Canapés	152 I. U.
Pea or Navy Bean Soup	284 I. U.	Broiled Lamb Chops	147 I. U.
Roast Stuffed Shoulder of Lamb	279 I. U.	Broiled Scallops	142 I. U.
Peanut Butter-Pineapple Canapés	272 I. U.	Asparagus and Mushrooms on Toast	135 I. U.
Liver Canapés	228 I. U.	Beef-Liver Loaf	129 I. U.
Dried Fruit Canapés	206 I. U.		

Tuna-Tomato
Casserole .... 126 I. U.
Baked Eggs, Mush-
room Sauce .... 120 I. U.
Creamed Eggs .... 119 I. U.
Salmon Loaf .... 118 I. U.
Stuffed Baked Fish... 115 I. U.
Liver-Vegetable
Soup .... 114 I. U.
Creamed Mush-
rooms with Green
Peppers .... 114 I. U.
Beef Meat Loaf...... 113 I. U.

Fish Stuffing................. 113 I. U.
Brunswick Stew.......... 111 I. U.
Liver-Beef Spaghetti 109 I. U.
Broiled Lamb-Liver
Patties .... 104 I. U.
Oatmeal Spice
Cookies .... 100 I. U.
Beef-Rice Casserole 92 I. U.
Veal Stew .... 91 I. U.
Cottage Cheese
Salad .... 82 I. U.
Braised Veal Cutlets 71 I. U.
Whole Wheat Waf-
fles .... 65 I. U.

RECIPES HIGH IN VITAMIN C

Approximate Vitamin C content per portion, measured in International units.

Fruit Juice Beverages
Steamed Clams .... 3,063 I. U.
Vitamin Butter .... 2,137 I. U.
Beef-Kidney Stew ... 1,537 I. U.
Liver-Beef and
Spaghetti .... 1,406 I. U.
Manhattan Clam
Chowder .... 1,310 I. U.
Spinach and
Mushrooms .... 1,288 I. U.
Quick-Cooked
Greens .... 1,128 I. U.
Mixed Greens Salad 1,108 I. U.
Chinese Chop Suey 1,102 I. U.
Kale and Onions...... 1,097 I. U.
Cottage Cheese and
Pepper Salad .... 1,030 I. U.
Red Cabbage and
Apples .... 964 I. U.
Orange Ice .... 960 I. U.

Vegetable Gelatin
Salad .... 889 I. U.
Coleslaw (Cabbage) 883 I. U.
Asparagus Salad........ 831 I. U.
Corn with Green
Peppers .... 809 I. U.
Potato Salad .... 809 I. U.
Turnips and Greens 804 I. U.
Vitamin C Mayon-
naise .... 802 I. U.
Fresh Fruit Plate...... 783 I. U.
Creamed Eggs with
Pimiento .... 766 I. U.
Beef-Rice Casserole 761 I. U.
Shrimp Creole .... 761 I. U.
Creole Squash............. 755 I. U.
Brunswick Stew .... 754 I. U.
Meat-Vegetable
Soup .... 752 I. U.
Vegetable Soup
Stock .... 747 I. U.

Continental Scrambled Eggs	733 I. U.
Italian Spaghetti Sauce	713 I. U.
Chicken and Sweetbreads à la King	707 I. U.
Tripe Creole	693 I. U.
Cream of Spinach Soup	684 I. U.
Creamed Mushrooms with Green Peppers	671 I. U.
Pimiento-Bean Loaf	671 I. U.
Cantaloupe Salad	670 I. U.
Turnips with Peas	663 I. U.
Tomato Salad	656 I. U.
Stuffed Baked Fish	638 I. U.
Cream Cheese Salad	637 I. U.
Asparagus and Mushrooms on Toast	620 I. U.
Borsht	617 I. U.
Creole Sauce	601 I. U.
New England Clam Chowder	591 I. U.
Brussels Sprouts and Celery	578 I. U.
Tomato Sauce	578 I. U.
Cream of Asparagus Soup	577 I. U.
Spinach and Egg	554 I. U.
Chicken Canapés	536 I. U.
Broiled Tomatoes	532 I. U.
Liver-Vegetable Soup	530 I. U.
Lettuce and Tomato Sandwich	475 I. U.
Chard Leaves and Potatoes	465 I. U.
Liver-Beef Loaf	453 I. U.
Broiled Lamb-Liver Patties	408 I. U.
Cauliflower au Gratin	403 I. U.
Black Bean Soup	396 I. U.
Spring Consommé	394 I. U.
Peas and Lettuce	393 I. U.
Cream of Celery Soup	389 I. U.
Grapefruit Salad	388 I. U.
Baked Stuffed Heart	380 I. U.
Beef-Liver Loaf	369 I. U.
Date Cup	362 I. U.
Cream of Mushroom Soup	362 I. U.
Tongue Creole	361 I. U.
Fish Roe	354 I. U.
Parsley Butter	351 I. U.
Spanish Steak	332 I. U.
Reducing Dressing	329 I. U.
Quick-Cooked Rhubarb	322 I. U.
Fruit Gelatin Salad	318 I. U.
Scrambled Eggs and Brains	315 I. U.
Tuna Fish with Cheese	312 I. U.
Carrot-Raisin Salad	309 I. U.
Parsnip Loaf	306 I. U.
Broiled Scallops	291 I. U.
Beef Stew	288 I. U.
Lemon Butter	285 I. U.
Creamed Oysters and Celery	281 I. U.
Beef Meat Loaf	274 I. U.
Leek-Potato Soup	273 I. U.
Cheese Egg Canapés	261 I. U.
Pear (Peach or Pineapple) Salad	260 I. U.
Lentil Soup	253 I. U.
Waldorf Salad	250 I. U.

RECIPES HIGH IN VITAMIN G

Approximate Vitamin G content per portion, measured in Milligrams.

Chicken Livers with Mushrooms	3.42 Mg.	Baked Ham with Fruit	.6 Mg.
Liver-Vegetable Soup	3.2 Mg.	Quick-Cooked Greens	.59 Mg.
Baked Stuffed Heart...	2.8 Mg.	Baked Oysters	.56 Mg.
Liver-Beef Loaf	2.72 Mg.	Veal Stew	.50 Mg.
Liver-Beef Spaghetti...	2.5 Mg.	Roast Prime Ribs of Beef	.5 Mg.
Beef-Kidney Stew	2.4 Mg.	Broiled Steak	.49 Mg.
Black Bean Soup	1.5 Mg.	Scrambled Eggs and Brains	.47 Mg.
Pea or Navy Bean Soup	1.43 Mg.	Stuffed Baked Fish	.47 Mg.
Beef-Liver Loaf	1.4 Mg.	Spanish Steak	.47 Mg.
Liver Canapés	1.3 Mg.	Baked Cheese Omelet	.46 Mg.
Chard Leaves and Potatoes	1.29 Mg.	Veal Loaf	.46 Mg.
Broiled Lamb-Liver Patties	1.2 Mg.	Asparagus and Mushrooms	.45 Mg.
Pimiento-Bean Loaf ...	1.1 Mg.	Beef Stew	.45 Mg.
Kale and Onions	.93 Mg.	Brunswick Stew	.45 Mg.
Roast Stuffed Shoulder of Lamb	.91 Mg.	Cheese Fondue	.44 Mg.
Broiled Lamb Chops	.76 Mg.	Ham and Cheese Casserole	.43 Mg.
Lamb-Fruit Grill	.76 Mg.	Baked Eggs, with Mushroom Sauce	.43 Mg.
Chinese Chop Suey	.7 Mg.	Broiled Fish	.42 Mg.
Creamed Oysters and Celery	.64 Mg.	Beef Meat Loaf	.41 Mg.
Spinach and Egg	.7 Mg.	Cottage Cheese Salad	.4 Mg.
Meat-Vegetable Soup	.7 Mg.	Pear (Peach or Pineapple) Salad	.4 Mg.
Eggnog	.64 Mg.	Creamed Eggs	.4 Mg.
Spinach and Mushrooms	.63 Mg.	Corn and Tomato Soufflé	.35 Mg.
Broiled Pork Chops...	.60 Mg.		
Roast Spareribs	.60 Mg.		

INDEX TO DISCUSSION

French cooking, 23
Freshness of foods, indication of vitamin content, 27
Fricasséeing, 38

G

Garnishing, 71
German cooking, 23
Glucose, 14
Grains, cereals and breads, refining of, 56-59
Grating, 71
Grilling, 70

H

Handling of foods, 32, 33
Hay fever, 17
Hives, 17

K

Kitchen equipment, 39, 40
Kneading, 71

L

Lactic acid, 14
Lafayette, 22
Larding, 71
Leavening agents, 56
Liver, function, and Vitamin A, 44, 45
    Vitamin A in, 26, 42, 43
Louis XIV, 22

M

Madison, James, 22
Marinating, 72
Measurements and cookery terms, 67-73
Measuring dry ingredients, 67, 68
    fats, 68
    liquids, 68

Meats, ripening of, 34
Mincing, 72
Moist- and dry-heat cooking, 38
Moist-heat cooking, 37, 38

N

Nerves, effect of Vitamin B_1 upon, 14
Night blindness, 12, 13

O

Oil, Vitamin A soluble in, 48, 49
Oxidation and Vitamin A, 46
    and Vitamin C, 64

P

Pan-broiling, 36, 72
Pans, 39
Parboiling, 72
Paring, 72
Peeling, 72
Poaching, 72
Poisons, effect of Vitamin C upon, 16
Pot liquors, 72
    from "waste," 55
    Vitamin B_1 in, 54
    Vitamin C in, 61, 62
Preparation of foods for cooking, 32, 33
Puréeing, 72
Pyruvic acid, 15

R

Refrigerators, 39, 40
Richelieu, Duc de, and mayonnaise, 22
Ricing, 72
Ripening of meats, 34
Roasting, 36, 72
Roman cooking, 23

INDEX TO RECIPES

316